Japanese Racial Identities within US–Japan Relations, 1853–1919

Edinburgh East Asian Studies Series

Series Editors: Natascha Gentz, Urs Matthias Zachmann and David Der-Wei Wang

Covering language, literature, history and society, this series of academic monographs and reference volumes brings together scholars of East Asia to address crucial topics in East Asian Studies. The series embraces a broad scope of approaches and welcomes volumes that address topics such as regional patterns of cooperation and social, political, cultural implications of interregional collaborations, as well as volumes on individual regional themes across the spectrum of East Asian Studies. With its critical analysis of central issues in East Asia, and its remit of contributing to a wider understanding of East Asian countries' international impact, the series will be crucial to understand the shifting patterns in this region within an increasingly globalised world.

Titles available in the series:

Asia after Versailles: Asian Perspectives on the Paris Peace Conference and the Interwar Order 1919–1933
Urs Matthias Zachmann (Editor)

On the Margins of Modernism: Xu Xu, Wumingshi and Popular Chinese Literature in the 1940s
Christopher Rosenmeier

Politics and Policy in China's Social Assistance Reform: Providing for the Poor
Daniel R. Hammond

Japanese Racial Identities within US–Japan Relations, 1853–1919
Tarik Merida

www.edinburghuniversitypress.com/series/eeas

Japanese Racial Identities within US–Japan Relations, 1853–1919

Tarik Merida

EDINBURGH
University Press

Edinburgh University Press is one of the leading university presses in the UK. We publish academic books and journals in our selected subject areas across the humanities and social sciences, combining cutting-edge scholarship with high editorial and production values to produce academic works of lasting importance. For more information visit our website: edinburghuniversitypress.com

Edinburgh University Press Ltd
13 Infirmary Street
Edinburgh EH1 1LT

First published in hardback by Edinburgh University Press 2023

Typeset in 10/12pt Ehrhardt
by Cheshire Typesetting Ltd, Cuddington, Cheshire

A CIP record for this book is available from the British Library

ISBN 978-1-3995-0689-2 (hardback)
ISBN 978-1-3995-0690-8 (paperback)
ISBN 978-1-3995-0691-5 (webready PDF)
ISBN 978-1-3995-0692-2 (epub)

Contents

# *Acknowledgements*

Many people have supported and guided me throughout the process of writing this book. I would like to express my sincerest gratitude to Prof. Dr Urs Matthias Zachmann (Freie Universität Berlin) who since my undergraduate years has been a mentor and a role model, in matters of academic life and beyond. Prof. Dr Nakano Kōtarō from the University of Tokyo has equally inspired me during my research stays in Japan and I am ever grateful for his kindness, integrity and generosity. At Heidelberg University, where this work was originally submitted as a dissertation, Prof. Dr Hans Martin Krämer acted as my supervisor and provided me with invaluable help.

I also would like to extend my earnest appreciation to the Cluster of Excellence – 'Asia and Europe in a Global Context' (Heidelberg University) and the Japanese Society for the Promotion of Science for their generous financial support that enabled me to focus on my research as well as going on field trips to Japan and the United States.

At Edinburgh University Press Laura Quinn and Sam Johnson have supported me with their trust and advice. I would also like to thank the two anonymous reviewers who provided thoughtful comments on an early draft of this work.

Numerous colleagues, friends and family have made the writing of this book significantly more pleasant. I am indebted to Prof. Dr Judith Árokay, Dr Asa-Bettina Wuthenow, Imke Veit-Schirmer and Chihiro Kodama-Lambert for the kind-heartedness they have been offering me since my first steps in Heidelberg. My tutor, *senpai* and friend Isato has been standing at my side all these years and has helped me improve my Japanese.

My Japanese mother Keiko (and by extension the whole Yamagata family) has offered me a home when I was far from home. Never again will I meet such a kind and generous soul. My grandmother, Helene, not only nurtured my love for history but also supported me in every way possible so that I could chase an elusive dream, despite her having lost her youth to war and adulthood to work. She will never be able to hold this book in her hands, but I hope that it would have made her proud. To my mother Angelika, I can only humbly express my gratitude for everything that she has done for me.

And finally, Momoko, *ma douce amie*. Trying to enunciate the many ways in which she supports me would be futile. This book is dedicated to her.

Introduction: The Japanese Racial Anomaly

In the year 1850, a thirteen-year-old boy named Hamada Hikozō left Edo Bay on a junk bound for the south of Japan. One night, his ship was caught in a storm and severely wrecked. After days of drifting on the sea, he and fellow survivors were saved by an American vessel which brought them to San Francisco. In 1852, the castaways were told that the American government was sending them to Hong Kong to join the expedition of a certain Commodore Perry[1] who was supposed to take them home to Japan. Upon arriving in Hong Kong, however, Hamada decided to return to the United States. During his time there, he was baptised, met the American president, and went on becoming a citizen of the United States. Forty years after his shipwreck, Hamada, now known under his American name Joseph Heco, sat down and wrote his autobiography *The Narrative of a Japanese: What He Has Seen and the People He Has Met in the Course of the Last Forty Years.*[2]

Heco's description of his odyssey to the West offers us a rare glimpse into the life of a Japanese from the Tokugawa period (1603–1868) who was able to leave his country. There are several fascinating anecdotes in his work,[3] but one seems particularly striking: on a torrid July evening in a cabin on board the *Susquehanna* (one of Perry's Black Ships), he and his friends decided to go on deck to escape the heat. They saw no harm in their actions, but when the officer on watch duty saw them, 'he shouted out something in a loud voice. Then he kicked us with his shoes and pointed down for us to go below. Thus we were driven down to our quarters on the berth-deck like a herd of swine'.[4]

This was no isolated incident: Heco complained that the crew of the *Susquehanna* frequently tormented him and his fellow Japanese. Upon enquiring into the reason for this treatment to an interpreter, the latter explained that the crew had long been stationed in China and had 'become accustomed to deal with Chinamen'.[5] 'The Chinese are a greedy and cringing race', Heco explained,

> and to make money will submit to any treatment – even being kicked and beaten like beasts. Wherefore the people of the *Susquehanna* fancied that we were folks of the same spirit, or rather want of spirit, and they treated us in the same fashion as they treated the Chinese.[6]

There are two interesting aspects to the Japanese sailor's misadventure. One is that the crew of the Perry expedition was seeing the Chinese and the Japanese as one group of people and treated them the same way. The second is that Heco shared the American crew's prejudice towards Chinese people. And he therefore did not seem particularly pleased about being lumped together with them: 'But in this [treating the Japanese the same way as the Chinese] they were wrong', he objected, 'for in our childhood we had been taught that man must respect man as man and not treat him like a beast'.[7]

Joseph Heco's experience aboard the *Susquehanna* is but a short episode in one man's life. Yet, when considered in the global context in which Perry voyaged to Japan, Heco's mistreatment becomes representative of its time. At the time the Black Ships navigated across the Pacific, international relations had, as Paul Gordon Lauren suggested, long become interracial relations as well: The Age of Exploration had brought adventurers, merchants and missionaries from the emerging European nations in contact with a plethora of new people. As a result, the until then relatively homogeneous intra-European diplomatic relations became relations between different races.[8] The arrival of the Europeans proved catastrophic for the natives: a few generations after Columbus's 'discovery' of the New World, as many as eighty million of their bodies were covering the Americas, with extinguishing rates sometimes reaching 98 per cent.[9] The slaughter and failed enslavement of the American natives led the European ships to raid the African coast for coerced labour, initiating the Atlantic slave trade.

Avoiding the thorny question of what came first – colour prejudice or slavery – the experience of enslaving non-Whites gave already widespread theories of White superiority more credibility. As George M. Fredrickson argues, the two elements mutually reinforced each other and consolidated the idea that ruling over the 'coloured' was part of White people's fate.[10] Nevertheless, the category 'White', demands caution, as does that of the 'West', as they tend to overshadow the geographical and ethnic heterogeneity that composed them. In other words, not everyone was equally White (nor Western). The United States, for example, was made of a multitude of individuals that were legally White, but who faced exclusion on a societal level because they were considered inferior, such as the Irish, Italians, Eastern Europeans or Jews.[11] Yet, even a relative Whiteness was better than nothing, and the centuries after Columbus saw the consolidation of a colour line that firmly established who was civilised or not, which in turn defined who could enjoy rights or on the contrary be subjugated.

It was also these presumptions that had filled the sails of Perry's ships. To be sure, economic and political incentives were the main reasons behind the decision to send a naval squadron to Japan. Whales, which at the time were crucial for their oil and bones, were abundant in the waters surrounding Japan. Moreover, Japanese ports could provide welcome coaling stations for ships en route to China. Added to this was the need to negotiate some sort of legal protection for American shipwrecked sailors stranded on the Japanese coast.[12] These concrete incentives, however, were imbedded in ideological underpinnings that not only posited the superiority of the White race but also had a peculiar American component to it.

The westward expansion into the Pacific was fuelled by the same essence that had led British settlers from the eastern to the western coast of America. This almost mythological engine, known as 'Manifest Destiny', truly was, in the words of Walter LaFeber, 'the belief that Americans had God-given rights to spread both their new political institutions and successful commerce across the Continent . . . and to uplift . . . the benighted Europeans and Asians'.[13] Reginald Horsman has convincingly shown that this 'Manifest Destiny' also had a strong racial connotation, as Americans justified it not only in terms of technological and political superiority but also explicitly on the conviction of Anglo-Saxon superiority.[14] Worldwide geopolitical developments as well as the belief in a peculiar American destiny led the people arriving from the West to Japan to identify not only by their nationality, but also by the colour of their skin. The 'opening' of Japan in the mid-nineteenth century, therefore, did not occur on a neutral racial basis. An intriguing visual representation of this fact could be found in Perry's use of African Americans throughout the negotiations with the Japanese officials.

Perry landed in Kurihama on 14 July 1853, with letters written by the American president for the Japanese officials. One hundred Marines as well as 100 sailors surrounded him as he walked towards the reception hall.[15] At his side were his personal bodyguards: two African Americans. The *Narrative* of the expedition describes the event as follows:

> On either side of the Commodore marched a tall, well-formed negro, who, armed to the teeth, acted as his personal guard. These blacks, selected for the occasion, were two of the best-looking fellows of their color that the squadron could furnish.[16]

Those very Blacks handed the letters to the Japanese officials: 'The two stalwart negroes followed immediately . . . took out the letters and, displaying the writings and the seals, laid them upon the lid of the Japanese box.'[17]

In what reads as an attempt to reassure the readership, the *Narrative* states that 'all this, of course, was but for effect'.[18] Yet, the symbolism that lies behind the use of the two 'stalwart negroes' is still worth exploring. As Jeffrey Keith rightly points out, the description of the bodyguards emphasises their physical strength, threatening potential and Blackness. However, these three factors could easily be tamed by an unarmed, White officer.[19] Perry was in fact displaying White supremacy. And while they might seem anecdotal, the interactions between Japanese, Whites and Blacks at Kurihama are a reminder that the meeting of the United States and Japan was not merely a meeting between two countries, but also between several races. It also illustrates that the interactions between these races cannot be understood outside the context of White supremacy.

On the (ir)relevance of studying race

From an academic point of view, one could legitimately ask if nowadays writing a book using the word 'race' is truly advisable. Therefore, a brief clarification on (and legitimisation of) the use of the concept in this work seems necessary. In the social sciences, the claim that race should not be used as an analytical concept has been consistently made from the first half of the twentieth century onwards.[20] The biological value of the concept has long been discredited and most scholars today employ it as a social construct in which 'the facts of biological difference are secondary to the meanings that are attributed to them and, indeed, to imagined biological difference'.[21] Somatic differences such as hair type or skin colour therefore are not relevant per se, but are made so through a 'process of signification whereby certain somatic characteristics are attributed with meaning and are used to organise populations into distinct groups that are defined as "races"'.[22] It is with this meaning that the concept is mostly being used within academia today.

Some scholars have cast doubts on the wisdom of this approach. According to them, the problem emerges from the relationship between the common-sense meaning of race; that is, the everyday uses and meanings of it as a marker of biological differences, and the theoretical discussions on it.[23] Miles and Brown for example condemn the fact that social scientists from North America and Europe were employing 'uncritically the common sense notion of "race," reified it and then attributed it with the status of a scientific concept'.[24] The sociologist and feminist Colette Guillaumin wrote that, 'Whatever the theoretical foundations underlying the various interpretations of "racial" relations', the very use of this type of distinction implies 'the acceptance of some essential difference between types of social relations, some, somewhere, being specifically racial'.[25] Miles and Brown thus argue that 'social scientists have prolonged the life of an idea that should be consigned to the dustbin of analytically useless terms'.[26] In other words, race exists because people continue using the term.[27]

The opponents of this line of thinking, on the other hand, stress the inescapability as well as the potential value of the concept.[28] Indeed, race possesses a practical value for social activism, as well as for social identification: it was transformed in 'a discourse of resistance', and 'certain somatic characteristics (usually skin colour) have been signified as the foundation for a common experience and fate as an excluded population, irrespective of class position and cultural origin'.[29] St Louis perfectly summarises the tensions between the two approaches – post-racial and racial:

> On the one hand, there is the correct intention of developing an assiduous critique of the pragmatic affiliations and alliances based on the collectivization of monolithic racial group identities and interests. On the other hand, there is the equally worthy aim of building formal and informal political associations capable of recognizing, presenting and addressing the injustices experienced by sectors of society that understand themselves as racial groups whether 'imagined' or 'real'.[30]

The academic discussions surrounding the usage of race have an undeniable social relevance, and any scholar writing about the subject will be confronted with it. And while theoretical discussions about race in contemporary societies remain mainly the subject of the social sciences, scholars from other disciplines cannot ignore these due to their actuality and immediate societal significance.

Nonetheless, it is necessary to situate the present work outside the territory of contemporary conceptual and political discussions. There are two reasons for this: first, this book is a study of the history of the concept of race and is concerned with understanding the process through which racial identities were constructed in specific historical contexts. Hence, it is foremost situated in the past and does not prioritise finding a solution for contemporary issues. Second, the problem of defining race is facilitated by the fact that in the period under analysis here – that is from the late nineteenth to the early twentieth century – race was not an abstract concept but a concrete 'scientific' fact with a consensual definition.[31] Hence, as Charles W. Mills wrote, 'that race should be irrelevant is certainly an attractive ideal, but when it has not been irrelevant, it is absurd to proceed as if it had been'.[32] Which leads us to the premise of this book: the normality of race. In this work, race needs to be understood as a tangible biological fact, in the way people of the nineteenth century defined it. Without this understanding, describing the attitudes, decisions and events that constitute this book would not be conceivable. This is also the reason why I omit quotation marks when referring to the concept itself or racial categories.[33]

Subject and scope

This book is about the various interpretations of Japanese racial identities in the period between the arrival of Commodore Perry in 1853 and the Paris Peace Conference of 1919. It is the importance of both events, not only for the various Western interpretations of the Japanese as a race, but also for the conceptualisation of race by the Japanese, that informed their choice as the temporal boundaries of this work. As explained above, the coming of Perry's ships signalled that the relations between Japan and the West were to possess a racial dimension. The Paris Peace Conference of 1919, conversely, was a watershed not only in global history but also in the context of racial discourse. The conference gave a glimpse of hope after the world had been ablaze for four years. The promise of a new world made by the American President Woodrow Wilson (1856–1924) and his Fourteen Points was heard all over the globe, especially by people in European and American colonies, to whom ideas of 'self-determination' and 'equality' should have sounded particularly sweet.[34] Wilson's ideas were quickly picked up in the non-Western world to push for the liberation from colonialism, with protest movements launching in the process.[35] The Japanese had other hopes: sitting at the Parisian negotiation table as one of the winning nations, the conference could have been a final seal of approval for their recently gained status as a great power. Instead, it proved the contrary.

The period between the two events saw the emergence of Japan as a 'modern' imperialist power. Railways and telegraph poles appeared inside the Japanese landscape, streetlights illuminated Western-style buildings, and talks of 'civilisation and enlightenment' filled discussion rooms.[36] Further, military boots started marching on foreign ground. The transformation of Japan from a 'backwards' feudal state to a 'modern' nation left Western observers rightly impressed. The problem was that from a racial perspective, nothing of this was supposed to happen. The attributes of modernity which were believed to make a nation civilised (often referred to as the 'standard of civilisation') were believed to be the prerogative of the White race only.[37] More than that, the standard was used to justify the colonial expansion of White nations and was therefore entangled in a 'history of subordinating and extinguishing alien cultures'.[38] This 'right' to expand or subjugate in the name of the standard was based on, amongst other things, possessing a state guaranteeing certain rights and a modern military force capable of defending that very state.

By 1905, Japan not only had both, but had also proven that it was not lagging behind Western countries. Inspired by the Prussian and British models, the Meiji Constitution was promulgated on 11 February 1889. The first Diet was convened the next year. In 1873, the Conscription Law had made military service obligatory for all male subjects. The army was modernised along Prussian lines, the Navy along British ones. The first baptism of fire followed in 1894 when war erupted against China, with a swift victory the next year. A mere ten years later, the victory against Russia left no doubts that Japan was now a great power in the Far East. With the obvious slight anomaly of not being White.

This anomaly of being coloured and modern at the same time had serious implications for both Japan and the racial paradigm it was moving inside. The Japanese, who had modernised according to a standard that classified them as inferior, now wanted recognition as an equal. Stefan Tanaka remarked that Japan faced a dilemma in its modernisation process: 'How to become modern while simultaneously shedding the objectivistic category of Oriental and yet not lose an identity.'[39] Seen from a racial perspective, the dilemma can be described as follows: how to become modern while shedding the category of Oriental and gaining a new and strategically more advantageous identity in the process. This was the crucial question indeed, as the association with the Oriental/'coloured' races was a serious barrier to the desired equality with the West. The most straightforward way to annihilate this barrier was to prove that the Japanese were 'better' than the rest.

For the West, the implications of the Japanese exception were perhaps even more far-reaching. What Joseph Henning wrote for the American conception of Japan holds true for the West as a whole: 'Japan's success . . . undermined the widespread American conception that modern civilization and progress were inseparable from Christianity and Anglo-Saxon ancestry.'[40] It also made clear that the Japanese could not be treated the same way as the rest of the 'coloured' people. As the only non-White nation having achieved modernity, Japan became a threat to the very fabric of White supremacy.

White supremacy, as George M. Fredrickson describes it, refers to 'attitudes, ideologies, and policies associated with the rise of blatant forms of white or European dominance over "nonwhite" populations'.[41] However, he continues, White supremacy implies more: 'It suggests systematic and self-conscious efforts to make race or color a qualification for membership in the civil community.'[42] While the foci of Fredrickson's study are the particulars cases of the North American and South African societies, his characterisation of White supremacy also applies to the domain of international relations at the turn of the twentieth century. There too, race or colour became qualifications for membership of the international community of civilised nations. Whiteness became 'a transnational form of racial identification, that was . . . at once global in its power and personal in its meaning, the basis of geo-political alliances and a subjective sense of self'.[43]

In a rather ironic reiteration of history, the historian of Japan today faces the same conundrum as the characters in this study, separated by more than a century: what to do with a nation that has achieved all the qualifications for membership in the community of great powers but one – Whiteness. The problem is even deeper: after the First Sino-Japanese War, Japan became a colonial power itself. By mimicking the colonial enterprise of the West, that is justifying its expansion with civilisational and racial superiority, one could argue that Japan expanded the sphere of White supremacy.[44]

As with the riddle, the answer to it remains the same as 100 years ago: one stretches the meaning of Whiteness. I argue that at the end of the nineteenth century, the Western powers and Japan jointly created a negotiation zone in which the latter could temporarily receive the status of 'honorary White'. This enabled Japan to escape the subordinate status that was common for 'coloured' people and receive preferential treatment. It also enabled the preservation of the racial status quo and to cope with the anomaly of having a 'coloured' race equal to Whites. The aim of this book, therefore, is to explain how such a zone was created, how it functioned, and how the Japanese racial identity was negotiated inside of it. In the process, I would like to deconstruct the usual view of race relations between Japan and the West as a strict dichotomy between the 'yellow' and the White race. In the same line of thought as Carol Gluck, who called for an understanding of Meiji that goes beyond the binaries of modernity versus tradition and West versus East,[45] racial interactions between Japan and the West must be seen as more than the opposition of two hermetically closed racial categories.

Coming close to what I would like to express with the idea of a negotiation zone, Henning wrote that in the particular case of the United States, Americans had to devise new ways to adapt the Japanese into the categories of 'White' and 'Christian', thereby distinguishing them from other Asians.[46] What Henning underestimated, however, is the active role the Japanese played in renegotiating their racial identity. Accepting Japan into the sphere of White supremacy was not a one-sided process, with the Western nations bestowing Japan with a new identity. The Japanese side insisted on being differentiated from non-Whites and used the very criteria the Western nations used to categorise people into races to underscore their demand.

To really accommodate this Japanese anomaly inside the context of White supremacy, it is necessary to rethink our understanding of what that supremacy was. Fredrickson's definition unfortunately does not leave enough space to include Japan. For our needs, Charles W. Mills's definition of the concept proves more helpful: Mills does not see White supremacy as solely an ideology, but as a whole political system, 'a particular power structure of formal or informal rule, socioeconomic privilege, and norms for the differential distribution of material wealth and opportunities, benefits and burdens, rights and duties'.[47] Individuals can be part of this political system and receive its benefits by subscribing to what he called a 'Racial Contract'.

Briefly summarised, the racial contract is a set of agreements between individuals designated by racial criteria as White to categorise 'the remaining subset of humans as "nonwhite" and of a different and inferior moral status, subpersons, so that they have a subordinate civil standing in the . . . white-ruled polities'.[48] The racial contract thus 'establishes a racial polity, a racial state, and a racial juridical system, where the status of whites and nonwhites is clearly demarcated, whether by law or custom'.[49] The purpose of this state is to ensure that Whites retain control over non-Whites.[50] Seen as such, White supremacy is less about colour than about the capacity to subordinate. As Mills write, 'Whiteness is not really a color at all, but a set of power relations'.[51]

With this understanding, fitting Japan into the sphere of White supremacy does not seem particularly irrational. It was in fact tempting to use Mills's Racial Contract as the theoretical framework of this book. The argument would have been that Japan subscribed to the racial contract, thus acknowledging that Whites were superior, and by emulating White powers extended the sphere of White supremacy. Mills does indeed point to Japan as White supremacist power.[52] However, not on the ground that it was accepted by Western powers – except for the Nazi regime – but because it had enough power to force a racial contract of its own on other non-Whites. Hence, according to him, Japan was a White power in the context of its interactions with Nazi Germany and its own colonies, but non-White according to the global racial contract signed by nations of European origin.[53] This approach postulates two strictly opposite sides defined by their race, with one side oppressing the other. One is therefore either White or non-White, but there is no room for fluidity in-between.

This binary view is problematic as, if one accepts the argument that Japan was part of the sphere of White supremacy, the implications would be that it was unconditionally accepted as a White power. However, on the contrary, because Japan did not have the 'somatic advantage', it was in constant need to prove that it was worthy to join the club of civilised nations. It may have become a member, but only a second-rank one at best. At the same time, while Japan as a nation may have received preferential treatment, Japanese individuals, in the form of immigrants for example, were far from receiving the treatment usually guaranteed by the racial contract. White nations treated Japanese immigrants the way they treated other 'coloured' immigrants coming to their countries. The 'honorary Whiteness' of Japan, therefore, was a fragile thing limited in scope.

The problems regarding the monolithic view of the Japanese race are representative of historical studies on Japan. Most of the works on race inside Japanese history[54] contain one limitation that has to do with the heterogeneity of the concept of race and the problem of seeing race relations as a dichotomy: they treat race as a monolithic and essentialist concept, and ultimately ignore its heterogeneous and negotiated quality. Rotem Kowner, for example, asserts that at the beginning of the twentieth century, 'scholars no longer suggested any substantial distinction between the peoples of the "Mongoloid race," and the Chinese and Japanese in particular'.[55] He further comments that in the United States, 'Chinese, Japanese and Koreans . . . were seen invariably as members of a single large mass, whether "Orientals," "Mongols," the "Yellow race," or worse – "Chinamen," "Japs," and "chinks"'.[56] The description Kowner made of the early twentieth-century conception of the Asian race as a conglomerate of Japanese, Chinese and Koreans is accurate. But it is only one side of the story. It was certainly not the perception of the Japanese and the Chinese as alike that made missionary and scholar Sidney L. Gulick (1860–1945) ask in 1903:

> We have thought that no 'heathen' nation could possibly gain, much less wield, unaided by Westerners, the forces of civilized Christendom. We have likewise held that national growth is a slow process, a gradual evolution, extending over scores and centuries of years. In both respects our theories seem to be at fault. This 'little nation of little people', which we have been so ready to condemn as 'heathen' and 'uncivilized', and thus to despise, or to ignore, has in a single generation leaped into the forefront of the world's attention. Are our theories wrong? Is Japan an exception?[57]

Michael Weiner's 'two-tiered' conception of the Japanese race seems helpful here: he describes the conceptualisation of the Japanese race (by Japanese ideologues) as based on the idea of a 'conflict between the white and yellow "races"', while at the same time, 'it assumed distinct and immutable differences in intellectual and cultural capacities between the Yamato *minzoku* and those of China and Korea'.[58] Thus, Japanese ideologues could maintain the racial categorisation built by Western racial thinkers, while at the same time define themselves as superior to other Asians.[59]

Weiner's definition of the Japanese race according to either the domestic (imperial) or the international context is correct but lacks nuance in placing Japan inside the Western racial ideology of the time. Despite the strict hierarchisation of races by Western ideologues[60] and the theoretical association of the Japanese and the Chinese, geopolitical expediencies often overshadowed the theoretical discourse. Likewise, at least in its dealings with the West, the Japanese certainly did not readily identify themselves, as Weiner argues, as 'belonging to the same "racial" stock as Koreans and Chinese'.[61] As shown in Chapter 3 of this work, Japanese statesmen often targeted their efforts at proving that the Japanese were different from other Asians and closer to Whites.

We cannot, therefore, define the Japanese racial identity based on an oppositional relationship between White and 'yellow'. Quite the contrary, for the most part of a century after Perry's arrival, there was no consensus at all about what the Japanese really were; there existed as many different interpretations of them for as many different actors involved.

Any scholar concerned with issues of race in modern Japan will ultimately reach a crossroads where his research will diverge into two distinct – of course linked, but different – directions: race in the Japanese domestic context on one side, and race in the international context on the other. In the domestic context, the subject of study is the way in which the Japanese saw themselves as a race and how this affected their view of the racial 'others' inside their empire. At the international level, the matter of enquiry is how the Japanese were seen as a race – primarily by the Western powers. This distinction is crucial: depending on which level one chooses the meaning and relevance of race for Japan changes considerably. And most importantly, the authority Japan had over the concept changes too. In its dealings with the West, Japan's range of manoeuvre was severely limited: the White race set the standard and the Japanese had to cope with it, willingly or not. Inside its own empire, however, it was Japan that dictated its own set of rules. In both cases, interactions were tainted by a clear racial component, but race had an independent dynamic and a different meaning. As will be explained throughout this work, another layer is added when distinguishing between Japan as a nation and the Japanese as individuals. Both were not synonymous and the interpretation of what exactly Japan was as a race varied considerably depending on which one mattered most.

To fully appreciate the complex interplay of racial thinking, realpolitik and pragmatism characteristic of Japan's position inside the sphere of White supremacy which made the racial identity of Japan such a composite entity, I would like to propose the notion of a 'Racial Middle Ground'.

Theoretical framework – the racial middle ground

A racial middle ground,[62] is a negotiation zone inside a racial dichotomy – in the context of this book a White versus a 'coloured' one. Inside this zone, the group that is usually categorised as the inferior race and therefore subjected to different treatment can temporarily leave its inferior status and receive preferential treatment. Through this, that group can avoid, or at the very least be better protected against, abuses that are usually reserved for members of their group. In a White versus 'coloured' dichotomy, such abuses entail slavery, colonialism, physical violence and other types of discriminatory treatment.

The scope of a racial middle ground depends on several factors, such as the actors involved (individuals or states), and the political and economic context. The most important factor, however, is that of bargaining power: the race which leaves the inferior category must possess a certain quality that makes the revaluation of its racial identity by the other race necessary. Such a quality could be the gaining of political, economic or military significance which would make subjugation too difficult and therefore cooperation more desirable (diplomacy over war). Another one could be a certain usefulness for the dominant race which would justify differential treatment, for example the overseeing of other 'coloured'. The creation of a racial middle ground therefore rests on a bilateral agreement: in the White versus 'coloured' dichotomy, Whites agree that a specific group of 'coloured' is superior, more threatening, or more useful than the 'rest', while this group (becoming 'honorary Whites') accepts the inherent premise of White supremacy that Whites are superior and 'coloured' inferior. The creation of the middle ground thus always involves three actors: the 'upper race', the 'race in the middle' and, equally important, the 'race at the bottom' (which only serves as a reference point and remains a passive actor).

To preserve its privileged position, the 'race in the middle' needs to constantly remind others of its (threatening or otherwise) potential, or its usefulness to the upper race that justifies its differential treatment. This implies distancing itself from the 'race at the bottom', for example by emphasising the savageness of the 'other', the denial of racism, the self-imposed segregation from the 'inferiors', the denial of its own 'colour', or the attempts to 'biologically' turn into the 'upper race' (with eugenics for example).

The creation of a racial middle ground is before all else a pragmatic act, made to pursue amongst others political or economic incentives. Factors such as prestige can be added to the motivations on part of the 'race in the middle'. This means that in essence, the middle ground is a zone in which racial concerns are temporarily set aside for the sake of more pressing issues.

A few clarifications on the scope of this negotiation zone are necessary. First, while the degree to which the middle ground is accepted depends on several factors, it only applies to specific issues and does not grant universal equality. Likewise, those factors only matter to a limited number of actors, and are not representative of their race as a whole. The issue of foreign immigration is telling in this regard: while the government of a White nation might negotiate on an equal level with the government of a 'coloured' one (because the latter is rich in natural resources for example), the White nation can refuse the entry of immigrants from the same 'coloured' nation because it represents a threat to the racial purity of the country. In this case, the racial middle ground only affects interstate relations, and equality on a diplomatic level does not mean equality on an individual one.

If we now imagine that the government of the same White nation accepts immigrants from the 'coloured' nation because of the same economic incentives, it does not guarantee that the citizen of this same White nation will equally accept the immigrants. The interests of state and civil actors do not always overlap: the government might have been willing to renegotiate the racial status of the 'coloured' nation for concrete economic incentives, while the citizen of the country might be more concerned with an alleged racial threat to their society, or with losing their employment to cheaper foreign labour. In this case, the individuals from the 'race in the middle' will be accepted on the state level, but that will not necessarily prevent them from being lynched by angry mobs. It is therefore crucial to look at what issues and what actors are involved in the creation of a racial middle ground to understand the reason for its existence as well as its scope.

Which leads us to the matter of agency: while the negotiation zone can be seen as an abstract space where racial identities are temporarily renegotiated, the creation of this space is made by real individuals. The preconditions that made the creation of this middle ground necessary might be independent from purposeful individual action (for example political, institutional or demographic change), but, in the end, it is human decision and action that actively launch the creational and maintenance process. The racial middle ground, therefore, needs active 'agents' to be successfully built.

In a nutshell, the negotiation of the Japanese racial identity in terms of this middle ground can be described as follows: the modernisation of Japan occurred during the high age of imperialism, in which geopolitical as well as scientific evolutions had put the White race at the top of a racial hierarchy and confined the 'coloured' races to the bottom. Due to its 'civilisational' progress, Japan did not fit in this model anymore, thus threatening the racial order. The Japanese, conscious of their difference, insisted on being treated as a great power, which implied being differentiated from other 'coloured' races. Western powers, or, more precisely, the agents of the Western powers, granted this request by creating a racial middle ground in which the difference of Japan could be acknowledged, and the Japanese elevated to a status above the 'coloured' races – in the middle – without threatening the racial status quo. The Racial Middle Ground can thus be used to deconstruct the common dichotomic view of race relations that confines the history of interactions between Japan and the West to a confrontation between 'yellow' and White. Clarifying the process through which the Japanese anomaly was incorporated into the Western racial framework enables us to highlight the intermediate place that the Japanese temporarily occupied, as neither completely 'coloured' nor entirely White.

While most of the works on the topic tend to give a monolithic view of the Japanese racial identity, some scholars have seen beyond this and have documented the dilemma represented by Japan.[63] These studies show that racial identities can be subjected to compromises and that, despite the existence of biologically defined categories, there always remained some room for negotiation. They do, however, lack a comprehensive theoretical framework that can be used to analyse the process by which these racial identities can be renegotiated. By applying the Racial Middle Ground to Japanese history,[64] I hope to widen our understanding of how racial identities are being constructed by considering the influence of pragmatism on human decisions.

Focus and sources

This book is as much a study of diplomatic as of social history. The racial middle ground under analysis here was primarily a matter of interstate diplomacy, in which state actors of both sides – Western and Japanese – negotiated together. However, these negotiations sometimes spilled into the public sphere; not only because they also took place inside the pages of newspapers or in public talks, but also because they had a direct connection to the societal level. The anti-Japanese movement in the United States at the turn of the twentieth century (more details are provided in Chapters 4–7), for example, was as much a cause for, as a product of, the middle ground. And while there was an obvious distinction between Japan as a nation and the Japanese as individuals, both entities could not be separated.

The reader will notice that from Chapter 4 onwards, the focus of the study noticeably shifts to US–Japan relations. Several factors make these relations the most illustrative example of the wider negotiation zone that was built between Japan and the Western nations. Saying that race had a pivotal role inside American society during the time frame of this work is an understatement. Especially the southern part of the country was built on a racial order with legally sanctioned segregation separating White and Black Americans. Added to that was the widespread animosity directed towards Chinese immigrants which escalated to their exclusion in 1882. American society therefore not only possessed certain attitudes towards Asians, but also towards non-Whites in general.[65] This was certainly the case for most Western nations, but unlike for Great Britain or France for example – which both had their colonies outside the mother country and hence had only limited contact with non-Whites – a great number of non-Whites were living in the United States and were therefore an integral part of the American social structure. As the country became a popular destination for the emigration of Japanese at the turn of the twentieth century, immigrants were naturally confronted with this racial situation. And exactly these 'domestic' non-Whites were to become the 'race at the bottom' the Japanese tried to avoid.

To this was added the geopolitical importance of the United States. While the nation was not the sole relevant actor in world politics, it was one of the only Western ones that remained influential in the Far East after the Russo-Japanese War (alongside the British).[66] From a geopolitical perspective, interactions between the US and Japan were therefore inevitable.[67] This is where the racial middle ground gained its importance: there was bound to be a clash between a strict racial ideology that dictated the societal order at home and a realpolitik that tried to avoid war. The racial middle ground temporarily enabled the mediation between these two conflicting agendas.

American society of the turn of the twentieth century also best exemplifies the importance of the 'race at the bottom' in the creational process of the negotiation zone. The country was not lacking in candidates for that position. Be it African Americans, Native Americans or Chinese immigrants, all were subjected to legal and societal pressure which relegated them to the position of racially undesirable people. In terms of theoretical racial classification, the similarities between the Japanese and the Chinese, as members of the 'yellow' race, would have made the Chinese as the reference point obvious. However, in the specific context of the US, African Americans proved to be a more significant standard to assess the success of the renegotiation of Japan's racial identity.

Black Americans, more than any other domestic minority, were the racial 'other' per se inside the post-Civil War society, and the question of their status as citizens would remain (and still is) a central point of discussion inside the American political and societal discourse. Most of the civil rights issues that were debated with reference to Black citizens were of direct relevance to Japanese immigrants. A comparison between the treatment of the two groups can therefore give a measure of the success of the middle ground in elevating the Japanese to a status above that of other 'coloured' races. The Japanese attitude towards African Americans, conversely, exemplifies how the 'race in the middle' uses the 'race at the bottom' to enhance its position inside the predominant racial hierarchy.

There also is a desire for novelty that informed the choice of Black Americans as the 'race at the bottom'. While not in terms of the Racial Middle Ground, the strivings of the Japanese to separate themselves from the Chinese in the United States have been extensively researched.[68] And while the interactions between Japanese and African Americans did gain a certain popularity in academic circles in recent years, most of the research focuses on the African American view of the Japanese, thus creating a one-sided narrative of their common history.[69] The choice of Black Americans was therefore made to offer a convincing alternative to the Chinese, as well as to introduce new sources for future research on the topic of Japanese and African American interactions.

Lastly, the event that led to the demise of the negotiation zone, the Paris Peace Conference, was chaired by President Wilson. His personal role in the ending of the racial middle ground offers further legitimacy for the choice as the United States as a main character in the events described in this study.

To give the most inclusive overview of this negotiation zone, this study relies on a multitude of different sources. For the numerous opinions of White Americans about Japan, it draws widely on US newspapers and periodicals. Broadsheets, magazines, such as the *North American Review*, or journals such as the *Annals of the American Academy of Political and Social Science* were the theatre of fierce discussions about the Japanese racial identity and its meaning for not only the United States but also for the White and Christian West in general. Additional types of sources, such as personal letters or memoirs, are used in a less systematic, more cursory way. For the Japanese side, newspapers such as the *Asahi shinbun*, *Yomiuri shinbun* and *The Japan Times* provided an entry point to the opinion of the Japanese public on racial issues. So did other periodicals such as the popular magazine *Taiyō*. I also used governmental sources, such as diplomatic correspondences available in the *Nihon gaikō monjo* (Documents on Japanese Foreign Policy), to explain the evolution of the idea of a racial middle ground within the Japanese government.

Structure of the book

This book is divided into two parts. The first part, comprising the first two chapters, offers a preliminary framework for a discussion on the concept of race inside Japanese history. It is important to understand that it was only after their country was forcibly 'opened' to the West that the Japanese gained knowledge of the concept of race and understood its dangerous implications. The acceptance of race in the Meiji period was facilitated by the fact that early modern Japanese society was far from immune to prejudice and possessed its own patterns of differentiation. Contrary to race, however, these were not grounded in 'biological' factors.

Chapter 1 thus gives an overview of these early modern patterns of differentiation and compares them to a differentiation based on race. Some scholars made the argument that instances of racial discrimination could be found in early modern Japan. A close analysis of these arguments, however, will show that they entail too many conceptual hurdles. Instead, this study proposes several alternatives that anchor the differentiation of people in early modern Japan firmly to the framework of domestic thought.

The second chapter retraces the import of the concept of race in Meiji Japan. With Perry's arrival in 1853, Japan became part of an international struggle in which knowing one's opponent became crucial. The translation of Western books became a source of such knowledge and in the process a way to understand the West, its institutions and its customs. Most of the geography works translated at the beginning of the Meiji period contained a section about race, a fact that made the importance of the concept obvious to translators. Yet, race was before all a hegemonic discourse, a Western tool which under the cover of scientific legitimation offered a rationale for imperialism. And according to this discourse, the Japanese were quite obviously on the losing side. Chapter 2 thus shows how Japanese translators managed to navigate between a legitimate Western 'scientific' concept on one side and the unease felt by introducing an idea that posited one's own inferiority. Neither of the first two chapters claims to be exhaustive. Their aim is to serve as a starting point for the present study and for further research on the topic.

Part II comprises five chapters which reconstruct the racial middle ground, from its inception to its demise. Chapter 3 describes the specificities of the negotiation zone between Japan and the West. It also explains that the need for a special status for the Japanese was born out of racial insecurity that made them doubt their chances of survival against the White race. Discussions on interracial contact in the early Meiji period are used to illustrate this.

The fourth chapter deals mainly with two wars. The First Sino-Japanese War (1894–5) is the potential beginning of the racial middle ground. As a civilisational test under the watchful eyes of the West, the war was the opportunity for Japan to prove that it had left 'coloured' Asia behind. However, the massacre of Chinese civilians and soldiers alike after the siege of Port Arthur in December 1894 led to questions regarding the ability of Japan to join the ranks of civilised nations. Western reactions to the massacre show that in this case though, the Japanese were seen as Western proxies and as such were allowed to mistreat people considered to be inferior. This leniency extended to the Russo-Japanese War (1904–5). Through the work of the agents of the middle ground, racial considerations were momentarily put aside in a conflict that otherwise would have been seen as a war between the 'yellow' and the White race. The racial middle ground thus reached its most complete form by rendering race obsolete.

Chapter 5 centres on the California Crisis that was caused by the decision to exclude Japanese children from White schools in San Francisco. The decision led to an international crisis, in which the American President Theodore Roosevelt (1858–1919) became Japan's strongest agent of the middle ground. By intervening on behalf of the Japanese, Roosevelt enabled them to escape the customary treatment of non-Whites in the United States, but also created a dissonance between the special position of the Japanese and the American racial order. This is emphasised in Chapter 6 with the reaction of African Americans to the events in California. The chapter also deals with the Japanese views of Black Americans as the 'race at the bottom'. Finally, Chapter 7 looks at the Paris Peace Conference and explains why the event represents the end of the negotiation zone described in this work. It shows that for both the Western and the Japanese side the middle ground became obsolete and other alternatives became more viable.

Notes

1. From the 1630s to 1854, maritime prohibitions (*kaikin*) issued by the Japanese authorities forbade travelling abroad and limited contacts with foreign countries. In 1852, the US naval officer Matthew Calbraith Perry (1794–1858) commanded a squadron of vessels (including two steamships, the famous 'Black Ships') over the Pacific with official orders to force an end to the Japanese seclusion policy. For details on the maritime prohibitions, see Tashiro Kazui, 'Foreign Relations during the Edo Period: Sakoku Reexamined', *Journal of Japanese Studies* 8, no. 2 (1982): 283–306. For an entertaining account of the Perry expedition, see Peter Booth Wiley, *Yankees in the Land of the Gods: Commodore Perry and the Opening of Japan* (New York: Viking, 1990).
2. Joseph Heco, *The Narrative of a Japanese: What He Has Seen and the People He*

Has Met in the Course of the Last Forty Years, ed. James M. A. Murdoch, 2 vols (Yokohama Printing and Publishing, 1892, 1895).

3. For an in-depth analysis of Heco's *Narrative*, see Hsuan L. Hsu, 'Personality, Race, and Geopolitics in Joseph Heco's "Narrative of a Japanese"', *Biography* 29, no. 2 (Spring 2006): 273–306.
4. Heco, *The Narrative of a Japanese*, 116.
5. Ibid., 115.
6. Ibid.
7. Ibid.
8. Paul Gordon Lauren, *Power and Prejudice: The Politics and Diplomacy of Racial Discrimination*, 2nd ed. (Boulder, CO: WestviewPress, 1996), 10.
9. Ibid., 13.
10. George M. Fredrickson, *White Supremacy: A Comparative Study in American and South African History* (New York: Oxford University Press, 1981), 93.
11. For details see for example Gary Gerstle, *American Crucible: Race and Nation in the Twentieth Century* (Princeton, NJ: Princeton University Press, 2001); Noel Ignatiev, *How the Irish Became White* (New York: Routledge, 1995).
12. See Wiley, *Yankees in the Land of the Gods.*
13. Walter LaFeber, *The Clash: U.S.-Japan Relations Throughout History* (New York: W. W. Norton & Company, 1997), 4–5.
14. See Reginald Horsman, *Race and Manifest Destiny: The Origins of American Racial Anglo-Saxonism* (Cambridge, MA: Harvard University Press, 1981).
15. Francis L. Hawks, *Narrative of the Expedition of an American Squadron to the China Seas and Japan, Performed in the Years 1852, 1853, and 1854, under the Command of Commodore M. C. Perry, United States Navy, by Order of the Government of the United States* (Washington: Beverley Tucker, 1856), 254.
16. Hawks, *Narrative of the Expedition of an American Squadron to the China Seas and Japan, Performed in the Years 1852, 1853, and 1854, under the Command of Commodore M. C. Perry, United States Navy, by Order of the Government of the United States*, 255.
17. Ibid., 256.
18. Ibid., 255.
19. Jeffrey A. Keith, 'Civilization, Race, and the Japan Expedition's Cultural Diplomacy, 1853–1854', *Diplomatic History* 35, no. 2 (2011): 190.
20. For a detailed review of works built around this line of argument, see Robert Miles, *Racism after 'Race Relations'* (London: Routledge, 1993), 27–52.
21. Robert Miles and Malcolm Brown, *Racism*, 2nd ed. (London: Routledge, 2003), 88.
22. Ibid., 88–9.
23. For a comment and summary of the work of 'post-racial' thinkers, see Brett St Louis, 'Post-Race/Post-Politics? Activist-Intellectualism and the Reification of Race', *Ethnic and Racial Studies* 25, no. 4 (2002): 652–75.
24. Miles and Brown, *Racism*, 90.
25. As cited in ibid.
26. Ibid.

27. It is necessary to point out that the opponents of the use of 'race' do not imply that suppressing the word from the language equals suppressing the problems stemming from the concept, such as racism. Their critique is aimed solely at the value of 'race' as an analytical term. As Guillaumin has written: 'Saying that "race does not exist" . . . is a truth. But it is merely an intellectual truth. For its enunciation does neither suppress nor even reach racism. Believing that by saying this, racism would suddenly become obsolete is a daydream.' Colette Guillaumin, 'Avec ou sans race?', *Le Genre Humain* 2, no. 11 (1984): 217–18.
28. As St Louis comments on the issue: 'How might a post-racial imagination that trades on the theoretical and conceptual bankruptcy of race and is committed to its erasure retain efficacy in a civil society and political culture largely arranged around its immense practical currency?' Louis, 'Post-Race/Post-Politics?', 661.
29. Miles and Brown, *Racism*, 91. Miles and Brown criticise this approach as it is their sense that it implies an acceptance of the European discourse on race and therefore legitimises it.
30. Louis, 'Post-Race/Post-Politics?', 660.
31. There may have been disagreement about the number of racial categories and about the reasons for the differences between the races. Scientists, however, did not doubt that mankind could be separated into discrete biological categories. More details on this are given in Chapter 1 of this work.
32. Charles W. Mills, '"But What Are You Really?": The Metaphysics of Race', in *Blackness Visible: Essays on Philosophy and Race* (Ithaca, NY: Cornell University Press, 2015), 41. Mills wrote the above quoted line to denounce the invisibility of the topic of race inside contemporary Western philosophy. The question of ignoring it, however, is also crucial for this book.
33. Despite the comment on the temporal focus of this work, it is not possible to entirely escape current societal issues. I will therefore capitalise the racial markers White and Black but use a lowercase letter and quotation marks for racial epithets such as 'yellow' and 'coloured'.
34. For details on the impact of the Wilsonian rhetoric on Asia, Africa and the Middle East, see Urs Matthias Zachmann, ed., *Asia after Versailles: Asian Perspectives on the Paris Peace Conference and the Interwar Order, 1919–33* (Edinburgh: Edinburgh University Press, 2017). Also see Erez Manela, *The Wilsonian Moment: Self-Determination and the International Origins of Anticolonial Nationalism* (Oxford: Oxford University Press, 2007).
35. Manela, *The Wilsonian Moment*, 9.
36. For the technological development of Japan, see Tessa Morris-Suzuki, *The Technological Transformation of Japan: From the Seventeenth to the Twenty-First Century* (Cambridge: Cambridge University Press, 1994).
37. The standard of civilisation and its relationship with race will be further discussed in Chapter 3 of this work. For details on the general working process of the standard, see Gerrit W. Gong, *The Standard of 'Civilization' in International Society* (Oxford: Clarendon Press, 1984).
38. Antony Anghie, 'Francisco De Vitoria and the Colonial Origins of International

Law', *Social & Legal Studies* 5, no. 3 (September 1996): 333. Also see Brett Bowden, 'The Colonial Origins of International Law. European Expansion and the Classical Standard of Civilization', *Journal of the History of International Law* 7 (January 2005): 23.

39. Stefan Tanaka, *Japan's Orient: Rendering Pasts into History* (Berkeley: University of California Press, 1993), 3.
40. Joseph M. Henning, *Outposts of Civilization: Race, Religion, and the Formative Years of American-Japanese Relations* (New York: New York University Press, 2000), 137.
41. Fredrickson, *White Supremacy*, xi.
42. Ibid.
43. Marilyn Lake and Henry Reynolds, *Drawing the Global Colour Line: White Men's Countries and the International Challenge of Racial Equality* (Cambridge: Cambridge University Press, 2008), 3.
44. For the history of Japanese colonialism, see Ramon Hawley Myers and Mark R. Peattie, *The Japanese Colonial Empire, 1895–1945* (Princeton, NJ: Princeton University Press, 1984).
45. See Carol Gluck, 'Re-Présenter Meiji', in *La nation en marche: Études sur le Japon impérial de Meiji*, ed. Jean-Jacques Tschudin and Claude Hamon (Paris: Philippe Picquier, 2007), 9–40.
46. Henning, *Outposts of Civilization*, 5.
47. Charles W. Mills, *The Racial Contract* (Ithaca, NY: Cornell University Press, 1997), 3.
48. Ibid., 11.
49. Ibid., 13.
50. Ibid., 14.
51. Ibid., 127.
52. See ibid.
53. Ibid.
54. The following list is not exhaustive but it does contain major works that help to understand the significance of race inside Japanese history: Oguma Eiji, *A Genealogy of 'Japanese' Self-Images*, trans. David Askew (Melbourne: Trans Pacific Press, 2002); Frank Dikötter, ed., *The Construction of Racial Identities in China and Japan* (Hong Kong: Hong Kong University Press, 1997); Michael Keevak, *Becoming Yellow: A Short History of Racial Thinking* (Princeton, NJ: Princeton University Press, 2011); Michael Weiner, *Race and Migration in Imperial Japan* (London: Routledge, 1994); Richard Siddle, *Race, Resistance, and the Ainu of Japan* (London: Routledge, 1996); Rotem Kowner and Walter Demel, *Race and Racism in Modern East Asia: Western and Eastern Constructions* (Leiden: Brill, 2013); Rotem Kowner, '"Lighter than Yellow, but not Enough": Western Discourse on the Japanese "Race", 1854–1904', *The Historical Journal* 43, no. 1 (2000): 103–31; Takezawa Yasuko, ed., *Jinshu gainen no fuhensei o tou: Seiyōteki paradaimu o koete* (Tokyo: Jimbunshoin, 2005); Tessa Morris-Suzuki, *Re-Inventing Japan: Time, Space, Nation* (New York: M. E. Sharpe, 1998); Urs Matthias Zachmann, 'Race Without Supremacy: On Racism in the Political Discourse of Late Meiji Japan, 1890–1912', in *Racism in*

the Modern World: Historical Perspectives on Cultural Transfer and Adaptation, ed. Manfred Berg and Simon Wendt (New York: Berghahn Books, 2011), 255–79.

55. Rotem Kowner, 'Between Contempt and Fear: Western Racial Constructions of East Asians since 1800', in *Race and Racism in Modern East Asia*, 90.
56. Ibid.
57. Sidney L. Gulick, *Evolution of the Japanese: Social and Psychic* (New York: Fleming H. Revell, 1903), 25. Also cited in Henning, *Outposts of Civilization*, 146.
58. Michael Weiner, 'The Invention of Identity: Race and Nation in Pre-War Japan', in *The Construction of Racial Identities in China and Japan: Historical and Contemporary Perspectives*, ed. Frank Dikötter (Hong Kong: Hong Kong University Press, 1997), 110. In the same vein, Yukiko Koshiro does mention a 'double racial consciousness': one as equals to Whites and one as superiors to Asians. See Yukiko Koshiro, *Trans-Pacific Racisms and the U.S. Occupation of Japan* (New York: Columbia University Press, 1999).
59. Michael Weiner, 'The Invention of Identity', 110.
60. More details can be found in Chapter 1.
61. Weiner, 'The Invention of Identity', 110.
62. The influence of Mill's *Racial Contract* on the idea of the Racial Middle Ground is evident and I gladly acknowledge my debt to his work. As he did, I chose to capitalise Racial Middle Ground when referring to the theory of a negotiation space, and not to capitalise it when referring to the negotiation space itself. Readers familiar with historical studies on the North American continent will have recognised the similarities in name and essence between the Racial Middle Ground and historian Richard White's work on the interactions between North American natives and European settlers. White described his idea of a 'place in between' for the accommodation of the respective needs of the native population of the North American continent and various European settler groups around the Great Lakes as a 'Middle Ground'. See Richard White, *The Middle Ground: Indians, Empires, and Republics in the Great Lakes Region, 1650–1815*, 2nd ed. (New York: Cambridge University Press, 2011), xxvi. While White is primarily concerned with cultural exchange, his idea of a 'place in between' strongly influenced my idea of the Racial Middle Ground.
63. The already mentioned *Outposts of Civilization* by Henning is probably the most sophisticated study in this regard. Explaining a process similar to the one described in this book, Henning concluded that to accommodate the Japanese anomaly, 'many analysts pushed' the categories of Anglo-Saxon and Christian 'to their limits and resorted to intellectual contortions . . . Instead of accepting Japan as a modern power that disproved these beliefs, they stretched the terms "Christian," "Anglo-Saxon," and "white."' Henning, *Outposts of Civilization*, 163–4. While without doubt solid and well-documented, Henning's work is focused on the opinion of American missionaries in Japan, thereby (involuntarily) downplaying the geopolitical importance Japan had gained in the Far East. It was this importance more than anything that led to the renegotiation of the Japanese racial identity and also to concrete results and gains. The importance of what I called the 'race at the bottom' in the negotiation

process is also missing, as well as the distinction between Japan as a nation and the Japanese as individuals. My research therefore could be said to add additional layers to that of Henning. Gerhard Krebs is another scholar who described a nuanced view of the Japanese race in the context of the relations between Japan and Nazi Germany. See Gerhard Krebs, 'Racism under Negotiation: The Japanese Race in the Nazi-German Perspective', in *Race and Racism in Modern East Asia: Interactions, Nationalism, Gender and Lineage*, ed. Rotem Kowner and Walter Demel (Leiden: Brill, 2015). Rotem Kowner used the clever formula 'lighter than yellow but not enough' to describe the racial identity of the Japanese. However, here, too, it is implied that there was a hierarchy in which the Japanese could be but one thing at a time: White or something darker. See Kowner, '"Lighter than Yellow, but not Enough"', 103–31.

64. Outside the realm of academic research on Japan, one of the earliest utterances of fluid racial identities can be found in Frantz Fanon's *Black Skin, White Masks* (1952). Fanon's analysis, however, strongly posits a dichotomy between the Black and the White race, without accommodating space in the middle. See Frantz Fanon, *Peau noire, masques blancs* (Paris: Éditions du Seuil, 2015). Related to Fanon's work, there have been attempts to articulate the notion of a space in the middle – albeit not restricted to race but also encompassing notions of culture and identity – in the field of postcolonial studies. Homi K. Bhabha formulated his idea of 'interstices' as '"in-between spaces"' that offer a 'terrain for elaborating strategies of selfhood . . . that initiate new signs of identity, and innovative sites of collaboration, and contestation, in the act of defining the idea of society itself'. Homi K. Bhabha, *The Location of Culture*, 2nd ed. (London: Routledge, 2004), 2. Bhabha's approach cannot be separated from a certain notion of antagonism materialised as an asymmetrical relationship between two sides with clearly defined roles: oppressor and oppressed. This makes fitting the Japanese of the turn of the twentieth century inside Bhabha's interstices or mimicries difficult: it is problematic to set Japan on either the oppressing or the oppressed side, because from the 1890s onwards the Japanese were both at the same time. Other ideas of a race in the middle were expressed in scholarly works on the North and South American continents. See for example Ignatiev, *How the Irish Became White*; Sarah C. Chambers, 'Little Middle Ground: The Instability of a Mestizo Identity in the Andes, Eighteenth and Nineteenth Centuries', in *Race and Nation in Modern Latin America*, ed. Nancy P. Appelbaum, Anne S. Macpherson and Karin A. Rosemblatt (Chapel Hill: University of North Carolina Press, 2003).

65. For details, see for example Roger Daniels, 'Japanese Immigrants on a Western Frontier: The Issei in California, 1890–1940', in *East across the Pacific: Historical and Sociological Studies of Japanese Immigration and Assimilation*, ed. Hilary Conroy and T. Scott Miyakawa (Santa Barbara, CA: American Bibliographical Center-Clio Press, 1972).

66. The relevance of the United States for Japan goes well beyond the period immediately after the Russo-Japanese War. As the main Western enemy during the Pacific War and as the main occupational force in Japan because of this war, the importance of the United States as a reference point, be it as an enemy or an ally, cannot be

overstated. Readers interested in the continuous relationship between the Japanese and the Americans and the geopolitical ramifications of this relationship, as well as in the continuous importance of race inside of it, can consult Dower's two classic studies on the subject: John W. Dower, *War Without Mercy: Race and Power in the Pacific War* (New York: Pantheon Books, 1986); John W. Dower, *Embracing Defeat: Japan in the Wake of World War II* (New York: W. W. Norton & Co., 1999).

67. For the evolution of the United States as a power in the East and its confrontation with Japan, see Akira Iriye, *Pacific Estrangement: Japanese and American Expansion, 1897–1911* (Cambridge, MA: Harvard University Press, 1972); LaFeber, *The Clash*; Yamamuro Shin'ichi, *Fukugō sensō to sōryokusen no dansō: Nihon ni totte no daiichiji sekai taisen* (Tokyo: Jinbun shoin, 2011); Akira Iriye, 'Kyōsō aite Nihon: Sen happyaku kyūjūgo nen kara sen kyūyaku jūnana nen', in *Nihon to Amerika: Aite koku no imēji kenkyū*, ed. Hidetoshi Katō and Kamei Shunsuke (Tokyo: Nihon gakujutsu shinkōkai, 1993).

68. See the excellent study Eiichiro Azuma, *Between Two Empires: Race, History, and Transnationalism in Japanese America* (New York: Oxford University Press, 2005).

69. For research on the topic, see for example Reginald Kearney, *African American Views of the Japanese: Solidarity or Sedition?* (Albany: State University of New York Press, 1998); Yuichiro Onishi, *Transpacific Antiracism: Afro-Asian Solidarity in Twentieth-Century Black America, Japan, and Okinawa* (New York: New York University Press, 2013); David Wright, 'The Use of Race and Racial Perceptions among Asians and Blacks: The Case of the Japanese and African Americans', *Hitotsubashi Journal of Social Studies* 30, no. 2 (1998): 135–52; Yukiko Koshiro, 'Beyond an Alliance of Color: The African American Impact on Modern Japan', *positions: East Asia Cultures Critique* 11, no. 1 (Spring 2003); Ikuko Asaka, '"Colored Men of the East": African Americans and the Instability of Race in US-Japan Relations', *American Quarterly* 66, no. 4 (December 2014): 971–97; Marc Gallicchio, *The African American Encounter with Japan & China: Black Internationalism in Asia, 1895–1945* (Chapel Hill: University of North Carolina Press, 2000). Onishi's work is an exception as it does also include the Japanese side, but it is focused on the period after the First World War.

Part I: Race in the Japanese Context: Early Modern Patterns of Differentiation and the Introduction of Race in Modern Japan

Chapter 1

Patterns of Differentiation in Early Modern Japan

The practice of differentiating between individuals is a feature that knows neither spatial nor temporal limitations. With the organisation of human beings into societies came the development of oppositional relationships: there have been leaders and followers, rulers and ruled, worldly and spiritual authorities, those who owned the land and those who worked on it. There have been those who possessed social, economic and political capital, and those who did not. According to the context, the reasons why these relationships developed and were sustained varied greatly. Often, further differentiation occurred inside differentiation. For example, wielding a sword or a plough was not the only determining factor, but also if one was a man or a woman, or if one believed in one religion or the other. From the seventeenth century onwards, differentiation based on race was added to the equation.[1]

Being part of one group – whatever the group and the criteria for being included were – had a dual effect: it meant simultaneously belonging but also estrangement. At the risk of taking away the complexity from the matter, when the inclusion in or exclusion from a group entailed unequal treatment (in reference to other groups), then one talks not only of differentiation but also of discrimination. The simultaneous existence of several patterns of differentiation inside a given society makes the analysis of discrimination a convoluted undertaking, in which defining the concepts one uses becomes of crucial importance. An enquiry into Japanese history is no exception. Certainly, as in every society, there have been instances of economic, social, gender and racial discrimination. Equally certain, it is often difficult to distinguish between these, as the ways in which these occurred often overlapped. Yet, it is possible to do so, with the prerogative, however, to conceptually frame the object of enquiry. Not doing so invites the hazard of wrongly ascribing peculiar types of discriminations to the wrong causes.

Exemplary of this problem is the attribution of a racist character to the society of Tokugawa Japan. Historian Herman Ooms, for example, asserted the existence of an 'intra-race racism' aimed at the *eta* and *hinin* outcasts and fostered by the authorities.[2] The cultural anthropologist Takezawa Yasuko argued in a similar vein that these groups were at the margins of the Tokugawa society and were victims of racial discrimination.[3] The aim of present chapter is twofold: first, it enquires as to whether the argument of race in early modern Japan can hold up a conceptual scrutiny. Second, it presents alternatives which acknowledge the existence of societal differentiation in the period but which are situated outside the paradigm of race. Tokugawa Japan was not lacking in this regard: from the influence of Neo-Confucianism that dictated proper relations, to gender relations that envisioned women as inherently different from men, equality was hardly the norm in early modern Japan.

On the existence of race in early modern Japan

Despite the apparent remoteness of the concept of race from seventeenth-century Japan, it does not seem odd that scholars have tried to apply it to the Tokugawa societal system. The existence of harsh laws which specifically targeted outcasts does indeed point to the existence of systematic prejudice.[4] The fact that these individuals are described as outcasts itself already hints at an exclusion from 'regular' society. It is this assumption of a worse treatment than other members of the society that led some scholars to posit the existence of racial discrimination in Tokugawa Japan. Quoting a study of the Indian caste system, Ooms writes that '*all* systems of birth-ascribed stratification seem to include a claim that the social differences are reflected in biological (i.e. "racial") differences'.[5] For him, this applies to the outcasts as 'although the kawata[6] are indistinguishable from other Japanese, explicitly *racial* theories, which *differentiate*, and *racist* theories, which *discriminate*, have developed' to explain 'the origin of the kawata in order to justify discriminatory practices against them'.[7] The lack of distinguishing physical features and the 'construction of a racial theory' lead Ooms to envision a 'particular kind of intra-race racism, one based exclusively on descent'.[8]

Takezawa states that 'the theory of the alien racial origin of the burakumin can be found in pre-modern (medieval and early modern) literature' and there exist 'historical sources indicating the subsequent institutionalization of discrimination in statuary form by the sixteenth century'.[9] Takezawa framed this argument within her own understanding of race that she labelled 'race in the lower case'. It is worth quoting to some length, as it exemplifies the pitfalls of trying to retroactively apply the concept of race to history: Cases she refers to as 'race in the lower case' are,

> cases where differences observed in a particular society between socially differentiated groups are understood as those that are inherited over generations and cannot be changed (or easily changed) by the environment. These differences are represented in political, economic and social institutions accompanied by a clear hierarchy, and manifest an exclusive nature . . . 'race' is not a concept reducible to an 'ethnic group' or an 'other' defined by prejudice. Institutional changes in economics, religion, and politics come to mind as the main causes which transform prejudice into race accompanied by institutionalized discrimination.[10]

The major problem this understanding produces is that by applying it, possibly all social taxonomies can be said to be racial in nature. Socially significant differentiations based on gender and class, for example, also occur after a certain level of social stratification, and are influenced by political, religious or economic change. A clear hierarchy as well as the exclusion of the 'other' are present in both.[11] The exclusion of women from sacred places (*nyonin kinsei*) in the Tokugawa period is telling in this regard. Miyazaki Fumiko has documented that before 1872 female pilgrims were all, with some temporary exceptions, banned from sacred mountains without regards to their social status.[12] In the case of Mt Fuji for example, women could not access most climbing routes and hence neither the sacred places along them.[13] While the origin of the exclusion of women from sacred sites is uncertain, Miyazaki surmises that it was based on primarily religious concerns: the spread of the Blood Pond Sutra (*ketsubonkyō*) from the fourteenth century onwards strengthened the notion that women were polluted because they sullied sacred objects with bloodshed during their menstruation and childbirth.[14]

Pollution notwithstanding, economic incentives led to the readjustment of *nyonin kinsei* in the latter half of the Tokugawa period. After the *bakufu*[15] had relaxed travel restrictions for commoners, an increasing number of people (including women) went on pilgrimages to sacred places. In response, religious authorities in Yoshida (situated on the northern route to Mt Fuji) petitioned the *bakufu* office in charge of religious affairs to lessen the restrictions concerning female pilgrimage to sacred places. The incentives lying behind the petition were purely economic: the local religious authorities earned a substantial part or their income from the fees pilgrims had to pay for entering sacred places, for accommodation and for guidance. Offerings from pilgrims could not be overlooked either. Finally, local residents received their share too, as they provided clothing and food to the travellers.[16]

The *nyonin kinsei* gives us a representative example of the institutionalised discrimination of a particular group of people believed to have inheritable characteristics. Religious beliefs and social practices relegated them to the bottom of a hierarchy. However, economic, religious and political factors could influence their status. If one follows Takezawa's definition of 'race' cited above, then women in the Tokugawa period were a separate race and victims of racial discrimination. Ooms would probably agree to this approach, when he states that 'racism reveals the quintessential operations of the ascription of any inherent inequalities, such as those that prevailed in a "society of orders" like Tokugawa Japan'. Racism is therefore not 'a particular variety of discrimination; rather, all forms of discrimination produce effects like those of racism'.[17]

Both Takezawa's and Ooms's approaches are contemporary and common in the social sciences: they reduce alleged inherent characteristics (to avoid using the term 'biological') to social facts. What matters, then, is how alleged characteristics from a specific group are being perceived and acted upon by society, not if these characteristics truly exist or not. In this sense, one would not even need 'race' to have 'racism' and, as Ooms has argued, then 'all forms of discrimination produce effects like those of racism'.[18] Yet, the same is true for sexism or class discrimination. This very similarity between the effects of different types of discrimination is the reason why it is necessary to differentiate between them. As Fredrickson wrote, 'ideologies have content, and it is necessary to distinguish racist ideologies from other belief systems that emphasize human differences and can be used as rationalizations of inequality'.[19] If we then decide to look at the content of the ideology that was directed against early modern outcasts, the ascription of a racist nature to their differentiation becomes questionable.

An ideology of racism directed against outcasts would rest on following three requirements: that there existed a concept of race in the Tokugawa period; that individuals inside Tokugawa society identified themselves and others using this concept; and, finally, that outcasts were discriminated against because of their race while other members of Tokugawa society were not. The first one depends on which definition of race one uses. The sociological approach briefly described above is the result of a long quest to demystify the scientific validity of race that started in the 1930s.[20] However, while this approach is undeniably appropriate for contemporary issues of discrimination, its value for a historical perspective remains questionable, for while science today has enabled scientists to invalidate any scientific claims to race, the science from the seventeenth to the nineteenth century had done exactly the contrary.

The geopolitical repercussions of the meeting between European explorers and natives from the 'New World' have been described in the introduction of this book. Added to these, the meetings between different people had enormous scientific implications. The cascade of information brought back by the explorers eroded the foundations of uncertain medieval world views and led to the necessity of a renewed classification of mankind.[21] The first influential step was made by Swedish Botanist Carl von Linné (1707–78) who in 1735 presented a racial taxonomy of men in his *Systema Naturae*. Linné saw mankind divided into four races: Asians, Africans, Europeans and Americans (Native Americans). More important than his classification was his ascribing of inherent characteristics to each race: Africans were childlike and lazy, Asians greedy, Native Americans hot-tempered, and Europeans were civilised, intelligent and governed by law, not passion.[22] A hierarchy of races was now available, in which each race had distinct inherent and inheritable characteristics.

Other scientists produced their own racial division of the world, such as the French naturalist George-Louis Leclerc, Comte de Buffon (1707–88) in his *Histoire naturelle, générale et particulière*. Buffon was dubious of Linné's classification but agreed that there were differences between men and that Europeans were superior.[23] German physicist and anatomist Johann Friedrich von Blumenbach (1752–1840) extended Linné's classification and contributed in a significant way to the racial thinking of the time with his *De generis humani varietate nativa* (1775): in it he coined the terms 'Caucasian' and 'Mongolian' and explicitly lumped Japanese and Chinese together into the latter category.[24]

He also surmised that the 'Mongolians' had degenerated from the Caucasians and were now on the same level as Africans.[25] The question of whether it is possible to define the above-presented classifications as biological determinism is an ongoing debate. So is the correctness of seeing the creators of said classifications as the founders of scientific racism.[26] Such reflections seem secondary, however, when considering the already described geopolitical consequences of the Age of Exploration. There was no need for a scientific racism to ascribe inherent characteristics to native people that justified their submission in the eyes of European settlers. The same is true for the enslavement of Africans.

As the national heterogeneity of the individuals referred to above attests, classifying mankind had been an international venture. The shared experience of exploiting non-Whites and the successful international project of creating a White race whose members were bounded by their skin colour rather than by their nationality had transcended national borders. As Michael Keevak wrote, the taxonomies almost always implied that 'the European race, whether or not it was specifically identified as white, represented the highest or most civilized or most perfect human form'.[27]

The implications of the concept as developed by the scientists were in some regards similar to our present understanding of it, such as a dichotomic nature and its use as a legitimisation for power relations. However, it was still an entirely different concept due to its existence in a specific context. When looking at the race relations of a certain time, it is therefore necessary to apply the meaning that race had at that time and place. Which leads us to the Tokugawa period. For the longest part of the period there existed a 'scientifically' defined notion of race outside of the Japanese intellectual realm. Mentions of race in this context cannot ignore this point. As much as it would be problematic to call the early modern Japanese explorers in Ezo (nowadays Hokkaidō) 'conquistadors' or the European medieval knights 'bushi', labelling Tokugawa patterns of differentiation with the word 'race' can hardly be justified. It could be argued that reducing race to a category based on biological factors is too narrow, and for contemporary social issues this critique would be valid. Yet, until the second half of the twentieth century, that is exactly what race was. And, as Hannaford claimed, if it is difficult to legitimately speak of racism before the clear conceptual definition of race in the seventeenth century, then it is not difficult to acknowledge that seeking racial discrimination in a society where the concept did not even exist (while it existed elsewhere) is a misleading endeavour.[28]

The second requirement for an ideology of racism directed against outcasts is the self-identification of individuals within Tokugawa society with a racial identity. Race is not a one-sided concept, having at the same time an exclusionary but also an inclusionary function. As Miles exemplifies in a Black/White dichotomy, defining a group as 'White' automatically implies the creation of an 'other' that lacks the quality of being White. The same thing occurs by reversing the process: if the 'other' is deemed different because he is Black, the implicit assumption is that the 'self' is different because he lacks the characteristic of being Black. Thus, 'where ego identifies alter as a member of a particular "race" . . . ego is also engaged in a process of self-identification as a member of another "race"'.[29] In other words, there cannot be a racial 'other' if there is no racial 'self'.

This is where it becomes challenging to apply the idea of race to outcasts, as their differential treatment in the Tokugawa period did not lead to the strengthening of a collective racial identity of the differentiating side, foremost because no such identity existed in the first place. As David L. Howell reminds us, at the time 'social taxonomy was driven principally by occupation rather than some immutable characteristics such as heredity'.[30] The existence of race and of an 'intra-race racism' would entail that outcasts, as a peculiar race, were opposed to other racial groups inside early modern Japanese society. Which in turn would lead to the understanding that members of the remaining status groups saw themselves as having a distinct racial origin too. If 'outcast' was a race, then 'warrior', 'peasant' and 'townspeople' were races too.

If, for the sake of argument, one accepts the idea that status groups were indeed racial groups, it remains to be seen if outcasts were the sole object of a discriminatory treatment rooted in their origins. This is the third premise for the existence of a racist ideology in Tokugawa times. Both Ooms and Takezawa provided examples of the legal differentiation of outcasts and pointed to these as proof for their discrimination. However, focusing on these sources invites the danger of ignoring the fact that the differential treatment of individuals was the norm inside Tokugawa society. As a Japanese authority on the subject put it succinctly: 'Discrimination (*sabetsu*) was the principle behind all social organization in early modern Japan; equality was seen as neither natural nor proper.'[31] The societal organisation of early modern Japan was intrinsically unequal in character, a fact that was true not only for inter-status group relations but also for relations inside the status groups as well. Saitō Yōichi and Ōishi Shinzaburō go as far as to write that,

> more than the differences between the different status groups, the singularity of the Edo period status system was the strong inequality between the ranks inside the status groups. There existed huge differences in rank among the *samurai*, the peasants and the townsmen. In this sense, the Edo period was a society of 'total discrimination' (*sōsabetsu no shakai*).[32]

When Tokugawa Ieyasu (1543–1616) established his *bakufu* in 1603, he had to build its foundations on the unpredictable terrain of loyalty between lord and retainer. Fully aware that loyalty was elusive as the wind, he sought to make treason an intolerable act partly by fostering the moral edification of his subjects.[33] Song Confucianism provided a good start. The teachings of the Southern Song philosopher Zhu Xi (1130–1200) for example, advocated self-cultivation, which was tied to moral discipline and learning. Central to this self-cultivation were the Five Relationships – between ruler and minister (lord and retainer), parent and child, husband and wife, older brother and younger brother, and between friends.[34]

The Confucian relationships were more than mere principles. These were seen as the natural law of things and as such had to be observed to avoid the collapse of society into chaos. The *Book of Changes* (*Yijin*) for example admonished: 'Heaven above, the lake below . . . Thus, the superior man discriminates between high and low, and thereby fortifies the thinking of the people.'[35] According to Confucian ideology then, asymmetrical relationships between humans were the proper way of things. This view was also advanced by Hayashi Razan (1583–1657), a neo-Confucian scholar and advisor to Ieyasu:

> It accords with the proper rules [*rei*] of heaven and earth that heaven is above and the earth below. Man is born with the proper rules of heaven and earth in his heart, so there is rank (high and low) and order (first and last) in all things. If we extend this spirit throughout heaven and earth, there will be no disorder between ruler and subject, high and low, or in any human relationship.[36]

While Confucian teachings clearly were but one tool used by the Tokugawa to assert their power, they did offer an ideological framework in which everyone had their proper place. Accordingly, keeping one's attributed place meant preserving the natural order of things, while not doing so meant threatening it, a thought that offered legitimacy and security to Tokugawa rule.[37]

However, ideology was evidently not enough, and the 'natural' order of things had to be preserved through more tangible measures. The long-standing peace initiated by the unification of the country under Tokugawa rule enabled the flourishing of commerce. Merchants, living in growing cities prospered and started to behave and consume in ways deemed inconsistent with their status. These challenges to the social order led to the promulgation of sumptuary regulations to all classes (*ken'yakurei*) that forbade the wearing of 'extravagant' clothes.[38] The prohibition of clothes might seem trivial, but it is important to remember that clothing was one of the only immediate visible markers (alongside hairstyle) of social standing. The social 'other' was not visible as such and therefore had to be made apparent.[39] Peasants did not fare substantially better regarding their legal treatment, as epitomised by the famous statement by a *bakufu* official 'sesame seeds and peasants are very much alike. The more you squeeze them, the more you can extract from them.'[40] They too saw their lifestyle restricted by sumptuary laws, as they had to focus on their work as food providers for the other status groups. Ordinary farmers had to wear cotton as silk was forbidden to them. Horse-riding was prohibited, and their diet was to consist of grains and as little rice as possible. Even the size of their housing was fixed by law.[41]

While at the top of the hierarchy in terms of social prestige, the warrior status group may indeed have been the most unequal: everything regarding their behaviour, clothing and even their resting place during audiences in Edo castle was defined by their income. The domains with the highest income were those wielding 500,000 *koku* and amounted to a mere seven houses out of the roughly 266 from the mid-nineteenth century. This means that the wealth and power of the warriors was in the hands of 2.6 per cent of them.[42] Conversely, some of the outcasts, as leather suppliers, benefited from their close relationship with the warrior elite and were able to accumulate considerably more wealth than some of their patrons.[43]

The brief description above shows that differentiation between and inside the status groups was an integral part of the Tokugawa order. In this sense, the treatment of outcasts, while certainly harsh, was in essence not different from that of the other status groups. This also begs the question of the appropriateness of the word 'discrimination' when referring to said treatment, for if everything was discriminatory, in the end, nothing was. And while differentiation (inter- and intra-status groups) between individuals was omnipresent, it was not based on biological or ethnic factors, but on occupational differences that were fostered by social and political incentives and made tangible through specific legislation. John Whitney Hall's classic categorisation of Tokugawa society as a 'container society' is helpful here: According to Hall, the individual was confined into social containers which limited his free will, but at the same time protected him by 'limiting the arbitrary exercise of authority upon him'.[44] The outcast 'container' was certainly the target of harsh legislation and societal pressure, but it also guaranteed a certain degree of legal protection, as well as a specific role inside society. In the words of Hall, 'rule by status assured an equality of treatment under law appropriate to the status of each individual'.[45]

If we go back to the three requirements necessary for applying the idea of racism to the Tokugawa period – the existence of race, the self-identification with race, and the discrimination of outcasts based on race – it must be acknowledged that too many contextual and conceptual hurdles stand in our way. The simultaneous existence of a well-defined concept of race in the emerging European nations makes a direct comparison with Tokugawa patterns of differentiation mandatory. Yet, even stretching the meaning of race to force a racial component into the conceptualisation of the status groups is difficult: due to both the exclusionary and inclusionary function of race, describing one status group as a race implies that the other groups were races too. Finally, the omnipresence of differentiation as a pillar of the political and social structure of Tokugawa society calls into question the notion of discrimination itself – racial or not.

This does not mean that a comparison between the concept of race and early modern patterns of differentiation is unreasonable. Quite the contrary, this task is necessary to 'transcend the Western paradigm of race', as originally intended by Takezawa. To that aim, it is more fruitful to momentarily liberate ourselves from the concept of race and examine how exactly 'others' in early modern Japan were constructed and perceived. The status system was but one of many patterns of differentiation. Only by understanding why and how these differed from a racial ideology will it be possible to transcend the Western paradigm.

Confucianism and the 'Middle Kingdom'

The introduction of the concept of race in modern Japan did not occur in a vacuum, nor did race claim an empty space. We have seen that the social differentiation of 'others' (individuals, occupational groups, etc.) in early modern Japan was deeply entrenched in everyday practice. The practice was imbedded in a broader ideological framework that dictated not only societal but also international relations. This ideological framework varied greatly according to the prevalent schools of thoughts in Tokugawa Japan, but the essence remained the same: domestic society as well as the world were divided into hierarchies. As Ronald P. Toby observed, 'Edo-period Japanese, whether of Neoconfucianist or Nativist persuasion, to a greater or lesser extent accepted the idea of a normative hierarchy of peoples, and applied this normative mapping to a Japan-centred perception of the world.'[46]

The importance of Confucian thought with its emphasis on proper relations and as a tool for social regulation has already been mentioned. To this, one can briefly add that Confucian scholars also possessed a Chinese-inspired world view, the Middle Kingdom, which ordered human beings on two levels: a societal level, composed of literates and commoners, and the geographical realms, composed of a civilised centre and layers of barbaric peripheries. The criteria for being part of the first category in both realms were to possess proper rituals and rules of behaviour, as well as erudition in the Confucian classics.[47] Without the knowledge of rituals or the classics, commoners and people living outside the civilised centre needed the intervention of erudite scholars to escape their alleged state of ignorance. This cultural elevation was achieved through 'ritual edification', which was 'centred on making one's activities accord with one's hereditary social-status designation. In short, ritual edification was designed to produce submissive adherence to the existing social hierarchy.'[48]

It is not difficult to notice the similarities between the Confucian-inspired world view and one racial in character: both were simultaneously exclusive and inclusive, and posited a centre (civilisational for the former, racial for the latter). In both instances the centre was superior to the peripheral (biological) 'other'. The origin of the exclusion in both cases, however, hinders us from equating them: with race, the 'other' was discriminated because of alleged inheritable and unchangeable characteristics. Exceptions, such as the one that is the topic of this book, existed, but, as a rule, once categorised into an inferior race, individuals could hardly change their status. In the Sinocentric world view, however, the criteria for being civilised were to possess the right form or knowledge. Something one could, theoretically, learn and internalise. With race then, it mattered who one was; with knowledge, how one behaved.

This distinction is of crucial importance, as it explains why Tokugawa scholars could study Confucianism in the first place. Japanese scholars of Confucianism had to acknowledge that the rituals and classics were of Chinese origin. They could not, however, agree that only the Chinese were able to master them. Nor could they accept the fact that the Japanese were doomed to remain on the barbaric periphery. Indeed, this would have meant more than mere cultural subordination: the acceptance of China as the civilised Middle Kingdom implied the acceptance of the country as a political centre.[49] This world view was pivotal to China's foreign relations, and a strict adherence to it would have made Japan a tributary state to the Middle Kingdom.[50] Consequently, Japanese Confucians had to separate the centre of civilisation from China to either universalise it or claim it for Japan.[51]

The most legitimate (and straightforward) manner to do this was to look for confirmation in the classics themselves. Wakabayashi has shown that the scholar Itō Jinsai (1627–1705), for example, followed liberal interpretations of passages from Confucius's *Analects* to underscore Japanese claims to cultural achievements with the authority of Confucius himself, and thereby managed to displace the centre of civilisation from China to Japan.[52] These were, in the words of Wakabayashi, 'amazing philological acrobatics'.[53] Yet, they exemplify that Japanese Confucianists were able to adapt the Chinese idea of a Middle Kingdom in order to escape the subordinate status it implied for Japan. This, in turn, confirms that Tokugawa Confucians could not envision notions of civilisation and barbarism as deterministic. Regardless of how complicated and esoteric the Confucian rituals and classics were, it was possible to learn these.

After these additional details on the Confucian conception of 'otherness', we can turn to an example of differentiation at the societal level.

Gender and equality in early modern Japan

> On the slopes of this mountain, numerous areas are reserved for the practitioners. Hence, it goes without saying that women and other creatures such as cows, cats, monkeys, wild boars, white herons and chickens are warned to keep off . . . This mountain is not a place for women.[54]

This abstract from a pilgrimage guide to Mount Kōya from the year 1672 will surely surprise the reader. But while the equation of women with animals is rightly shocking, the fact that they could be banned from the sacred mountain seems consistent with the logic of the Tokugawa system already discussed in this chapter. The real cause of surprise in the above quote lies less in its content rather than in its scope: it was not some women who were excluded from Mount Kōya, but all women, regardless of status.

In this case, therefore, gender was a factor that transcended status, a distinctiveness that holds true for the whole Tokugawa world order: strictly speaking, in terms of ideology, women were envisioned differently from men regardless of their occupational group. This was a variable that women could seldom choose for themselves, but always stood in relation to a man, be it the father, the husband, or the son. In the words of Laura Nenzi, 'adult women . . . saw the foundation of their identity and the very meaning of their existence summarized, in legal discourse, as their being the dependents of men'.[55]

To understand why women were relegated to the periphery of the Tokugawa order, we have to turn to religious, political and societal factors. Until the last two decades, it was customary to see the Tokugawa period as the darkest period in history for Japanese women. Even in 2001, Mikiso Hane, for example, asserted that 'by the Tokugawa period the status of women, especially upper-class women, had reached is nadir'.[56] The diffusion of Confucianism and Buddhism, as well as the ascendancy of the warrior class in medieval Japan, led to the transformation of the woman from a semi-divine being who was 'brave, strong, intelligent, wise, and clever' in the Yayoi Period to an individual who had 'completely lost her freedom and her rights (marriage, divorce and property rights)' in the Edo period.[57]

Increasingly, this notion has since come under attack and several scholars have convincingly reassessed the position of women in early modern Japan.[58] Whether the examples brought forward in recent scholarship on the topic should be seen as mere exceptions or as the norm remains outside the scope of this study. They show, however, that there often was a discrepancy between the prevalent ideologies and actual social practice. It is indeed hard to deny that at least ideologically, women were seen as peculiar entities, almost always inferior to and in opposition to men. In the Tokugawa period, therefore, there existed a prevalent discourse about women that could or could not, according to the context, have actual influence on the treatment of women in general.

This was certainly the case for issues of immediate concern to the Tokugawa. Neo-Confucian scholars had tied the government to the households in its service inside a 'natural' relationship. The household of the warriors became an extension of the *bakufu*'s authority and, as such, betraying the household head also meant betraying the *bakufu*. As Dan Fenno Henderson wrote, state authority 'was analogous to the authority of the feudal master and also of the father, because the feudal state and the family were the same thing on different levels'.[59] This interconnectedness had also evident consequences for the status of women in both the educational and the legal realm. Women, too, were educated along Confucian lines. And while the inculcation of morality, filial piety and obedience was not restricted to them, as a group women were at the bottom of a hierarchy of obedience. The already-mentioned Five Relationships offered a general framework for submission, but, inside them, women had to submit even more. By following the *sanjū* (Three Followings), a woman was dependent her whole life: as a young girl she submitted to her father, as a wife to her husband, as a widow to her eldest son.[60]

The Confucian education of women in the Tokugawa period was based on moral guides (*jokun*), which young girls would recite and copy to learn the Japanese syllabary.[61] Among those guides, *The Greater Learning for Women* (*Onna daigaku*, written in the eighteenth century) was the most widespread.[62]

The content of the book reflects neo-Confucian concerns with loyalty and filial piety, as well as with a woman's place inside the household:

> It is the chief duty of a girl living in the parental house to practice filial piety. But after marriage, her chief duty is to honour her father-in-law and mother-in-law . . . Never should a woman fail, night and morning, to pay her respects to her father-in-law and mother-in-law. Never should she be remiss in performing any tasks they may require of her.[63]

The text was also quite clear about the role of a wife: 'The way of the woman is to obey her man.'[64]

While in matters of gender and education, the analogy between *bakufu* and household can be observed in the moulding of women into obedient and loyal wives, its implications were also obvious in the legal realm. Since the status of women was inevitably tied to shogunal politics, the legal treatment of women evolved concurrently to political trends.[65] Concerning household matters, the legal treatment of women was consistently worse than that of men. The institution of marriage for example 'had important symbolic significance; it stood for social order, and the relationship between man and wife served as a metaphor for the relationship between governors and governed'.[66] Accordingly, a treason to this institution, mirroring a treason to the state, was seen as a particularly hideous crime and adultery was thus punished with severity. Guilt, however, was closely tied to gender: from medieval times and throughout the Tokugawa period, the crime of adultery was dependent on the marital status of the female involved. An infidel husband could therefore not commit adultery in the legal sense (except if he was to have an affair with a married woman, in which case his crime was committed against the husband of his lover, not his own wife), while an adulterous wife was sentenced to death (as was her lover).[67] A samurai who had been betrayed by his wife had the right to cut down her and her lover on the spot.[68] This right was later extended to commoners as well. As Stanley mentioned, taking revenge on one's adulterous wife was in fact an extension of shogunal authority, with husbands acting as substitutes for the government.[69]

Leaving Confucian thoughts and politics behind, religion was another realm in which women were marginalised because of their alleged inherent flaws. Buddhism, for example, as an ascetic religion that implied restraint from worldly pleasures, was incompatible with women and their 'seductive nature'. According to the Lotus Sutra, women needed to transform themselves into men to achieve salvation.[70] The strong association of women with impurity (because of the blood shed during menstruation and childbirth) gave them the 'privilege' of their very own hell, described in the Blood Bowl Sutra (*Ketsubon kyō*). According to the Sutra, women go to hell because they pollute the earth with their blood, and because they wash their stained clothes in rivers, from which the water was later used to make tea for holy men.[71] This inherent impurity would send them to the Blood Pond filled with menstruation blood, from where they could only reach salvation by reciting the Blood Bowl Sutra.[72]

As with the legal treatment of women, their sacral perception did not distinguish between statuses. In 1821, a temple published the following explanation for the Blood Bowl Sutra:

> All women, even those who are the children of high families, have no faith and conduct no practices, but rather have strong feelings of avarice and jealousy. These sins are thus compounded and become menstrual blood, and every month this flows out, polluting the god of the earth in addition to the spirits of the mountains and rivers. In retribution for this, women are condemned to the Blood Pool Hell.[73]

The above discussion demonstrates that during the Tokugawa period, an ideological discourse encompassing religious, political and social factors constructed the identity 'woman'. This discourse defined them by their quality of not being men, which should remind the reader of Miles's description of the process of racial identity creation mentioned above. Moreover, the characteristics that allegedly defined women were 'natural' (to avoid the use of 'biological') and inheritable. Yet, despite this undeniable similitude, it would be a mistake to ascribe the differentiation of women in early modern Japan to a racial ideology. As Fredrickson has criticised the use of the term 'racism' to characterise biases against gender or sexual orientation, 'usually . . . the act of racializing the Other seizes upon differences that are "ethnic" in some sense'.[74] Women were not seen as 'ethnically' different. But a certain political ideology that emphasised loyalty and obedience differentiated them as an integral part of the household. Religious beliefs, which included contempt for impurity, cemented the idea of women as inherently different.

The case of women gave us the example of differentiation at the societal level. As a last example, it is time to turn to the differentiation of elements situated outside of Tokugawa society.

Hairy barbarians: Ainu, foreigners and Japanese civilisation

The Confucian standard of civilisation described earlier worked well enough as an intellectual exercise inside a circle of scholars. It also served as a regulation mechanism for early modern Japanese society. It was, however, hardly applicable when applied to elements foreign to Tokugawa society. These elements were 'outside' in the sense that, unlike the different status groups or women, they did not directly yield to the political authority of the *bakufu*. To this was added their physical appearance, customs and societal organisation that set them apart from the containers of early modern Japanese society. Yet, setting them apart as 'barbarians' because of their lack of erudition was difficult, as according to the same logic Japanese commoners would have been equally uncivilised.[75]

Therefore, a new standard was applied to foreign elements that 'focused on easily manipulated customs' and in the process made civilisation a 'matter of everyday life'.[76] Interactions between the Japanese and the Ainu[77] exemplify the working of this standard. Inside these, the differentiation of the latter was not only an intellectual exercise, but also an integral part of domain politics.

The existence of the Ainu remained peripheral to the *bakufu* for the greater part of the Tokugawa period. It was for a particular clan, the Matsumae, that they became of crucial importance. The Matsumae domain had a peculiar position inside the *bakufu* structure: situated at the southernmost part of Ezochi (or Ezo; nowadays Hokkaido) and surrounded by poor agricultural land, its existence as a domain did not derive from rice income or from military force as was usually the case. Instead, it drew legitimacy from its geographical location as a frontier domain and subsequent access to trade with the Ainu.[78] Through the latter, the domain could acquire local products that were hardly obtainable outside of Ezochi, such as hawks, eagle feathers and pelts. The Matsumae were granted monopoly on this trade and without it, and by extension without the Ainu, they had no reason for their existence. This made two things crucial for the domain: first, that the Ainu subsisted, and, second, that they retained their 'foreign' characteristics that justified trade with them. This in turn meant emphasising, or as Walker has even suggested, 'manufacturing' the alleged barbaric features of the Ainu.[79]

It is not surprising to observe that these barbaric features were the exact opposite of what Japanese civilisation was supposed to be. The tradition of female tattoos, unkempt hair and unshaved beards, diet (without rice), clothing folded on the left rather than on the right, all these were the visual markers that set the Ainu apart from the Japanese.[80] Conversely, in order to accentuate the alterity of the Ainu, the Matsumae forbade everything that would have made them 'pass' for Japanese: straw raincoats and footwear for example, which were the apparel of Japanese farmers, were prohibited. So too was the use of the Japanese language.[81] In this sense, it did not really matter who the Ainu really were, but how they looked and behaved. This is reminiscent of both the Confucian inspired world view of the Middle Kingdom and the sumptuary regulations presented earlier in this chapter. And, indeed, Matsumae-Ainu relations became a small-scale replica of the Middle Kingdom order, except that the more practical standard of customs and appearances was applied instead of the elitist standard of erudition.

This was not the only resemblance. To symbolise its central status inside the civilisational order, the *bakufu* made 'peripherical' nations enter a tributary relation with it.[82] The Matsumae did the same with the Ainu through the so-called *uymam* ceremonies. These were, depending on the side, interpreted as tributary missions or as simple trading ceremonies. On a yearly basis, Ainu delegations would visit the seat of the Matsumae at Fukuyama Castle to exchange gifts and trade. Yet, as Walker suggested, *uymam* were 'audiences and gifts exchanges that had more political connotations than did simple exchanges of goods'.[83]

These occurred according to a strict protocol which aimed at symbolising the political subordination of the Ainu: Matsumae officials seated on an elevated position, while Ainu elders stayed in an outer chamber and the remaining Ainu stayed at the entrance porch. Likewise, Matsumae weapons and armour were arranged in the audience chamber as a display of military power.[84]

The differentiation of the Ainu as well as their theatrical subordination were therefore decisive factors for the political and economic structure of the Matsumae domain. That the characteristics which made them barbarians were arbitrary and not inherited is only confirmed by the ease with which the *bakufu* replaced them in later years. When the central government assumed control over Ezochi in the nineteenth century, it launched a strict policy of assimilation to turn the Ainu into Japanese. This entailed reversing exactly those features and practices that the Matsumae officials had fostered to reinforce Ainu alterity: the Ainu now had to shave and cut their hair, fold their clothes the 'right' way and use Japanese as their official language.[85] This shows not only the artificiality of 'Ainu barbarism' but also that, as Tessa Morris-Suzuki has suggested, 'Japaneseness' was not 'a matter of race or inheritance, but something which could be acquired by the adoption of the "right" customs'.[86]

The Tokugawa government took a similar approach to that of the Matsumae in its dealings with the Ryūkyū Kingdom (nowadays Okinawa Prefecture). Initially an independent kingdom tributary of China, it was invaded by the Satsuma domain in 1609 and became a tributary to both Satsuma and the *bakufu*. As with the *uymam* ceremony in the case of the Ainu, the importance of tribute missions from Ryūkyū were their symbolic meaning as a representation of the submission of a foreign power by the Japanese authorities.[87] The Tokugawa therefore insisted that the members of the tribute mission looked as foreign as possible.[88] Again, the crucial matter for the *bakufu* was not the foreignness of the Ryūkyū people per se, but their foreign appearance.

While the otherness of both the Ainu and the people from the Ryūkyū kingdom were necessary for political purposes and thus consciously emphasised, some elements that came into contact with Japan from the sixteenth century onwards were so drastically different that no doubts could remain concerning their alterity. The arrival of Europeans in 1543 deeply impacted the Japanese interpretation of the outside world. The 'Iberian eruption', as Toby has labelled it, made the reappraisal of the hitherto common and now obsolete cosmology of *sangoku* (three realms)[89] necessary. Missionaries, soldiers and traders from Portugal, Spain and Holland became an ordinary sight in Japan's port cities. This also gave Japanese artists the opportunity to depict these foreigners, and their work remains a useful source to investigate how early modern Japanese envisioned people from the West.

Interestingly, Europeans were quickly interpreted inside the same framework as other foreign elements. Keiko Suzuki has shown that at the popular level of *ukiyo-e* (woodblock prints), Westerners were included in the category of *tōjin*, which, originally designating Tang Chinese, evolved over time to form 'a general category of foreigner that included both Westerners and non-Westerners'.[90] There was a certain derogatory notion to the term: a *tōjin* denotated a simple-minded person (and could also be applied to Japanese), whereas a *kettōjin* (hairy *tōjin*) was used to disparage foreigners specifically because of their facial pilosity.[91] On *ukiyo-e* prints, a curious blend of attributes was used to standardise foreignness: Korean and Chinese envoys wore Iberian plum hats and frilled collars and spotted beards. Chinese palaces could be represented with Western architectural elements and with a Dutch flag floating above. Even the Ainu were sometimes depicted with Iberian shirts.[92] Japanese artists therefore depicted Europeans in the same framework already used to represent the foreignness of elements living outside the Tokugawa sphere of control. In this sense, Europeans were not seen as particularly different from other foreigners and were quickly incorporated into well-known tropes of difference.[93]

The first chapter of this book was centred on the question of the existence of race in early modern Japan. Political incentives had led to the separation of the society into distinct status groups. Due to the 'ethnical' homogeneity of the groups, the authorities had to artificially create differences to identify the social 'other' and to confine him to a certain function. Clothing and hairstyles thus became the most convenient and important outward markers of social belonging, and it is on them, not on any 'biological' features, that differentiation was based.

A few alternatives were given to counter the narrative of racial identities in Tokugawa Japan. First was an overarching ideological framework that divided the world into civilised and barbarians, in which the defining criteria was erudition in the Confucian classics and knowledge of the proper rituals. Then there was the complicated case of gender. Morris-Suzuki argues that the 'sharpest line of exclusion' in Tokugawa times was 'directed not at "foreigners" as such, but at Christianity'.[94] But, in fact, it was probably women who were, ideologically speaking, most targeted by exclusion. The 'problem' of Christianity could be resolved by means of apostasy. And even if the descendants of former Christians were monitored for several generations, the belief in the Christian doctrine was not seen as something inherent.[95] Likewise, Christian faith as such was not the problem but rather the political and ideological threat it could represent. The identity of 'woman', on the other hand, was an issue that had deep roots in political and religious thought. Through this, women were created as the opposite of men and relegated to an inferior role inside society.

Lastly, the interpretation of elements foreign to Tokugawa society was briefly explained. The Matsumae domain fostered the differentiation of the Ainu to create a negative of Japanese civilisation: Ainu hairstyles and clothing, diet, dwellings and language were seen as markers of barbarity. That the *bakufu* chose and 'corrected' those very markers for its assimilation policy once again underlines the artificiality and shallowness of the factors that drove social distinction in early modern Japan. The same holds true for the otherness of people from the Ryūkyū Kingdom. Europeans, despite their radical alterity, were incorporated alongside other non-Japanese elements. The different patterns of differentiation in early modern Japan had in common that they were created and maintained through the political authority that derived from the Tokugawa.[96] This would change after an epistemological turn occurred in Meiji-Japan, which would supplant ancient notions of civilisation and barbarism with the introduction of a world view based on race.

Notes

1. For the timeless rejection of an 'other' from any given community, see for example Immanuel Wallerstein, 'Universalisme, racisme, sexisme: les tensions idéologiques du capitalisme', in *Race, nation, classe: Les identités ambiguës*, ed. Étienne Balibar and Immanuel Wallerstein (Paris: La Découverte, 1997), 42–53. Also see the first chapter of Lauren, *Power and Prejudice*.
2. Herman Ooms, *Tokugawa Village Practice: Class, Status, Power, Law* (Berkeley: University of California Press, 1996), 244–312. The *eta* and *hinin* were groups that were considered defiled because their occupation often brought them in contact with death and blood. Frequent occupations were leather workers or executioners. For details, see Timothy D. Amos, *Embodying Difference: The Making of Burakumin in Modern Japan* (Honolulu: University of Hawaii Press, 2011).
3. Takezawa Yasuko, 'Transcending the Western Paradigm of the Idea of Race', *The Japanese Journal of American Studies* 16 (2005): 5–30. For her work in Japanese, see: Takezawa, *Jinshu gainen no fuhensei o tou*.
4. For details on laws aimed at outcasts, see for example Amos, *Embodying Difference*.
5. Ooms, *Tokugawa Village Practice*, 247; emphasis in the original.
6. The term '*kawata*' was used by the leather workers to refer to themselves, instead of the derogatory *eta*. See ibid., 244.
7. Ibid., 247; emphasis in the original.
8. Ibid.
9. Takezawa, 'Transcending the Western Paradigm of the Idea of Race', 10.
10. Ibid., 8.
11. Members of the Victorian bourgeoisie, for example, sometimes saw the alleged differences of the workers in Britain as so profound that they emitted serious doubts regarding their belonging to the same White race. Workers were excluded from the production of a 'superior' White identity and were often compared, with regard to their 'quality', to Blacks and 'browns' from the colonies. Upper-class Victorians thereby excluded them from the 'superior' identity of the White bourgeoisie. See Alastair Bonnet, 'How the British Working Class Became White: The Symbolic (Re)formation of Racialized Capitalism', *Journal of Historical Sociology* 11, no. 3 (1998): 316–40. In the same vein, Balibar writes of the racialisation (*racisation*) of the working class with the attribution of characteristics such as 'material and spiritual misery, criminality . . . physical and mental retardation'. Étienne Balibar, 'Le racisme de classe', in *Race, nation, classe: les identités ambiguës*, ed. Étienne Balibar and Immanuel Wallerstein (Paris: La Découverte, 1997), 272–88.

12. See Fumiko Miyazaki, 'Female Pilgrims and Mt. Fuji: Changing Perspectives on the Exclusion of Women', *Monumenta Nipponica* 60, no. 3 (2005): 339–91.
13. The religious and political authorities erected checkpoints at strategic locations to monitor the pilgrims. Ibid., 353–4.
14. Ibid., 341–43. For more details on the Blood Pond Sutra, see Momoko Takemi, '"Menstruation Sutra" Belief in Japan', *Japanese Journal of Religious Studies* 10, no. 2–3 (1983): 229–46.
15. The *bakufu* ('tent government') was the political structure of the military government headed by a shogun. It was founded in the twelfth century and lasted until the second half of the nineteenth century.
16. Miyazaki, 'Female Pilgrims and Mt. Fuji', 354–5.
17. Ooms, *Tokugawa Village Practice*, 287.
18. On 'racism without race', see for example Miles, *Racism after 'Race Relations'*. Ooms also quotes Étienne Balibar to support his argument. For Balibar's approach to 'racism without race', see Balibar, 'Y a-t-il un "néo-racisme"?', in *Race, nation, classe: les identités ambiguës*, 24–41.
19. George M. Fredrickson, 'Racism, History of', in *International Encyclopedia of the Social & Behavioral Sciences*, ed. James D. Wright (Amsterdam: Elsevier, 2015), 853.
20. For a succinct summary of the history of research on race and racism, see ibid., 852–6. For a longer study on this topic, see Ivan Hannaford, *Race: The History of an Idea in the West* (Baltimore, MD: The Johns Hopkins University Press, 1996).
21. For details about medieval world views of mankind and the influence of the Age of Exploration on these, see George M. Fredrickson, *Racism: A Short History* (Princeton, NJ: Princeton University Press, 2015).
22. Michael L. Krenn, *The Color of Empire: Race and American Foreign Relations* (Washington, DC: Potomac Books, 2006), 4.
23. Ibid.
24. Keevak, *Becoming Yellow*, 64–5.
25. Ibid., 62.
26. See Stephen Jay Gould, *The Mismeasure of Man* (New York: Norton, 1981); Ashley Montagu, *Man's Most Dangerous Myth: The Fallacy of Race*, 6th ed. (Walnut Creek, CA: AltaMira Press, 1997). For a study focused on the intellectual history of race, see Hannaford, *Race*.
27. Keevak, *Becoming Yellow*, 62.
28. In the introduction to his work, Hannaford gives the useful advice to his readers 'not to accept the postulates of race as "givens" but to examine the past without the intellectual baggage acquired since the end of the seventeenth century'. Hannaford, *Race*, 4.
29. Miles, *Racism after 'Race Relations'*, 58.
30. David L. Howell, *Geographies of Identity in Nineteenth-Century Japan* (Berkeley: University of California Press, 2005), 34. People were divided into four status groups: warriors, peasants, artisants and merchants. For the limits of this clear-cut

clasification, see Daniel V. Botsman, *Punishment and Power in the Making of Modern Japan* (Princeton, NJ: Princeton University Press, 2005), 59–61.

31. As cited in ibid., 31.
32. Saitō Yōichi and Ōishi Shinzaburō, *Mibun sabetsu shakai no shinjitsu* (Tokyo: Kodansha, 1995), 5.
33. For the importance of punishments for the preservation of the political and social order in Tokugawa times, see Botsman, *Punishment and Power in the Making of Modern Japan*.
34. For details on the importance of Song Confucianism for the moral education of subjects in the Tokugawa period, see Ronald P. Dore, *Education in Tokugawa Japan* (London: The Athlone Press, 1984). Details on the Five Relationships can be found in Willem Boot, 'Confucianism in the Early Tokugawa Period', in *Sources of Japanese Tradition*, ed. Wm. Theodore de Bary, Carol Gluck and Arthur E. Tiedemann (New York: Columbia University Press, 2005). Also see Watanabe Hiroshi, *A History of Japanese Political Thought, 1600–1901*, trans. David Noble (Tokyo: I-House Press, 2012), 13–15.
35. As cited in Maruyama Masao, *Studies in the Intellectual History of Tokugawa Japan*, trans. Mikiso Hane (Princeton, NJ: Princeton University Press, 1974), 197.
36. As cited in ibid., 200.
37. Botsman warns us that 'while it would be foolish to discount the significance of Confucian influences, it would also be a mistake to assume that the emphasis given to protecting hierarchies in the Tokugawa period can be attributed to a single source'. Botsman, *Punishment and Power in the Making of Modern Japan*, 31.
38. Donald H. Shively, 'Sumptuary Regulation and Status in Early Tokugawa Japan', *Harvard Journal of Asiatic Studies* 25 (1964–1965): 124.
39. Shively retells a famous incident of the period: The procession of Shogun Tsunayoshi (1646–1709) was on its way to Ueno when the shogun himself saw a beautifully dressed woman followed by equally exquisitely dressed servants. Believing her to be the wife of a *daimyō* (domain lord), he sent an aide to enquire her name. When it turned out that the woman in question was in fact the wife of an Edo townsman who had made a fortune in the brokerage business, he had the man and his wife banished from Edo and confiscated their property; ibid., 129. Interestingly, these laws were not designed to hinder commoners from accumulating wealth, but more the display of such wealth to preserve the social status quo. See Howell, *Geographies of Identity*, 64.
40. Mikiso Hane, *Peasants, Rebels, and Outcastes: The Underside of Modern Japan* (New York: Pantheon, 1982), 8.
41. Shively, 'Sumptuary Regulation and Status in Early Tokugawa Japan', 153–5.
42. Saitō and Ōishi, *Mibun sabetsu shakai no shinjitsu*, 6.
43. Amos, *Embodying Difference*, 83–4.
44. John W. Hall, 'Rule by Status in Tokugawa Japan', *The Journal of Japanese Studies* 1, no. 1 (Autumn 1974): 45.
45. Ibid., 45.
46. Ronald P. Toby, *State and Diplomacy in Early Modern Japan: Asia in the Development of the Tokugawa Bakufu* (Princeton, NJ: Princeton University Press, 1984), 211.

47. Bob Tadashi Wakabayashi, *Anti-Foreignism and Western Learning in Early-Modern Japan: The New Theses of 1825* (Cambridge, MA: Harvard University Press, 1992), 18.
48. Ibid., 19.
49. Kate Wildman Nakai wrote that 'no Tokugawa Confucian was prepared to accept the connotation in Chinese usage that peripheral peoples should acknowledge some degree of political subordination to *chū*=China'. Kate Wildman Nakai, 'The Naturalization of Confucianism in Tokugawa Japan: The Problem of Sinocentrism', *Harvard Journal of Asiatic Studies* 40, no. 1 (June 1980): 181–2.
50. For a detailed analysis of the Middle Kingdom world view and its importance for Chinese foreign relations, see John K. Fairbank, ed., *The Chinese World Order: Traditional China's Foreign Relations* (Cambridge, MA: Harvard University Press, 1968). Also see Toby, *State and Diplomacy in Early Modern Japan*, 170.
51. For a broader analysis of the Japanese efforts to adapt Confucian thought to Japan, see Wakabayashi, *Anti-Foreignism and Western Learning*, 17–57; Wildman Nakai, 'The Naturalization of Confucianism in Tokugawa Japan'; Harry D. Harootunian, 'The Functions of China in Tokugawa Thought', in *The Chinese and the Japanese: Essays in Political and Cultural Interactions*, ed. Akira Iriye (Princeton, NJ: Princeton University Press, 1980), 9–36.
52. Wakabayashi, *Anti-Foreignism and Western Learning*, 22–30.
53. Ibid., 26.
54. As cited in Laura Nenzi, *Excursions in Modernity: Travel and the Intersection of Place, Gender, and Status in Edo Japan* (Honolulu: University of Hawaii Press, 2008), 60.
55. Ibid., 50.
56. Mikiso Hane, *Modern Japan: A Historical Survey*, 3rd ed. (Boulder, CO: Westview Press, 2001), 38.
57. Christiane Langer-Kaneko, 'Zur Geschichte der Erziehung und Bildung der Frau in Japan, reflektiert an ihrer Rolle in der Gesellschaft', in *Japan – Ein Land der Frauen?*, ed. Elisabeth Gössman (München: Iudicium Verlag, 1991), 93.
58. See for example Dorothy Ko, JaHyun Kim Haboush and Joan R. Piggot, eds, *Women and Confucian Cultures in Premodern China, Korea, and Japan* (Los Angeles: University of California Press, 2003); Nenzi, *Excursions in Modernity*; Harald Fuess, *Divorce in Japan: Family, Gender, and the State, 1600–2000* (Stanford, CA: Stanford University Press, 2004).
59. Dan Fenno Henderson, 'The Evolution of Tokugawa Law', in *Studies in the Institutional History of Early Modern Japan*, ed. John Whitney Hall and Marius B. Jansen (Princeton, NJ: Princeton University Press, 1968), 222.
60. Langer-Kaneko, 'Zur Geschichte der Erziehung und Bildung der Frau in Japan', 93.
61. For a fascinating insight into the daily life of a girl and her education in the Tokugawa period, see Yamakawa Kikue, *Women of the Mito Domain; Recollections of Samurai Family Life*, trans. Kate Wildman Nakai (Tokyo: University of Tokyo Press, 1992).
62. The book is attributed to scholar Kaibara Eikken (1630–1714). For more information, see Martha C. Tocco, 'Norms and Texts for Women's Education in Tokugawa

Japan', in *Women and Confucian Cultures in Premodern China, Korea, and Japan*, ed. Dorothy Ko, JaHyun Kim Haboush and Joan R. Piggot (Los Angeles: University of California Press, 2003), 197–8.

63. Kaibara Ekken, 'The Great Learning for Women', in *Sources of Japanese Tradition: Volume 2, 1600–2000*, 2nd ed., eds Wm. Theodore de Bary, Carol Gluck and Arthur E. Tiedemann (New York: Columbia University Press, 2005), 264.
64. Ibid.
65. For details, see Amy Stanley, 'Adultery, Punishment, and Reconciliation in Tokugawa Japan', *The Journal of Japanese Studies* 33, no. 2 (Summer 2007): 309–35; Diana E. Wright, 'Female Crime and State Punishment in Early Modern Japan', *Journal of Women's History* 16, no. 3 (Fall 2004): 10–29.
66. Stanley, 'Adultery, Punishment, and Reconciliation in Tokugawa Japan', 311.
67. For adultery in medieval times, see ibid., 313. For the Tokugawa period, see Botsman, *Punishment and Power in the Making of Modern Japan*, 30.
68. Stanley, 'Adultery, Punishment, and Reconciliation in Tokugawa Japan', 315.
69. Ibid., 319.
70. Bernard Faure, *The Power of Denial: Buddhism, Purity, and Gender* (Princeton, NJ: Princeton University Press, 2009), 91–118. As already pointed out, Buddhist ideology also was not always consistent with social practice. The case of *nyonin kinsei* was already mentioned. In Shin Buddhism, wives of priests could have an important role as proselytisers and caretakers of the temple. Several schools of Buddhism also seriously discussed the possibility of salvation for women. For Shin Buddhism, see Jessica Starling, 'Domestic Religion in Late Edo-Period Sermons for Temple Wives', *The Eastern Buddhist* 43, no. 1/2 (2012): 271–97. For the issue of salvation for women, see Kenji Matsuo, *A History of Japanese Buddhism* (Kent: Global Oriental, 2007), 132–48.
71. Takemi, '"Menstruation Sutra" Belief in Japan', 230.
72. Ibid.
73. As cited in ibid., 235. Early modern Shintō had the same concern with impurity: women were considered pure when young virgins, but after becoming an adult, menstruation, childbirth and sexual intercourse made them unclean. See Karen Ann Smyers, 'Women and Shinto: The Relation Between Purity and Pollution', *Japanese Religions* 12, no. 4 (July 1983): 13.
74. Fredrickson, *Racism*, 139.
75. As Howell pointed out, the scholar Yamaga Sokō (1622–1685) actually argued that commoners and barbarians were alike. See Howell, *Geographies of Identity*, 138.
76. Ibid.
77. The Ainu form a minority group inside Japanese society that originally settled the northernmost island of the country. Officially recognised as indigenous since 2008, their history of interactions with non-Ainu Japanese may date back to the eighth century. From the seventeenth century onwards, the Ainu population has steadily been oppressed through violence and assimilation policies by the non-Ainu majority. For an overview of Ainu history, see Siddle, *Race, Resistance, and the Ainu of Japan*.

78. Brett L. Walker, *The Conquest of Ainu Lands: Ecology and Culture in Japanese Expansion, 1590–1800* (Berkeley: University of California Press, 2001), 39–47. Also see Howell, *Geographies of Identity*, 140.
79. Walker, *The Conquest of Ainu Lands*, 204. Also see David L. Howell, 'Ainu Ethnicity and the Boundaries of the Early Modern Japanese State', *Past & Present*, no. 142 (February 1994): 75.
80. Siddle, *Race, Resistance, and the Ainu of Japan*, 42; Howell, *Geographies of Identity*, 141–3.
81. Tessa Morris-Suzuki, 'A Descent into the Past: The Frontier in the Construction of Japanese History', in *Multicultural Japan: Palaeolithic to Postmodern*, ed. Donald Denoon et al. (Cambridge: Cambridge Universtity Press, 2001), 84.
82. For details on the tributary relations with the Tokugawa *bakufu*, see Toby, *State and Diplomacy in Early Modern Japan*, 85–9.
83. Walker, *The Conquest of Ainu Lands*, 205.
84. Ibid., 214–17.
85. Siddle, *Race, Resistance, and the Ainu of Japan*, 41.
86. Morris-Suzuki, 'A Descent into the Past', 85.
87. Ibid., 84.
88. Ibid.
89. The 'three realms' were *Wagachō* ('Our Land', i.e. Japan), *Kara* (China and Korea) and *Tenjiku* (India) as the land of Buddha. See Ronald P. Toby, 'Three Realms/Myriad Countries: An "Ethnography" of Other and the Re-bounding of Japan, 1550–1750', in *Constructing Nationhood in Modern East Asia*, ed. Kai-wing Chow, Kevin M. Doak and Poshek Fu (Ann Harbor: University of Michigan Press, 2001), 18. Also see by the same author 'Imagining and Imaging "Anthropos" in Early-Modern Japan', *Visual Anthropology Review* 14, no. 1 (Spring-Summer 1998): 19.
90. Keiko Suzuki, 'The Making of *Tōjin*: Construction of the Other in Early Modern Japan', *Asian Folklore Studies* 66, no. 1/2 (2007): 85.
91. Ibid., 86.
92. For details on the prints with examples, ibid., 93–6.
93. As Suzuki has written, 'as far as *ukiyo-e* is concerned, a Western *tōjin*'s appearances are hardly marked by any specific anomaly or bestialization. The most distinguishable physical features of *tōjin* are beards and mustaches, which are regarded as almost sine qua non for them', ibid., 96.
94. Morris-Suzuki, *Re-Inventing Japan*, 82.
95. Readers interested in apostasy in early modern Japan can consult Ikuo Higashibaba, *Christianity in Early Modern Japan: Kirishitan Belief and Practice* (Leiden: Brill, 2001). For further information on Japanese Christians, see Charles Ralph Boxer, *The Christian Century in Japan, 1549–1650* (Berkeley: University of California Press, 1951); George Elison, *Deus Destroyed: The Image of Christianity in Early Modern Japan* (Cambridge, MA: Harvard University Press, 1988).
96. Morris-Suzuki writes that, while a coherent ideology of race cannot be found in the period, the exclusion of people 'tended to be explained primarily in terms of submission to the power of the state'. Morris-Suzuki, *Re-Inventing Japan*, 82.

Chapter 2

The Translation of Race in the Meiji Period

Of all the 'Western things' Japan imported over the decades following the arrival of the Black Ships, race has to be the most complicated. The very nature of the concept itself, its function as a pillar for the structure of White supremacy, as well as its intrinsically exclusive nature should have been enough to persuade the Japanese to ignore it. Moreover, we have seen in the previous chapter that Japan already had patterns of exclusion which were in their function similar to race. Thinking in the framework of domestic intellectual thought, then, the introduction of the concept does not make much sense, and even appears to be rather counterproductive. Following up on what was argued in the previous chapter, the early history of race in Japan cannot be separated from coeval developments in the West, as the country became part of an international struggle in which race played a pivotal role. Retracing parts of that history is the aim of the present chapter.

Introducing modernity: the translation of race in the early Meiji period

On 6 April 1868, the Charter Oath was read aloud before the Emperor in the Kyoto Imperial Palace. Comprising five articles, the Oath was designed to set the future course of Japan and to usher the country into a new era of Western-inspired modernity. The last article famously required that 'Knowledge shall be thought throughout the world so as to strengthen the foundation of imperial rule'. This rapidly became a priority, for the opening of treaty ports and the unequal treaties imposed on Japan made the acquisition of information about the Western nations not only unavoidable but also of paramount importance: only by having a substantial knowledge of these nations could Japan hope to escape the fate of its neighbour China after the Opium Wars (1839–42 and 1856–60).[1] Knowledge came either from the Western people themselves in the form of foreign consultants and teachers (*o-yatoi gaikokujin*), or was acquired by Japanese going abroad as emissaries or exchange students. It also came to Japan through the translation of Western works. Translation, therefore, became a means to understand the West, its institutions, history, geography and arts. Most of the geography works translated in the early Meiji period contained a section about race, a fact that made the importance of the concept palpable to the translators.

Translating race was more than a lexical issue: it meant adapting a new theory into a context that was very different from the one it originated in.[2] Obviously on the losing side according to this theory, the translators engaging with it certainly felt uneasy. This raises the question of why they chose to do so anyway. The most plausible reason can be traced back to the meaning of translation for Meiji Japan mentioned earlier. Added to this were the similarities between the Western concept and the Japanese patterns of differentiation. The core of the idea, namely that mankind was composed of different groups that could be ranked inside a hierarchy, should indeed not have been much of a surprise to the Japanese. As Louise Young comments on the development of Japanese racial chauvinism in East Asia and the acceptance of Western racial thinking: 'Western racial categories made sense precisely because they resonated with home-grown notions of hierarchy'.[3] Already in Tokugawa times, society was not intended to be equal and foreign policy did not envision international relations as consisting of relations between equal partners. In this sense, the introduction of Western racial thinking in Meiji Japan was less a change and more a continuation of the same ideology of difference. What changed were the justifications for the differences among human beings: certain groups of people were not different and inferior because of their lack of education or rituals anymore, but because of what they were.

One may add that this was not the first time the Japanese adopted a world view for another. The Middle Kingdom world view of Tokugawa times had replaced an ancient view that divided the world into the realms of humans and demons.[4] A shift in the conceptualisation of the world was therefore neither new, nor exceptional, but only the logical consequence of Japan changing its reference point from China to the Western nations. Race was an integral part of the rational Western sciences, as opposed to the 'evil customs of the past' the Charter Oath admonished to break off with. The introduction of race in Japan thus gives us an example of a knowledge transfer in the context of imperialism that was not entirely forced. Despite its problematic implications, the concept was greeted with acceptance because it fitted rather well into indigenous conceptions of 'otherness', but also because the Japanese on the receiving end considered their own knowledge primitive and the new one necessary for their survival.

Of course, a little reworking was necessary. As their Confucian predecessors had struggled with the inherent Sinocentric features of the Middle Kingdom, the Japanese who engaged with the concept of race could not accept all of its Eurocentric assumptions. The problem was not the idea itself. Nor even the premise that there was a superior race. The problem was that according to Western scientists, racial characteristics were biologically fixed and therefore inheritable and unchangeable, which meant that the Japanese were doomed to remain part of an inferior race. It was thus necessary to take what was useful and at the same time reject any deterministic notions to redefine race into a concept that suited the Japanese aspirations.

Adapting the concept of race

In contemporary Japan, the word *jinshu* is used to express the idea of race as we understand it nowadays and is composed of the two characters for human 人 (*jin/hito*) and sort/category (*shu/tane*).[5] It seems that this composite was in circulation before its modern usage, with meanings such as 'human' or 'seeds of humankind'.[6] There is no consensus about which particular translator disseminated the modern idea of race into Japan. Tessa Morris-Suzuki credits the Meiji intellectual and educator Fukuzawa Yukichi (1835–1901), while according to Takezawa, one of the first intellectuals to use the Chinese character for what is now read *jinshu* was Tokugawa period scholar Watanabe Kazan (1793–1841).[7] When comparing the respective influence of both scholars in terms of publications, readership and legacy, it is safe to assume that while he might not have been the first to use it, Fukuzawa Yukichi was substantially more influential in disseminating the idea of race among the Japanese public. It is also a measure of his influence that his definition was still being quoted fifty years later.[8] Starting his career as a translator, his works were highly readable and explicitly aimed at the education of common people, which contributed to their popularity. Furthermore, his books were on the official textbooks lists of the Meiji government for use in the new education curriculum.[9]

More than the translator however, the factor that influenced the introduction of race was the context in which the concept was translated. Three years before Perry's arrival, the Scottish anatomist Robert Knox wrote: 'I . . . am prepared to assert that race is everything in human history . . . Literature, science, art, in a word, civilization depend on it.'[10] While Knox wrote his work out of personal bigotry,[11] it is true that race had penetrated every sphere of people's life. From the plantations in the American South, to the opium dens in Shanghai, race was a force that determined power relations in the mother land and in the colonies, judging on the basis of arbitrary characteristics who had the right to enjoy civil rights and who did not, or who had the right or the ability to own a nation. It was in this context that the Japanese encountered the concept of race. And while the Japanese thinkers who engaged with it were certainly aware of its harmful potential, denying its manifestations must have seemed difficult: leaving a contemporary critical approach aside, it was White officers who had commanded the steamships that came to Japan, White diplomats who had forced their terms upon the nation because of their technological superiority, and White experts who were invited to teach the Japanese to 'become modern'. At the time race was translated, White supremacy was not a myth, but a fact that was revealing itself to the Japanese in the form of steamships, trains and telegraph poles. Fukuzawa Yukichi was aware of this situation, foremost because he had witnessed it first-hand.

Before the advent of the Meiji period, Fukuzawa had travelled abroad on three occasions, first in 1860 as a member of the First Japanese Embassy to the US, then in Europe from 1861 to 1862 and finally again to the United States in 1867.[12] During his travels in 1860, Fukuzawa witnessed the global racial situation. Be it in Hawaii, Panama or elsewhere, he and the other members of the Japanese embassies observed how Whites systematically dominated non-Whites.[13] Unsurprisingly, then, his commented translations of Western works reproduce a White supremacist world view as found in the original works. *Sekai kunizukishi* (World Geography) is a fitting example of this. Written in 1869 'to teach women and children how the world is built',[14] the work introduced a world view that was new to most Japanese, not only because it was based on Western geography, but also because it was divided along racial lines.[15]

Before going into details, a brief commentary on the nature of the work is necessary. While penned by Fukuzawa, *Sekai kunizukushi* is a mainly a commented translation of the book *A System of Modern Geography* (first published in 1843) by American geographer Samuel Augustus Mitchell (1790–1868). Mitchell, who was not only a geographer but also an entrepreneur, founded a publishing company that became famous for its pocket maps.[16] His maps, however, were no mere neutral topographical advisers, but reflected mid-nineteenth-century American prejudices.[17] The same is true for his *A System of Modern Geography*: the book is not simply an account of the location of different countries and information about the people living there, but presented to its reader a geography of civilisation. The preface to the work makes it clear that geography and politics (including race) were intertwined: 'Geography is twofold: Physical and Political. Physical Geography is valuable mainly because it makes Political Geography more intelligible.'[18] The political features of geography included 'the population, as to race and descent, as well as to numbers'.[19] There were, according to Mitchell, a total of five races: the 'Caucasian or White race', the 'Mongolian or Yellow race', the 'African or Black race', the 'Malay or Brown race' and the 'American or Red race'.[20] Mitchell also posited a hierarchy amongst them, as he explains that 'the various races differ in color, form, feature, and mental capacity'.[21]

The detailed description of the races leaves no room for doubts regarding the composition of that hierarchy: the Caucasian race was not only the fairest, but also the 'most improved and intelligent of the human family, and seem[s] capable of attaining the highest degree of progress and civilization'.[22] Members of the Mongolian race were of a 'yellow complexion' and with oblique eyes. They were 'patient and industrious, but limited in genius and slow in progress. The Chinese and the Japanese comprise a large portion of the Mongol race.'[23] The Black race was 'strong and active in body, but indolent in habit, and [has] not attained to any high degree of civilization'.[24] Roughly the same was true for the Malay race while the American race was 'tall and well formed, but revengeful and warlike'.[25]

This classification was nothing new to the Western reader. The Japanese reader, however, discovered a new division of the world much more complex than the until then usual division into civilised and barbarian. Notions of civilisation were also to be found in Mitchell's work, but these were inseparable from notions of race. The work explained that mankind could be divided into two classes: 'Savage' and 'Civilized'.[26] The criteria for being part of the civilised greatly differed from those we saw in ideas of civilisation in early modern Japan. Rituals did not matter to Mitchell. A society was civilised if it built 'cities and towns' and if its people were living in 'durable and comfortable houses'. Then, this society was enjoying 'the blessings conferred by order, industry, morality and religion'.[27] The two classes of 'savage' and 'civilised' could be further divided into five categories: 'Savage', 'Barbarous', 'Half-Civilized', 'Civilized' and 'Enlightened'.[28]

There is no need to go further into details concerning the categories here. Suffice to say that in Mitchell's work, race and civilisation were intertwined: only White nations were civilised and enlightened, while only coloured nations were composing the 'Savage', 'Barbarous' and 'Half-Civilized' categories.[29] Some leniency is given for variation inside the categories, but trespassing was not allowed: 'Some nations are more savage than others . . . and among those which are called enlightened, some are much more so than others. The division . . . is exact enough for practical purposes.'[30]

According to this deterministic view, Japan was ranked among the 'Half-Civilized' nations: 'The Half-Civilized state is a decided improvement, in life and manners, upon the barbarous state.'[31] A certain level of agricultural skill could be found, as could be cities and town and a fair level of literacy. 'Half-Civilized nations, however, are jealous of strangers, and treat their women as slaves. China, Japan, Turkey, and Persia are the principal countries of this class.'[32] Eurocentric assumptions notwithstanding, for the Japanese who were just starting to walk on the road of modernisation, *A System of Modern Geography* was an accessible guidebook on how to become 'modern', that is 'civilised'. It contained information about what to do and possess in order to be a first-rank nation, all based on 'modern' and 'rational' science. And race, as an integral part of it, needed to be taken into account.[33]

Accordingly, *Sekai kunizukishi* contains the same racial classification as its main source.[34] There is, however, one point in which Fukuzawa's translation substantially differs: where Mitchell explicitly points at the Chinese and the Japanese as members of the Mongolian/Asian race, Fukuzawa conspicuously left Japan out. Asia was comprised solely of China, India, Persia, Turkey and Russia.[35] This is not the only striking absence of Japan: in the Appendix of *Sekai kunizukushi*, Fukuzawa picks up Mitchell's definition of Political Geography and its correlated division of the world into civilised and uncivilised and the subdivisions savage, barbarian, half-civilised and enlightened,[36] but chose again to leave Japan out.[37]

This is even more striking considering that the descriptions of other races and nations contain almost all information found in the original work. Thus,

Fukuzawa's description of Africa is far from flattering: in the North lived some Europeans, but amongst them were Blacks, whose customs were 'extremely barbarous'.[38] The South of Africa was populated by the 'Hottentots' who were 'incredibly stupid' and belonged 'the lowest ranks of humanity'.[39] While the interiors of the continent were almost uncharted, it was known, according to him, that Ethiopians had no education and were raw-spirited, while the Blacks from a place called 'Nyam Nyam' were killing people and eating their flesh.[40] Although rather far-fetched, the clear distinction between Black and White in Fukuzawa's description of Africa is also a testimony of his racial awareness, which is omnipresent in his work. Europe is described as the paragon of civilisation: after specifying that its composition was 90 per cent White, Fukuzawa engages in a laudation of the different countries composing it: England was full of wisdom and Prussia had no illiterate people amongst its people.[41] In the case of North America, Fukuzawa once again explicitly separates the indigenous population from the White settlers: in the North lived a race called 'Eskimo', which had no scripture and was 'extremely stupid'. Native Americans did not fare better, as they were gruesome in nature and hunted wild animals to wear their skin. Fukuzawa also specifies that the White settlers segregated the natives from their cities and were increasingly expelling them, so that their numbers were declining.[42]

It is evident from the content of *Sekai Kunizukushi* that Fukuzawa introduced Mitchell's White supremacist world view without much opposition, and thereby presented to his readers a world divided along colour lines. However, considering that the work is a commented translation, it is legitimate to question whether *Sekai Kunizukushi* reflects Fukuzawa's personal opinion on race. Fukuzawa's constant use of the expression *to iu* ('it is said that') at the end of his phrases reinforces the idea that the content of the book is indeed no more than a mere translation which does not imply his agreement.[43] The conspicuous absence of Japan inside the five racial categories lends further credibility to this assessment. However, despite all these clues, it is important to remember the aim of Fukuzawa's work: the education of the Japanese people. Even if one decides that the ideas in the book do not entirely reflect Fukuzawa's own thoughts, this does not alter the case that these were diffused as factual through his translation. As Uchiyama stated, 'Fukuzawa, as the translator of the book, played a significant role in propagating a negative image of non-Western cultures'.[44]

It is notable that Fukuzawa Yukichi, while the most influential translator, was not the only one to introduce a racialised world view into Japan through translation and to adapt it in the process. The already mentioned *Yochi shōgaku* by Fukamauchi Motoi, likewise based on *System of World Geography*, also posits the existence of the five races as a fact. The Caucasians had a skin colour of 'egg white', 'their skeletal structure is evidently right, their face is extremely beautiful, and they are more skilled than the other races'. They were 'a race that is bound to reach the highest level of civilisation'.[45] Unlike his teacher, Fukamauchi included Japan as a member of the 'Mongolian race'. However, unlike the original source which conceded a certain level of intelligence to the Japanese but never saw them evolving towards high levels of civilisation, Fukamauchi's work declared that 'Mongolians' were 'a race that will advance towards enlightenment'.[46] The other races, however, did not benefit from the translator's adaptation: Ethiopians were lazy and made no progress towards civilisation, Malays had a very low level of enlightenment and [Native] Americans liked to fight but were declining in numbers.[47]

A similar strategy was adopted by another contemporary of Fukuzawa, Horikawa Kensai, who authored *Chikyū sanbutsu zasshi* (1872). The work is a translation of the French scholar Eugène Cortambert's (1805–81) book *Cours de Géographie comprenant la Description Physique et Politique et la Géographie Historique des Diverses Contrées du Globe* (originally published in 1846). The Japanese translation endorses Cortambert's threefold division of mankind into White, 'yellow' and Black, but adds some changes regarding the characteristics of the 'yellow races'. The French original claims that: 'Several of the yellow people, especially the Chinese, come from a very ancient civilisation and mastered lots of ingenious arts even before the Whites; but they remained stationary, and nowadays the White race outclasses them greatly.'[48] The Japanese translation, however, is less inclined to view the 'yellow race' as inferior, only reporting that 'the people of this race living in the Eastern part of Asia have developed a culture since ancient times, but the people in the northern parts are said to still possess barbaric customs'.[49] The characteristics of the two other races remain identical in both the original and the translation, which makes the changes for the 'yellow race' even more noticeable. In the translation, Whites were 'enterprising, smart and lead in matters of civilisation',[50] while the original states that the White race is 'active, enterprising and people on the top of civilisation belong to it'.[51] Likewise, the translation states that there was 'some civilisation' in the Black race, but 'it does not compare to that of the Whites. This is why Whites use them as servants or send them to the American colonies.'[52] The original likewise states that 'this race is less civilised . . . than the two first; a great number of Blacks, reduced to slavery at the hand of Europeans, were transported to the American colonies'.[53]

This brief analysis of the translations of Western geography works has shown that while the idea of a hierarchy of mankind was not surprising, the concept of race itself was new to the Japanese. The translations, mirroring their respective original works, include a section about race in which the division of mankind was acknowledged. The novelty (and legitimacy) of the concept lay in its Western 'scientific' foundations, which the Japanese needed to replace their 'evil customs of the past'. The translators equally accepted the idea that Whites were at the top of that hierarchy and that non-Whites were inferior. The attempts at adaptation on the part of Fukuzawa and his peers are proof that the translators understood the implications of the concept of race but could not agree with all the premises inherent to White supremacist thought. The motivations lying behind these changes are obvious: by challenging the notion that civilisation was defined by race, the translators were in fact arguing that race was not an obstacle for the Japanese people to reach the level of Western nations. The changes are not a denial of the superiority of White people, but only of the idea that civilisation was solely their prerogative.

Parts of the literature on the topic chose to ignore the dilemma caused by the translation of race. In his study on the transformation of the concept in modern Japan, Yonaha Jun dismisses *jinshu* in the early Meiji period as a mere translation meaning 'inhabitant'.[54] He argues that 'because imported in a fragmented way, the concepts of "*minshu*" [*Volk*] and "*jinshu*" of this period did not have a scientific definition'.[55] Furthermore, Yonaha claims that Fukuzawa Yukichi used *jinshu* as an all-encompassing term to differentiate people according to skin colour and regions and therefore did neither designate a race nor an ethnic group.[56] He is joined in his assessment by Sakano Teru, another historian of science, who asserts that *jinshu* only received its scientific value around the time of the birth of the Japanese Anthropological Association in 1884. Before that, it could designate an array of concepts like 'inhabitants', 'class', or 'group of people'.[57]

These assertions need to be relativised, as they downplay the importance race had in the international context. It was the whole point of race (also in the West) to categorise people according to their skin colour and regions of origin, which is one of the reasons why most of the racial categories are named after colours or continents thought to be representative of the races. If the Japanese translation of race cannot be 'scientific' for that reason, neither can be the Western concept.[58] We must also remember that *jinshu* originated from the translation of Western scientific works. The scientific value of these works was the reason why they were chosen in the first place. Therefore, *jinshu* was not a Japanese scientific concept, but a Western scientific concept translated into Japanese.

Fukuzawa's translation of race is in several regards interesting for this work, as it was in fact foreshadowing the creation of the racial middle ground. He did accept the existence of races and the idea that Whites were superior. However, he also set the Japanese apart from the other 'coloured' races and thereby tried to position them in a privileged position. The readers who read his translation could but think that Whites were superior and 'coloured' inferior. The question was what place Japan was to take inside this hierarchy. Fukuzawa's efforts to escape the mould of race were only an omen of what was to come for the Japanese government in the following decades, and what he did as an intellectual exercise, the government would attempt to do as a systematic policy. His work, therefore, was just the beginning of a Japanese quest to somehow cope with the influence of race on international relations.

Notes

1. For details on the unequal treaties, see Michael R. Auslin, *Negotiating with Imperialism: The Unequal Treaties and the Culture of Japanese Diplomacy* (Cambridge, MA: Harvard University Press, 2004). On the importance of the Opium Wars

during the Tokugawa period, see Bob Tadashi Wakabayashi, 'Opium, Expulsion, Sovereignty: China's Lessons for Bakumatsu Japan', *Monumenta Nipponica* 47, no. 1 (Spring 1992): 1–25.

2. This was the case for all the concepts that were introduced during the Meiji Restoration. In this sense, translation was not a mere linguistic task, but was in fact an engine for modernisation. On the importance of translation in the Meiji period, see: Douglas Howland, *Translating the West: Language and Political Reason in Nineteenth-Century Japan* (Honolulu: University of Hawaii Press, 2002); Maruyama Masao and Katō Shūichi, *Hon'yaku to Nihon no kindai* (Tokyo: Iwanami shoten, 1998); Kamei Shunsuke, ed., *Kindai Nihon no hon'yaku bunka* (Tokyo: Chūō kōronsha, 1994).
3. Louise Young, 'Rethinking Race for Manchukuo: Self and Other in the Colonial Context', in *The Construction of Racial Identities in China and Japan: Historical and Contemporary Perspectives*, ed. Frank Dikötter (Hong Kong: Hong Kong University Press, 1997), 160.
4. Howell, *Geographies of Identity*, 131.
5. I will not deal with the difference between *jinshu* (race) and *minzoku* (most aptly translated with the German word *Volk*, but sometimes also translated with race) as the distinction is not relevant for the present discussion. Michael Weiner and Tessa Morris-Suzuki have written about it in respectively: Weiner, 'The Invention of Identity', 96–116; Morris-Suzuki, *Re-Inventing Japan*.
6. Takezawa Yasuko, 'Translating and Transforming "Race": Early Meiji Period Textbooks', *Japanese Studies* 35, no. 1 (2015): 6–8.
7. Morris-Suzuki, *Re-Inventing Japan*, 85; Takezawa, 'Translating and Transforming "Race"', 8.
8. See for example Kamata Ekichi, 'Jinshu sabetsu teppai mondai', *Nihon no kanmon* 4, no. 45 (June 1919): 17–18; Yuhara Motoichi, 'Jinshu mondai yori miru kōkyū heiwa no yōken', *Taiyō* 25, no. 2 (February 1919): 88–94. It is telling that Fukuzawa's definition was used in a time when the problems with race were acute (see Chapter 7 of this work).
9. Akiko Uchiyama, 'Translation as Representation: Fukuzawa Yukichi's Representation of the "Others"', in *Agents of Translation*, ed. John Milton and Paul Bandia (Amsterdam: John Benjamins Publishing Company, 2009), 67–8.
10. Robert Knox, *Races of Men: A Fragment* (Philadelphia, PA: Lea and Blanchard, 1850), 7.
11. Knox is often presented as the 'founder of British racism'. For details on his views on race, see Michael Denis Biddiss, 'The Politics of Anatomy: Dr Robert Knox and Victorian Racism', *Journal of the Royal Society of Medicine* 69, no. 4 (1975): 245–50.
12. Uchiyama, 'Translation as Representation', 66.
13. See John G. Russel, 'The Other Other: The Black Presence in the Japanese Experience', in *Japan's Minorities: The Illusion of Homogeneity*, ed. Michael Weiner (London: Routledge, 2009): 84–115.
14. Keiō gijuku, ed., *Fukuzawa Yukichi zenshū*, vol. 1 (Tokyo: Iwanami shoten, 1969–71), 581.

15. I will not deal with Fukuzawa's later works on race, such as those on the betterment of the Japanese race written in the 1880s. The aim in this chapter is to focus on the introduction of race as a new concept at the beginning of the Meiji period. In the 1880s, however, race was already an integral part of the societal discourse. Readers interested in the meaning of race in Fukuzawa's later works can consult: Ameda Eiichi, 'Fukuzawa Yukichi no "maruhadaka no kyōsō" to "jinshu kairyō" no shisō', *Tōyō bunka kenkyū* 2 (2000): 385–418.
16. Brian James McFarland, 'From Publisher to Pocket: Interpreting Nineteenth Century American History through the Pocket Maps of Samuel Augustus Mitchell', MA thesis (University of Texas at Arlington, 2002), 4.
17. Ibid.
18. Samuel Augustus Mitchell, *A System of Modern Geography: Political, Physical and Descriptive* (Philadelphia, PA: E. H. Butler and Co., 1865), 3.
19. Ibid.
20. Ibid., 32.
21. Ibid.
22. Ibid., 33.
23. Ibid.
24. Ibid., 34.
25. Ibid.
26. Ibid., 35.
27. Ibid.
28. Ibid.
29. Ibid., 35–8.
30. Ibid., 38.
31. Ibid., 37.
32. Ibid., 38.
33. This assumption finds confirmation in another translation of Mitchell's work, *Yochi shōgaku* [A Short Study of Geography] by Fukamauchi Motoi (1846–1901). Fukamauchi, who was a Keiō Gikuju trained translator, commented that the racial classification introduced in the work can be found in several other books and was part of a science called *jinruigaku* (anthropology) and that it was therefore necessary to learn it. See Fukamauchi Motoi, *Yochi shōgaku*, vol. 1 (Tokyo: Meizankaku, 1874), 18.
34. Keiō gijuku, *Fukuzawa Yukichi zenshū*, 591.
35. Ibid., 591–600.
36. The terms Fukuzawa used to translate the words of Mitchell are interesting: 'Political Geography' is translated as *ningen no chigaku*, which literally means 'geography of mankind'. Likewise, 'civilised' and 'enlightened' are translated as *bunmei kaika* (civilisation and enlightenment), an expression that became one of the slogans of the early Meiji period.
37. Fukuzawa only mentions China, Turkey and Persia. Keiō gijuku, *Fukuzawa Yukichi zenshū*, 664.
38. Keiō gijuku, *Fukuzawa Yukichi zenshū*, 601.

39. Ibid., 604.
40. Ibid.
41. Ibid., 630–1.
42. Ibid., 632.
43. This point was also observed by Uchiyama. See Uchiyama, 'Translation as Representation', 71.
44. Ibid., 74.
45. Fukamauchi, *Yochi shōgaku*, 16.
46. Ibid., 17.
47. Ibid., 17–18.
48. Eugène Cortambert, *Cours de géographie comprenant la description physique et politique et la géographie historique des diverses contrées du globe*, 13th ed. (Paris: Librairie Hachette et Cie., 1876), 42.
49. Horikawa Kensai, *Chikyū sanbutsu zasshi* (Tokyo: Izumiya ichibei, 1872), 6.
50. Ibid.
51. Cortambert, *Cours de géographie*, 42.
52. Horikawa, *Chikyū sanbutsu zasshi*, 6.
53. Cortambert, *Cours de géographie*, 42.
54. Yonaha Jun, 'Kindai Nihon ni okeru "jinshu" kannen no hen'yō: Tsuboi Shōgorō no "jinruigaku" to no kakawari o chūshin ni', *Minzoku kenkyū* 68, no. 1 (2003): 86.
55. Ibid.
56. Ibid.
57. Sakano Tōru, *Teikoku Nihon to jinruigakusha: 1884–1952 nen* (Tokyo: Keisō shobō, 2005), 95–6. Both Yonaha and Sakano explicitly use Fukuzawa's *Sekai kunizukushi* for their arguments.
58. For another critic of Sakano, see Takezawa, 'Translating and Transforming "Race"', 7.

Part II: A Racial Middle Ground: Negotiating the Japanese Racial Identity in the Context of White Supremacy

Chapter 3

Between Two Races – The Birth of the Racial Middle Ground between Japan and the West

In the previous chapter, we saw how Fukuzawa Yukichi translated the concept of race and adapted it to suit the needs of modern Japan. This was a crucial step, as it acquainted the Japanese people with race and gave the Japanese elite an additional conceptual tool to understand the West. The nation was now aware that international relations were also conducted through the lens of race, and that Japan was at the bottom of a racial hierarchy alongside other 'coloured' people. However, this understanding makes us reach the crossroads mentioned in the introduction of this book. Fukuzawa's work is essential for further discussions about the conceptualisation of race at the domestic level. Yet, it is not enough to grasp the process behind the construction of the Japanese racial identity on the world stage. The reason is that, simply put, race was a game for which the rules were decided in the West. The adaptations Fukuzawa made to the concept did not influence the international racial standing of the Japanese inside. It is safe to assume that at the beginning of the Meiji period, policy makers in the West were not interested to know that some Japanese intellectual rejected biological determinism. In fact, keeping an international mindset, it is of secondary importance whether the Japanese even truly believed in the validity of race. The Western nations did, and that meant that if Japan wanted to have a place in international relations, it had to take the Western definition of it into account. The Japanese, however, were not forced to remain passive. If one continues the metaphor of a game, they may not have been able to decide the rules, but they were certainly able to influence the way in which these were interpreted.

As already mentioned, during the Meiji period, international relations had long become interracial relations as well. As the Australian Prime Minister Alfred Deakin (1856–1919) put it, the British Empire was 'divided broadly in two parts, one occupied wholly or mainly by a white ruling race, the other principally occupied by coloured races who are ruled'.[1] This pattern became so common that by 1914, less than one fifth of the world was free of European or American encroachment.[2] This clear-cut distinction between a ruling White race and ruled 'coloured' races worked well enough on paper and did find confirmation in most corners of the globe. Yet, by the turn of the twentieth century, fitting Japan into it became increasingly difficult. The theoretically 'yellow' Japan was less exhibiting the alleged characteristics of 'coloured' races, than presenting all the characteristics of a modern White nation: besides having preserved national sovereignty, by 1905 Japan had a modern government with a parliament and a constitution, a working diplomatic service, and a modern army that had proven its worth by defeating China and Russia successively. It had achieved what no other coloured nation had done before: reaching the 'standard of civilisation'.

Japan and the standard of civilisation: the problem of race against civilisation

A few years after the First Sino-Japanese War (1894–5), the American diplomat Thomas R. Jernigan (1847–1920) deemed, in reference to Japan, that

> when an Empire has, within a quarter of a century, turned its back upon Oriental customs and superstitions and written its name so brightly in modern history, it may justly claim the applause and respect of the world when it is about to take a place in the ranks of civilized nations.[3]

The meaning of Jernigan's assertion might seem straightforward, but it does invite several interrogations. Did the 'customs' and 'superstitions' the diplomat mentioned have a racial connotation? If not, should the ascendancy of Japan be seen in a civilisational framework devoid of any notion of biological determinism? This in turn would imply that all nations could be civilised, regardless of their racial belonging. To answer these questions, it is useful to enquire into the interdependence of the concepts of race and civilisation.

To be civilised in the nineteenth century, a nation needed to fulfil a set of prerogatives nowadays referred to as the 'standard of civilisation'. The classic – if contentious – study of the standard remains Gerrit Gong's *The Standard of 'Civilization' in International Society* (1984).[4] According to Gong, the expansion of Europe into the non-European world caused confrontations that were not only political, economic or military, but also civilisational in character. At the centre of these confrontations were different standards that nations used to monitor their relations between each other. During the nineteenth century, the standard applied by European nations became increasingly global and established itself as the sole valid one. By 1905, the European standard had evolved from rules into legal principles by which the Western nations identified themselves and used to regulate their international dealings. Briefly summarised, the standard entailed the following principles: (1) that a state was able to guarantee basic rights such as life and dignity, as well as the freedom of religion, commerce and travel; (2) a political bureaucracy capable of ruling the state and organising its defence; (3) a legal system that adhered to international law and consisted of courts on the domestic level; (4) a working diplomatic apparatus, and (5) the obedience to certain moral norms (rejection of polygamy, homosexuality and slavery).[5] These principles offered a civilisational scale in the form of a legal apparatus used to establish which societies were civilised or not. Furthermore, this standard 'was applied throughout the world' and 'became a catalyst for change both in the European international society and in the non-European countries which sought to enter it'.[6] The accuracy of this affirmation is hard to overstate in our case: it was precisely according to this standard that Japan launched its modernisation project, while it was the achievements of Japan based on this very standard that forced the Western powers to re-evaluate their image of the Japanese race.

However, Gong's analysis becomes questionable when he claims that 'at least in theory, the standard of civilization was colour-blind. It discriminated neither in favour of, nor against, non-white, non-European countries.'[7] Considering the domestic and international situations of most of the countries that were the bearers of the standard, this assumption invites some reflection. As noted above, when the world erupted in the first world conflict, only one fifth of the world remained free from European and American domination, a fact, one should note, that was justified with the standard of civilisation. This makes any claim of the standard's colour-blindness seem rather naive. It would be a mistake to underestimate the cohesive and rationalisation potential of racial identities in determining who had the right to live independently or not. Lake and Reynolds's assumption that most histories miss 'the significance of racial identifications to the construction of modern political subjectivities . . . in a process that shaped white men's sense of collective belonging to a larger community',[8] seems particularly appropriate here. Moreover, it should be stressed that the application of the standard to non-Western people, usually in the form of unequal treaties, was only one pattern of interaction with, and only restricted to a few, non-White people.[9] While the treaties had at least some sort of legal logic to them, dispossession and extermination were often favoured. The justification remained the same: the advance of civilisation through the actions of a superior race.

As Bowden has argued, European expansion was not merely a form of cultural or civilisational confrontation, but foremost 'an aggressive act involving what was usually the violent conquest and suppression of indigenous people'.[10] Examples illustrating this fact are not hard to find. The massacre of Native Americans (most of them women and children) at Wounded Knee in 1890, that is, only four years before the outbreak of Japan's first modern war, is but one instance of such interaction.[11] Commenting on the suppression of Native Americans as it had been the case at Wounded Knee, soon-to-be president Theodore Roosevelt (1858–1919) emphasised the 'race-importance' of the process: Whites were the vanguard of civilisation and hence their actions should not be judged 'by standards which would only be applicable in civilized townships and parishes', he claimed.[12] What mattered, was taking the land:

> Whether the whites won the land by treaty, by armed conquest, or, as was actually the case, by a mixture of both, mattered comparatively little so long as the land was won. It was all-important that it should be won for the benefit of civilization and in the interests of mankind.[13]

The relative protection granted by the standard, therefore, was only for a certain type of non-Whites.

Finally, the case of Japan itself casts doubts on the racial neutrality of the standard of civilisation. The very fact that, as Gong writes, 'Japan made it necessary that the standard be articulated in specific, legal terms'[14] and thereby contributed to the emergence of it, can be seen as proof that it was never expected from a coloured nation to reach it. The legal scholar Henry Wheaton (1785–1848) summarised this succinctly in his *Elements of International Law* (1836):

> Is there a uniform law of nations? There certainly is not the same one for all the nations and states of the world. The public law, with slight exceptions, has always been, and still is, limited to the civilized and Christian people of Europe or those of European origin. This distinction between the European law of nations and that of the other races of mankind has long been remarked by the publicists.[15]

Wheaton's assertion illustrates that Christianity and European descent were prerogatives of the standard.[16] It is also worth remembering that while the standard was under development, most nations of British descent such as the United States, Australia, Great Britain and Canada were enacting exclusionary laws aimed at Asians. If one adds to that the rejection of the racial equality proposal made by Japan at the Paris Peace Conference of 1919, despite Japan sitting at the negotiation table as a civilised great power, the colour-blindness of the standard becomes truly doubtful.[17]

The point is that, while we may have to distinguish the two notions from an analytical point of view, it is hard to separate race from civilisation in a historical perspective. At the very least, it is necessary to acknowledge that the parallel existence of several types of self-identification processes – civilisational and racial – as well as several types of interactions – 'legal/humanistic' and military – make the separation of the two concepts challenging. As much as civilisation was not a concept restricted to political, religious or cultural factors but also came to include ethnic features, race was not limited to a biological/ethnic concept but also encompassed differences in levels of civilisation. This is hardly surprising, as the scientific concept of race emerged during the phase of European expansion in which notions of civilisation, barbarism and savagery were crucial. Race did not only add a category for the classification of mankind, it also influenced the older ones by adding a biological dimension to them. As Miles and Brown have argued,

> the scientific discourse of race did not replace earlier preconceptions of the Other . . . For example, 'civilization' was initially considered attainable by all human beings given sufficient time and assistance, but this was challenged by the scientific idea that the human species was divided into permanent and discreet biological groups. As a result, savagery became a fixed condition of the 'Negro' or African 'race', a

> product of a small brain, and civilization became an attribute of large-brained 'white' people.[18]

In the nineteenth century, therefore, European civilisation/culture was synonymous with the European (that is, White) race, as much as Asian civilisation/culture was often synonymous with the 'Mongolian' or 'yellow' race.

The evolutions of Japan during the Meiji period made that dichotomy uncertain, as the Japanese were now becoming a people with what was believed to be obvious European features without European descent. Indeed, the anomaly of Japan cast so much doubt that in 1902 the French government wrote to the British Foreign Office to ask if the Japanese should be classified as White or non-White.[19] The question now is how to classify such a complex identity. This is where I would like to go back to the notion of Racial Middle Ground presented in the introduction of this work.

Japan, the West and the racial middle ground

The general function and creation process of a racial middle ground have been outlined in the introduction. It is now necessary to elaborate on some particularities of the one that Japan and the West created. First, based on the discussion above, the racial dimension of the interactions between Japan and the West should be taken for granted. This does not mean that factors such as culture or religion do not matter, but it implies that these were constantly imbued with a racial connotation. Therefore, in the analysis that follows and except when otherwise specified, 'Japan' or any other nation should also be understood as 'Japanese race' or any other race. Second, while the racial middle ground was a complicit act of creation between Japan and the West, its acceptance was entirely dependent on the latter. It was a matter of negotiation, but not between two equal partners. It was Japan that was looking for acceptance, not the other way around. The West, therefore, always had the upper hand in the negotiations.

Third, while the Western nations were always on top, Japan's position as a negotiating partner improved over time, which inevitably had an influence on the racial identity of the nation as well as on its position on the world stage. This increased the urgency of the racial negotiation zone for the Japanese to be accepted as a great power and for the West to uphold the fiction of White supremacy. Accepting Japan as a member of the family of civilised nations was equal to acknowledging that European ancestry was not a requisite to be civilised. Hence the necessity to accept Japan without losing the racial status quo. Fourth, while the primary reason for the Western nations to grant a racial middle ground to Japan was pragmatism, one can also observe a genuine interest in and appraisal of Japanese qualities, especially in comparison with other 'coloured' races. The fact that the Japanese had managed to do what other 'coloured' races could not was proof to some White people that maybe the Japanese were not that different from themselves. This led to some adaption regarding the traditional analogy between civilisation and European origin. This was no sign of universal racial tolerance, but merely an acknowledgement that the Japanese were different.

Turning to the question of agency, in our case the incentives shaping the actions of the agents were diverse.[20] On the Japanese side, the agents were mostly working on behalf of the government or were motivated by national pride. On the Western side, the incentives were more varied. Some worked for their government (or in some cases for the Japanese state), and others acted out of genuine sympathy and respect for the Japanese. There also were those who tried to reconcile the Japanese with the notion of Whiteness.[21] What all the agents of both sides had in common, apart from the fact that they were creating and maintaining the negotiation zone, was their attempts to frame Japanese actions in terms that the Western nations would understand and prioritise.

These terms were mostly defined by the standard of civilisation. The problematic of the racial neutrality of the standard aside, Japan recognised that it had to do something to avoid colonisation and adopted the standard as a compass to reach modernisation. Yet, as Ronald Dore commented on the notion of prestige in international relations, '"doing something" may require an open admission of backwardness, an overt acceptance of the demeaning status of pupil to the more advanced nations', something which is 'hard to reconcile with the patriot's pride'.[22]

The status of Japan as a 'pupil' was nowhere better symbolised than in the form of the so-called unequal treaties that the country signed from 1858 onwards. It was no secret that those treaties were a badge of inferiority forced upon nations deemed uncivilised. In a speech in the House of Representatives in 1893, the Foreign Minister Mutsu Munemitsu (1844–97) declared:

> In order to achieve the goal of treaty revision, ultimately we have to show the foreign countries actual proof for the fact that our progress, our civilization is truly a special case in all of Asia, and that we are a strong, civilized country; This is the chief goal for achieving treaty revision.[23]

Revising the treaties was equal to reaching the standard and, as such, to leaving the subordinate position of 'coloured' races. And indeed, in 1901, two years after the treaties had successfully been revised, the Japanese consul in Sydney admonished the Australian government that,

> the Japanese belong to an Empire whose standard of civilization is so much higher than that of Kanakas, Negroes, Pacific Islanders, Indians or other Eastern Peoples, that to refer to them in the same terms cannot but be regarded in the light of a reproach, which is hardly warranted by the fact of the shade of the national complexion.[24]

It took a long time and a middle ground for Japan to receive such acknowledgement. The efforts behind the creation of the negotiation zone were mostly informed by *realpolitik* – the need to restore and then preserve national independence. Yet, it also emerged from something less rational and more complex than diplomacy. It was grounded in racial insecurity; the feeling that the Japanese, as a race, were unable to compete with Whites. This was best observed in the debates that surrounded interracial contact.

Racial pessimism and the survival of the fittest

The threatening potential that Meiji Japanese attributed to interracial contacts can only be understood in light of two issues that strongly impacted Japanese society in the decades following the Meiji restoration. The first one, already touched upon, is the problem of the unequal treaties. The second is the introduction of social Darwinism.

The nature of the unequal treaties and the Japanese efforts to have them revised have already been thoroughly researched and only a brief summary will therefore suffice here.[25] From the 1850s onwards, Western powers imposed treaties on Japan that, while introducing the country to 'modern' forms of foreign relations, severely limited its sovereignty. Japan had to open several ports for commerce with foreign nations but saw its tariff autonomy restricted. The system of extraterritoriality that was part of the treaties made the foreigners in Japan immune to domestic law and answerable to their own nation's consular court only. The treaties were a constant reminder of Japan's inferior status, and their revision became the primary diplomatic objective of the Meiji period.[26] The domains in which the Japanese managed to maintain a semblance of sovereignty were those of foreign residence and travel. Japan, per treaty, had the right to restrict interior travel, that is, travel beyond the treaty ports, and to limit foreign residence to these same ports. A compromise was made under foreign pressure in 1873 and Japan allowed foreigners to travel further inland, but only for health and scientific purposes. This compromise, however, was only a temporary solution and the matter of foreign residence and travel would continue to be a contentious issue.

Parallel to the matter of the treaties, social Darwinism, as a new form of social thinking, was introduced into Japan. The work of Charles Darwin (1809–82) was introduced by Edward Sylvester Morse (1838–1925), a Harvard graduate who came to occupy the first chair of Zoology at the newly founded Tokyo Imperial University. His series of lecture given in 1877 offered the Japanese a first entry into evolutionary theory.[27] However, the lack of biological knowledge to fully comprehend Darwin's theory led most Japanese scholars to privilege the social dimension of it, and even biologists sought to apply it to social issues.[28] Spencerism became hugely popular, so much that Herbert Spencer (1820–1903) has been dubbed the 'most widely read and possibly the most influential Western social and political thinker in Japan during the 1880s'.[29] More than thirty translations of his work had appeared by the beginning of the twentieth century, the earliest one in 1884.[30]

The introduction and popularity of social Darwinism in Japan is easily understandable. Considering that it was equally popular in the West at the same time, and that the Japanese were copiously drawing from Western thought, introducing the idea had been inevitable. Moreover, social Darwinism provided a straightforward explanation for the events unfolding on the international arena. Notions of *seizon kyōsō* (struggle for survival) and *yūshō reppai* (survival of the fittest) resonated with Japan's efforts to protect national sovereignty.[31] Nevertheless, at the beginning of the Meiji period, the Japanese were seemingly on the losing side of this struggle for survival. And when it became apparent that the guarantee of free movement and residence of foreigners in Japan was a prerequisite for treaty revision, it was inevitable that they saw the issue through a Spencerian lens. The implications of mixed residence (*naichi zakkyo*) – foremost, contact with foreigners – gave birth to a whole array of feelings such as 'anxiety and curiosity, rejection and approval'.[32] Around 400 books were published on the topic, and *naichi zakkyo* became a central topic of public debate, perhaps even more than extraterritoriality and tariff restrictions.[33]

The discussions surrounding *naichi zakkyo* tended to focus on the issue of economic competition. Yet, there evidently was a racial component to this debate, as some feared that the Japanese as a race would not survive the association with Whites. Famous for this argument was renowned philosopher Inoue Tetsujirō (1855–1944) with his work *Naichi zakkyoron* (On Mixed Residence) from 1889.[34] Inoue saw mixed residence as a racial struggle and warned his readership that if it was allowed, 'all the people of Japan with no distinction regarding age or material wealth with find themselves directly struggling with Westerners'.[35] The Japanese were bound to lose that struggle because they were 'inferior in knowledge, economic power, physical constitution and in a multitude of other areas'.[36] Inoue had grave concerns regarding the physique of his compatriots compared to that of Western people: he warned that the Japanese facial structure was flawed, and that their heads were too big in relation to their body, a characteristic, he claimed, that could be found in all inferior races.[37] He also cautioned his readers that neither the physical characteristics of the Japanese nor their knowledge could be improved in a few decades.[38] If the Japanese were to measure themselves to Westerners now, it would be equal to 'a child challenging a trained grown man'.[39] It was therefore necessary to acknowledge that 'at the present, the Japanese race is inferior to the race of Western people'.[40]

Inoue tied the racial struggle to a political one, which would start as soon as mixed residence was allowed. His argument was that Western people had more knowledge about politics and would therefore be able to seize political power in Japan.[41] For him, it is a simple equation: it was equal to national and racial suicide. Invoking the authority of Machiavelli, he asserted that 'if several races mix in one country and several customs, religions and languages coexist, this country greatly loses its cohesive strength and becomes very hard to rule'.[42] The strength of a country lay in its national homogeneity, which was reflected in language, customs and appearance.[43] Inoue knew the outcome of this struggle:

'It does not happen that an inferior race rules a superior one.'[44] After the loss of their nation, the Japanese would undergo racial decline (*jinshu no metsubō*) as a result of interactions with White people. Quoting Darwin, he warned that the races of mankind were struggling against each other, with the result being that inferior races were quickly dying out.[45] The fate of Australian Aborigines and of the natives of New Zealand and North America was proof of this.[46]

Inoue's *Naichi zakkyoron* is an intriguing piece, as it asserts the inferiority of the Japanese race despite its author being, after all, Japanese himself. Its warnings about the impending doom of the Japanese race sound rather shallow, considering that Inoue wrote his book while living in Berlin. In fact, one reader later congratulated him for surviving his own mixed residence.[47] It seems, however, that Inoue did not consider himself a 'regular' Japanese. At the end of his book he anticipated criticism, and acknowledged that Japan, as a Far Eastern country that had successfully imported Western technology, was an exception.[48] Yet, according to him, the success of Japan was achieved by the government, and it was the 'common people' (*jinmin ippan*) he was worried about:

> Their physical, mental, and linguistic capacities are things that could not be improved as quickly as material things. Therefore, it is known to people with scientific knowledge that the Japanese are an inferior race compared to people from the West.[49]

The conclusion was that,

> the laws that apply to other inferior races apply to the Japanese too, this is why it is necessary to observe what changes occurred to other inferior races because of mixed residence when discussing the issue with regards to our country.[50]

In the end, mixed residence was enforced in 1899 and racial considerations were put aside for necessity. It would, however, be hasty to therefore dismiss race as irrelevant.[51] *Naichi zakkyoron* is less important for its influence on the result of the debates surrounding mixed residence than as a testimony of how insecure the Japanese were in their contacts with Whites.

The insecurities Inoue formulated should not be ridiculed as personal anxiety on his part, as these were shared not only by scholars but also by statesmen hardened by realpolitik. Prime Minister Itō Hirobumi (1841–1909), for example, instructed Kaneko Kentarō (1853–1942), a Harvard graduate, to ask Herbert Spencer himself if the mixing of Japanese with Westerners would be an advisable policy to improve the Japanese race. Spencer, in a letter from 1892, strongly advised against it:

> Respecting the intermarriage of foreigners and Japanese . . . it should be strictly forbidden . . . There is abundant proof, alike furnished by the intermarriages of human races and by the interbreeding, that when the varieties mingled diverge beyond a certain slight degree the result is inevitably a bad one in the long run.[52]

Considering the authority of Herbert Spencer amongst educated Japanese, it is not surprising then that intermarriage was not advocated as a state polity. But neither is the fact that it was considered in the first place. And while it was dismissed by politicians, miscegenation as a way of improving the race was a topic that received serious consideration amongst scholars during the Meiji period. Two texts, opposite in their argument, are famous for their study of the topic: *Nihon jinshu kairyōron* (On the Improvement of the Japanese Race, 1884) by journalist Takahashi Yoshio (1861–1937) and *Nihon jinshu kairyōron no ben* (Regarding the Improvement of the Japanese Race, 1886) by Katō Hiroyuki (1836–1916), a politician and president of the Tokyo Imperial University.[53] A brief look into the works will enable us to understand how race mixing was envisioned in Meiji Japan.

Both Takahashi and Katō saw Japan entering an era in which it would have to compete with other nations. And both saw the odds of winning as very low. For Takahashi, this competition was not a mere social reality but the biologically defined way of living beings: plants were struggling, animals were struggling, and so was mankind. In order to survive, living beings had to adapt.[54] Therefore, 'it is indeed no distortion of reality to say that the world of plants and animals is a battlefield where a struggle for survival takes places'.[55] In the 'savage' world, the struggle was based on physical strength, but in the civilised world, it was based on 'ambition, the acquisition of status, and self-interest aiming at transcending the others'.[56]

Both Katō (who explicitly endorsed Blumenbach's racial division) and Takahashi reasoned in terms of superior and inferior races and saw Japan as part of the latter: Katō unwillingly conceded that 'in a number of regards, it is already obvious that our Japanese race is inferior to the Western race'.[57] Takahashi tried to offer a more 'scientific' approach by comparing the weight, height and size of the head of the Japanese with those of Whites. According to him, the head of the Japanese was smaller in size and hence harboured a smaller brain.[58] Both Takahashi and Katō warned that in the struggle for survival, the stronger races inevitably exterminated the weaker ones.[59] How to avoid this fate for Japan was the issue on which their opinions diverged.

Takahashi was in favour of improving the Japanese race by intermarrying it with Whites. His logic was as follows: for him two factors influenced a race, habits (*shūyō*) and heredity (*iden*).[60] The two were mutually reinforcing, since habits were influencing the individual, and heredity his progeny.[61] Everything was inheritable, and people were passing on their mental and physical characteristics such as physique and affinity to arts, but also diseases.[62] In Japan, 'by selecting men and women, and wedding them, the children will be born with all necessary elements regarding mind and physique'.[63] Foreshadowing the racial middle ground created a few years later, Takahashi made it clear that racial miscegenation was only conceivable with the White race.[64] Race mixing needed to be monitored, as the aim of this artificial selection, Takahashi claimed, was the inheritance of positive features: 'That is why from the standpoint of reason and human nature one cannot condone intermarriage with lower races', and intermarriage should be promoted exclusively with 'members of the superior Western race'.[65]

The irony behind this position is hard to overlook. On the one hand, Takahashi was acknowledging that racial mixing with an inferior race was wrong. But on the other hand, he promoted the intermarriage of Whites and Japanese, and the latter he himself saw as inferior. Despite this obvious contradiction, it was not the reason why he earned criticism from Katō Hiroyuki. Katō, who explicitly aimed his critique at Takahashi,[66] had considerable doubts about the efficiency of race mixing. It could lead either to the proliferation or to the extinction of the race: seen, according to him, in the example of Tahiti, where Whites were marrying natives and thereby causing an increase of mixed-race children at an alarming speed.[67] Then there was the case of Jamaica, where after three generations of race mixing individuals were allegedly becoming infertile.[68] It was therefore difficult to know if miscegenation led to improvement or not.

The next problem, still according to Katō, was how to know from which side the child would inherit most – the paternal or the maternal side. There was no scientific consensus on the issue, but in the case of mixing between the White and the 'yellow' race, the maternal side seemed to be stronger. Therefore, if one planned to improve the Japanese race, Japanese men and Western women were to be married. This, Katō conceded, would logically create superior mixed-race children who would then be able to preserve national sovereignty and lead Japan on the path of civilisation.[69] However, Katō challenged his readership by asking: 'Do you want to leave the future of Japan in the hands of superior mixed-race children?'[70] This question is representative of the dilemma between accepting Japanese racial inferiority or trying to improve the race with outside help. Katō clearly favoured the former option:

> even if our Japanese Empire cannot preserve its independence, even if that means that our fellow Japanese country men cannot make any progress on the path of civilisation, or that our Japanese homeland falls into the hand of Western people, I oppose the policy of having mixed race children.[71]

Both Takahashi Yoshio and Katō Hiroyuki (as well as the previously mentioned Inoue Tetsujirō) were evolving within the Western scientific paradigm of race. They accepted notions of race, heredity and struggle for survival as scientific truths. All saw the Japanese as inferior in terms of a biological race and as such unable to win the struggle for survival. However, this inferiority was seen as temporary. In the same vein as Inoue, who saw the introduction of mixed residence not as impossible per se but as too early, both Takahashi and Katō believed in the potential of the evolution and adaptation of the Japanese race. For Takahashi, intermarriage with Western people was only a way to hasten this process of evolution. Oguma Eiji has argued that Takahashi had wanted to 'remodel the Japanese nation itself into a superior Caucasian nation' by mixing the blood of the 'Japanese with the Westerners as much as possible'.[72] However, Takahashi's aim was not to suppress the Japanese race, but to improve it, in eugenicist fashion, by suppressing what he saw as its deficient features.[73] His opponent, Katō Hiroyuki, accused him of wanting to destroy the Japanese, as intermarriage with Western people would lead to the transformation of the Japanese into Whites and hence to the disappearance of the Japanese race.[74]

It is noteworthy that the above-mentioned individuals were all convinced nationalists. Despite their acknowledgement of racial inferiority, all three in their own way were attempting to prepare Japan for the perceived upcoming struggle. Yet, the most conspicuous common aspect of their ideas is the deeply engrained racial insecurity they manifest. None of them sincerely believed that, at that point in time, the Japanese would be able to survive a confrontation with the White race. Hence the constant reminder of the fate that awaited inferior races in the struggle for survival. Kaneko Kentarō's exchange with Herbert Spencer is not merely an anecdote in this regard, but a measure of the authority of Western racial thinking in Meiji Japan and of its power on the self-identification process of the Japanese. In the end, however, despite serious discussions about the topic, it was not racial miscegenation but prowess in combat that made the Japanese reappraise themselves, and that made the Western nations reassess the Japanese race. The racial insecurity which led to the belief that the Japanese were not able to survive as a biological race faded away on the battlefields of the First Sino-Japanese War.

Notes

1. As cited in Lake and Reynolds, *Drawing the Global Colour Line*, 9.
2. Lauren, *Power and Prejudice*, 70.
3. T. R. Jernigan, 'Japan's Entry into the Family of Nations', *The North American Review* 169, no. 513 (August 1899): 226.
4. Despite its age, Gong's study remains the major work on what is now labelled the 'classical' standard of civilisation. This refers to the standard that was born out of the Westphalian states' system and was used to regulate international relations, first between the newborn European nations, and then with nations beyond Europe. Brett Bowden described the legacy and ongoing relevance of Gong's work as follows: 'Gong's book received something of a mixed reception at the time of its publication; it was a bit of an oddity in the field of international relations in that it dealt explicitly with the exclusivist nature of the European-cum-Western international society. More recently it has experienced a sort of second coming as a small but significant minority of international relations scholars became increasingly concerned about the historical and contemporary plight of the "Other."' See Brett Bowden, *The Empire of Civilization: The Evolution of an Imperial Idea* (Chicago: University of Chicago Press, 2009), 104.
5. Gong, *The Standard of 'Civilization' in International Society*, 14.
6. Ibid., 3–4.

7. Ibid., 53.
8. Lake and Reynolds, *Drawing the Global Colour Line*, 5.
9. Some of the other 'privileged' nations which interacted with the West through unequal treaties were China and the Ottoman Empire. For details, see Turan Kayaoglu, *Legal Imperialism: Sovereignty and Extraterritoriality in Japan, the Ottoman Empire, and China* (Cambridge: Cambridge University Press, 2010).
10. Bowden, 'The Colonial Origins of International Law', 2.
11. On 29 December 1890, a US Cavalry regiment committed a massacre on 150 Native Americans men, women and children on a reservation at Wounded Knee Creek in South Dakota. Twenty US soldiers were awarded the Medal of Honor for their actions.
12. Thomas G. Dyer, *Theodore Roosevelt and the Idea of Race* (Baton Rouge: Louisiana State University Press, 1980), 76.
13. Ibid.
14. Gong, *The Standard of 'Civilization' in International Society*, 29.
15. As cited in R. P. Anand, 'Family of "Civilized" States and Japan: A Story of Humiliation, Assimilation, Defiance and Confrontation', *Journal of the History of International Law* 5 (2003): 21. Interestingly, Wheaton's *The Elements of International Law* became the first textbook used by Japanese students of international law after the 'opening' of the country. See Harumi Goto-Shibata, 'Internationalism and Nationalism: Anti-Western Sentiments in Japanese Foreign Policy Debates, 1918–22', in *Nationalisms in Japan*, ed. Naoko Shimazu (London: Routledge, 2006), 68. For another work on the relationship between international law and colonialism, see Antony Anghie, *Imperialism, Sovereignty, and the Making of International Law* (Cambridge: Cambridge University Press, 2005).
16. Ceymil Aydin comes to the same conclusion in his analysis of pan-Asian and pan-Islamic movements: 'The new sense of Western self-reflection in relation to the non-Western world implied that no matter the success rate of non-Western reforms, non-Christian and non-white nations would never perfectly fulfill all the required standards of civilization because of defects in their racial makeup, religious dogmatism, or cultural character.' Cemil Aydin, *The Politics of Anti-Westernism in Asia: Visions of World Order in Pan-Islamic and Pan-Asian Thought*, Columbia Studies in International and Global History (New York: Columbia University Press, 2007), 40–1.
17. For another critic of the shortcomings of Gong's analysis, see Bowden, *The Empire of Civilization*, 105. Also see Shogo Suzuki, *Civilization and Empire: China and Japan's Encounter with European International Society* (London: Routledge, 2009). The exclusionary laws and the Paris Peace Conference are discussed in detail in Chapter 7 of this book.
18. Miles and Brown, *Racism*, 40–1.
19. See Lake and Reynolds, *Drawing the Global Colour Line*, 9.
20. It would be possible to argue that every person who lives on and benefits from a racial middle ground is in fact an 'agent', as that person's very existence is in a certain sense contributing to the formation and continued existence of the negotiation zone.

However, I would like to restrict the notion of 'agent' to people who actively engage in building and maintaining the middle ground as opposed to those who just passively benefit from it.

21. Henning has already presented the work of such agents in his studies. Concerning them, he wrote that 'when confronted with the perceived anomaly of a modern yet "heathen" Asian people, missionaries and scholars responded by emphasizing similarity rather than difference. They sought the evidence that the Japanese somehow were Christian and white.' Henning, *Outposts of Civilization*, 139.
22. R. P. Dore, 'The Prestige Factor in International Relations', *International Affairs* 51, no. 2 (April 1975): 194. The dilemma faced by the 'pupil' is exemplified by the President of the House of Peers Konoe Atsumaro (1863–1904), who as late as 1899 gave a speech at the Japan Society in London in which he conceded that Western people saw Japan as an 'Oriental monkey' for mimicking the West, but that Japan would nonetheless continue its efforts to learn the culture of superior countries. For details, see Urs Matthias Zachmann, *China and Japan in the Late Meiji Period: China Policy and the Japanese Discourse on National Identity, 1895–1904* (London: Routledge, 2009), 30.
23. 'Speech of Foreign Minister Mutsu Munemitsu in the House of Representatives', in *The Meiji Japan through Contemporary Sources*, vol. 3: 1869–1894, ed. Center for East Asian Cultural Studies (Tokyo, 1972), 185–6.
24. As cited in Lake and Reynolds, *Drawing the Global Colour Line*, 9–10.
25. See for example Auslin, *Negotiating with Imperialism*.
26. This inferior status was as much the reason for as the result of the treaties. The Western nations imposed serious legal restrictions, especially extraterritoriality, via the treaties because they believed that their own legal codes were superior and that the domestic legal system of the 'host country' was not developed enough to encompass foreigners from Western nations. For the 'logic' of the treaties, see Gong, *The Standard of 'Civilization' in International Society*.
27. Eikoh Shimao, 'Darwinism in Japan, 1877–1927', *Annals of Science* 38, no. 1 (1981): 93.
28. Unoura Hiroshi, 'Samurai Darwinism: Hiroyuki Katō and the Reception of Darwin's Theory in Modern Japan from the 1880s to the 1900s', *History and Anthropology* 11, no. 2–3 (1999): 239.
29. Michio Nagai, 'Herbert Spencer in Early Meiji Japan', *Far Eastern Quarterly* 14, no. 1 (November 1954): 55.
30. Weiner, 'The Invention of Identity', 105.
31. For the influence of social Darwinism on Japanese domestic issues, see Unoura, 'Samurai Darwinism'; Nagai, 'Herbert Spencer in Early Meiji Japan'. For the use of Spencer's theory to explain national success, see Weiner, 'The Invention of Identity', 109–10. In a recent study, G. Clinton Godart has relativised the common view of a smooth and uncontroversial acceptance of Darwinism in Japan. According to him, while the last years of the nineteenth century were characterised by a climate of intellectual openness and curiosity regarding new scientific ideas, the increasing militarism of the early twentieth century saw theories that could potentially put

the divinity of the emperor into question as threatening. See G. Clinton Godart, *Darwin, Dharma, and the Divine: Evolutionary Theory and Religion in Modern Japan* (Honolulu: University of Hawaii Press, 2017).

32. Inō Tentarō, *Naichi zakkyoron shiryō shūsei* (Tokyo: Hara shobō, 1992), 3.
33. Unoura Hiroshi, 'Shinkaron to naichi zakkyoron: Shinkaron juyō no ichi sokumen', *Kisato daigaku kiyōbu kiyō* (March 1988): 84. Zachmann has pointed out that the small number of foreigners living in Japan throughout the 1880s and 1890s make the intensity of the debate seem irrational. While this is undoubtedly true, it is also a measure of how insecure the Japanese were. See Zachmann, 'Race Without Supremacy', 263.
34. Inoue Tetsujirō, *Naichi zakkyoron* (Tokyo: Tetsugaku shoin, 1889).
35. Ibid., 10.
36. Ibid.
37. Ibid., 13.
38. Ibid.
39. Ibid., 15.
40. Ibid.
41. Ibid.
42. Ibid.
43. Ibid., 17.
44. Ibid., 20.
45. Ibid., 31.
46. Ibid., 35–43.
47. Henning, *Outposts of Civilization*, 128.
48. Inoue, *Naichi zakkyoron*, 49–50.
49. Ibid., 50.
50. Ibid., 51.
51. Zachmann for example dismisses the importance of race as follows: 'Thus, when mixed residence was finally introduced, it could be said that both pride and necessity had won over prejudice, and that race was hardly the issue'. Zachmann, 'Race Without Supremacy', 266.
52. As cited in ibid., 265.
53. Takahashi Yoshio, *Nihon jinshu kairyōron* (Tokyo: Ishikawa Hanjirō, 1884); Katō Hiroyuki, 'Nihon jinshu kairyōron no ben', *Tōkyō gakushi kaiin zasshi* 8, no. 1 (1886): 1–46.
54. Takahashi, *Nihon jinshu kairyōron*, 8.
55. Ibid., 9.
56. Ibid.
57. Katō, 'Nihon jinshu kairyōron no ben', 20–1.
58. Takahashi, *Nihon jinshu kairyōron*, 101–2.
59. Ibid., 10; Katō, 'Nihon jinshu kairyōron no ben', 1.
60. Takahashi, *Nihon jinshu kairyōron*, 29.
61. Ibid., 41.
62. Ibid., 31.

63. Ibid., 99.
64. Ibid., 100. Takahashi acknowledged that in ancient times Chinese and Koreans had mixed with Japanese, but since they were people of the same race (*dōitsu no jinshu*) no helpful effect was gained.
65. Ibid., 115. Takahashi pointed to the American state of Ohio which prohibited racial miscegenation between Whites and African Americans or Native Americans as a positive example of artificial selection.
66. Katō, 'Nihon jinshu kairyōron no ben', 4.
67. Ibid., 12.
68. Ibid., 13.
69. Ibid., 19–20.
70. Ibid., 22.
71. Ibid., 22–3.
72. Oguma, *A Genealogy of 'Japanese' Self-Images*, 143.
73. For details about eugenics in Japan, see Jennifer Robertson, 'Blood Talks: Eugenic Modernity and the Creation of New Japanese', *History and Anthropology* 13, no. 3 (2002): 191–216.
74. Hence Katō was against racial miscegenation. Weiner wrongly asserted that Katō's work is another example of Japanese arguing for race mixing. See Weiner, 'The Invention of Identity', 108; Michael Weiner, '"Self" and "Other" in Imperial Japan', in *Japan's Minorities: The Illusion of Homogeneity*, ed. Michael Weiner (London: Routledge, 2009), 6.

Chapter 4

Two Wars and First Successes: From the Port Arthur Massacre to the Treaty of Portsmouth

In July 1894, tensions between the Qing dynasty and Japan over the status of Korea erupted into war.[1] One week after the Japanese forces took the city of Port Arthur in late November 1894, a journalist for the French newspaper *Le Petit Journal* gave his comment on the siege of the city. He had not much sympathy left for the Chinese defeat:

> [The news of Port Arthur had] brought our [France's] joy to its pinnacle. Trained and armed in the European way, Japan is currently administrating a serious beating to the Chinese. Nothing better, and our dead from Tonkin will be avenged. I say: Will be, because I hope that it is not yet over; I even hope that the skinning of the great mastodon has yet just begun.[2]

The occupation of the main parts of China, he continued, will make civilisation in Asia do a leap forward of three centuries and it was quite the spectacle to see 'the beneficial invasion of the backwards and barbaric Orient by the progressive and modern Orient'.[3] Before the war, China, 'that amorphous monster, terrible as much as abject, the shame of humanity', was thought to be invincible. But the Japanese had shown 'that there was nothing in China. No authority, no intelligence, no military capacity'.[4] The French opinion, according to the journalist, could be resumed as follows:

> Go ahead, Japan! And no things by halves! The war until the end, until the final extermination, the sustainable material occupation, and foremost until the formal opening of China to European civilisation, willingly or not![5]

This article from *Le Petit Journal* is visibly tainted by resentment towards China: one decade prior to its publication, the French and Chinese armies had been clashing in French Indochina. Nevertheless, bitterness aside, the palpable sympathy towards Japan was not restricted to the French journalist, as Western public opinion often sided with the Japanese during the war.

There were several reasons for this tendency. The United States, for example, believed that a Japanese victory would lead to the advancement of progress and civilisation in Asia. It also believed that Korea would remain independent. The Americans also seemed to feel sympathetic towards what they saw as an underdog taking on a much bigger enemy.[6] Some British international lawyers supported Japan by providing legal justification for the war in the framework of international law, while at the same time presenting Japan as a civilised nation opposed to a barbaric China.[7] The Germans seem to have shared this enthusiasm for Japan: no less than 161 letters of congratulations and encouragement were sent from Germany to the Japanese Ministry of War during the conflict against China.[8] The tone of these letters did not differ greatly from the French article quoted above. One writer for example asserted that 'the shining victories of Japanese weapons over Chinese barbarity must fill the heart with satisfaction of every person with an interest in human civilisation'.[9]

The First Sino-Japanese War was indeed, in the words of Douglas Howland, 'a key moment at which the European founders of the "family of nations" did choose to expand their membership overseas and to bring Japan within the club'.[10] However, accepting Japan did also mean accepting a non-White newcomer who was, racially speaking, at the opposite end of White Christendom. The war, therefore, was also a test to judge whether the Japanese had shed their alleged racial defects and were worthy of joining the family. The developments in China made a successful completion of the test seem certain, until a massacre led to some reflections.

Early benefits of the racial middle ground: the Port Arthur Massacre

The fall of Port Arthur in November 1894 was at first praised as proof of Japan's successful march towards civilisation. The *Chicago Daily Tribune*, for example, concluded that: 'This much is certain – Japan has earned the right to be respected as one of the world's great nations and that it will in the future be treated with respect and consideration in all international relations.'[11] The same newspaper reported later that, 'all the naval and military experts consider the achievement of the Japanese as marvellous. They astonished everyone. They are equal to any European army or navy.'[12]

The problem was not the attack itself, which seem to have been unanimously lauded as a deed worthy of Europeans. It was what occurred in the wake of the battle that caused controversy: a few days after the siege, rumours started to circulate that the Japanese soldiers had committed a massacre upon entering the city. The *Los Angeles Times* told its readers that Chinese refugees were accusing the Japanese of murdering old and young once in the city.[13] On the same day the *Los Angeles Times* article appeared, a foreign correspondent for the London *Times* reached Hiroshima from Port Arthur to meet with Foreign Minister Mutsu to discuss the issue. He allegedly witnessed the massacre and asked Mutsu for explanations. His report was then published in *The Times* on 3 December.[14] However, it was through the report of another foreign correspondent, James Creelman (1859–1915), that the issue of the Port Arthur Massacre gained worldwide attention.

A journalist for the *New York World*, Creelman was famous for his penchant towards sensationalism.[15] On 11 December, he cabled his report to the *World*'s office in New York.[16] The next day it was on its front page:

> The Japanese troops entered Port Arthur on Nov. 21 and massacred practically the entire population in cold blood.
>
> The defenseless and unarmed inhabitants were butchered in their houses and their bodies were unspeakably mutilated. There was an unrestrained reign of murder which continued for three days. The whole town was plundered with appalling atrocities.
>
> It was the first stain upon Japanese civilization. The Japanese in this instance relapsed into barbarism.
>
> All pretenses that circumstances justified the atrocities are false. The civilized world will be horrified by the details.
>
> The foreign correspondents, horrified by the spectacle, left the army in a body.[17]

More sensationalist accounts with graphic details followed Creelman's original dispatch.[18]

The news of the massacre was more than problematic. As Sarah C. M. Paine observed, the Japanese troops had directed their efforts at exhibiting the high degree of civilisation of their country through gallant behaviour on the battlefield and humane treatment of non-combatants and prisoners alike.[19] The stories about Port Arthur contrasted starkly with the accustomed praise of the Japanese conduct of war. Yet, it is surprising to observe how ambivalent the Western reactions were to the tales of massacre. Where one would expect to find undisputed criticism, one finds on the contrary a great deal of sympathy towards the Japanese.

At the time when the massacre was but a rumour, the newspaper *The Atlanta Constitution* stated that the allegations of excessive slaughter were denied by Japanese officers, 'although it would have been excusable in consequence of torture and mutilation of Japanese soldiers'.[20] The paper was referring to something that contributed to demonise the Chinese as barbarians deserving of their treatment: on the way to besiege Port Arthur, the advancing Japanese troops apparently found the bodies of comrades severely mutilated, with their feet, hands and heads cut off. Some had been crucified and burned alive. The furore of the Japanese troops grew further when letters from Chinese officers demanding payment for the feet and hands of Japanese soldiers were found inside the city magistrate's office.[21] This alleged barbarity was sometimes compared to that, equally alleged, of Native Americans: *The Washington Post* reported that,

> Not only were some of the Japanese captives crucified and others burned alive at the stake, but their dead bodies were so horribly treated that the tales of Indian massacres in the early days of the frontier pale in comparison.[22]

The *Los Angeles Times* doubted the reports of the massacre altogether, but was quite certain of Chinese barbarity: again, equalling Chinese and Native Americans, the newspaper claimed that:

> It is quite possible that when maddened by the sight of atrocities that had been committed by the Chinese on their countrymen, the Japanese troops committed some excesses, but, in view of the record which the Japanese army has made hitherto during the war, it is hard to believe that the troops could have so suddenly changed their natures and gone into the business of wholesale butchery after the style of Apaches – or Chinese.[23]

The article then retells the story of a Korean village that had suffered under Chinese oppression but was liberated by the Japanese troops. This again would cast doubts on the allegations, and the Japanese behaviour was consistent with those of the other civilised nations of the world: 'The manner in which they have . . . overcome the most populous country on the face of the globe is one of the remarkable things of modern times', and it would place 'Japan in the front rank of civilized nations'.[24]

The comparison between the Chinese and Native Americans, and by extension of the Japanese with frontiersmen is not innocent. The Japanese advance into China was framed with the same ideology as the westward expansion of British settlers into the American continent: as the advance of civilisation into barbarian lands. In the eyes of the West, therefore, Japan, as a proxy for the Western nations, was bestowing civilisation upon the Chinese. The *New York Herald* could thus proclaim that Japan was on a *mission civilisatrice* and that it should be allowed to 'lift up her benighted neighbor into the sphere of modern life and utility'.[25] Japan was tasked with 'the breaking down of Chinese conservatism and the introduction of western civilization into the empire', heralded the *Chicago Tribune*, and it was therefore advisable to let Japan 'knock sense into the dull obstinate Chinese heads'.[26] The Japanese could not agree more: in an article written in English for the American public, the diplomat Kurino Shin'ichirō (1851–1937) explained that 'this war is in some measure a struggle between the forces of modern civilization and the *vis inertiae* of a conservatism the strongest and most stubborn the world has ever seen'.[27]

The outburst of violence could be condoned as an appropriate response to Chinese barbarity, and many newspapers argued that any Western power would have acted the same as Japan. A New York newspaper assured that the Japanese would give no quarter to the Chinese, 'and why should they? My own feelings were terribly roused at the horrible sight.'[28] To that, *The Washington Post* rhetorically responded: 'How many armies of Christian soldiery, we wonder, would have spared the authors of such fiendish barbarity under similar circumstances.'[29]

A final striking example can be found in a special correspondence of *Frank Leslie's Illustrated Weekly*. The journalist of the paper strongly denied the allegations of massacre and blamed the Chinese for the Japanese behaviour: 'They [the Chinese] were armed with German repeating rifles, and used express cartridges with explosive bullet – a thing no civilized nation would ever do.'[30] The reporter therefore asked:

> What would have been the conduct of any European army or an American army under the circumstances? Can anyone say that . . . soldiers from any country would not have committed excesses? I am only surprised that the Japanese committed so few . . . The whole responsibility of the killing rests upon the Chinese officers.[31]

The conclusion was that: 'Japan has done nothing which justifies people in saying that she has lost her right to enter the great family of civilized nation, and this war will remain the battle of civilization against barbarism.'[32]

The reaction of the American newspapers to the Port Arthur Massacre is reminiscent of Roosevelt's comment on the massacre of Native Americans mentioned in Chapter 3: the standard of civilisation used by nations of European descent could not be applied to the Chinese. The Japanese, as a substitute for Western nations, could therefore be excused for their excesses. The Port Arthur episode demonstrates that the West was starting to grant a racial middle ground to Japan, which gave it the licence to mistreat people considered as inferior. Japan was slowly becoming part of the sphere of White supremacy. The Chinese were in this case the 'subpersons', that Mills defines as 'humanoid entities who because of racial phenotype/genealogy/culture, are not fully human and therefore have a different and inferior schedule of rights and liberties applying to them'.[33] This enables behaviour towards them that would not be possible with persons, 'because they do not have the same rights as persons'.[34] On the middle ground, Japan was therefore allowed to do to Chinese what would have been unthinkable to do to Whites.

However, as the idea of a middle ground implies, Japan's acceptance into the sphere of White supremacy was not absolute and there always remained a level of distrust. Not everyone shared in the enthusiasm for the Japanese conduct, and if the war was seen as a test for the civilisational level of Japan, the massacre was to some a proof that the country had failed. A few voices expressed their concerns that Japan went back to its original state of 'Oriental barbarism'. The ambivalent feelings directed towards Japan are highlighted by the fact that the same newspapers which lauded Japan for its civilised behaviour could at the same time criticise it for its barbarism: 'The Japanese had shown that they are fully capable of the worst barbarities . . . It is to be feared that the Christian civilization of the Japanese is only a very thin varnish. Scratch it, and the barbarian is revealed.'[35]

The Washington Post republished criticism of Japan for endangering 'the admiration which Europe was so liberally extending to the Japanese'.[36] The mutilation of Chinese soldiers were 'carried on with every form that oriental brutality had ever invented', and the Japanese officers were 'totally losing their European veneer'.[37] Unfortunately for the Japanese, this opinion was not confined to the realm of news reporting: the American Consul General at Yokohama told the American Secretary of State Walter Q. Gresham (1832–95) in a private report that the Japanese were but children regarding civilisation. They had imitated Western civilisation before having undergone the necessary mental and moral growth and were not capable of understanding the legal fundaments of civilised countries.[38]

The entry of Japan into the family of civilised nations was a double-edged sword: on the one hand, it gave the Japanese licence to mistreat persons considered inferior as part of a *mission civilisatrice*. Despite the massacre, the American Senate unanimously approved the revision of the unequal treaty between the United States and Japan in 1895 – the year the First Sino-Japanese War ended.[39] At the same time, unlike other nation members of the club, Japan did not have the inherent racial advantage and therefore needed to constantly prove its adherence to the White standard. There always remained the apprehension that its 'true nature' lurked beneath the surface and would eventually show itself. The Japanese were painfully aware of this, despite the further successes of the racial middle ground that came in the following decade.

'Yellow fears' of 'yellow peril': race and the Russo-Japanese War

Amongst its numerous geopolitical repercussions, the First Sino-Japanese War had several effects on Japan. The racial insecurity of the former years faded away and gave way to the self-confidence of a first-rate nation (*ittō koku*).[40] Second, it was proof to the Western nations that the Japanese were an exception amongst 'coloured' people, and that Japan was turning its back on the 'Orient'. The Japanese were keen to emphasise this: the already mentioned Kurino commented shortly after the war that the observer of Japanese history will not fail to discover

> the sincere purpose which actuates the only Asiatic people who have sought to improve their condition and to strengthen their position as an independent and self-respecting nation, by voluntarily adopting and practically utilizing the elements of Western progress and civilization.[41]

The discussions surrounding the Port Arthur Massacre show that the Western powers agreed with this statement.

The signing of the Anglo-Japanese Alliance on 30 January 1902 further confirmed Japan's newly gained status. The alliance recognised the respective interests of Japan and Great Britain in the Far East, and guaranteed support in a war with more than one power.[42] The symbolic significance of the pact is hard to overstate. As an astute Japanese witness of the events observed, 'the fact that the alliance was made between two different races and two different religions makes it truly special in the history of modern diplomatic relations'.[43] At least at the diplomatic level, Japan was now on par with Great Britain. The Japanese public rejoiced accordingly: the *Asahi shinbun* claimed that 'both Houses [of the parliament] are welcoming it [the alliance] with standing ovations, and the people too are looking forward to it with thundering applause'.[44] The former (and future) Prime Minister Ōkuma Shigenobu (1838–1922) deemed the alliance a diplomatic victory for Japan which was cause for celebration not only for statesmen but also for the Japanese people as a whole.[45]

In our case, the alliance highlights how realpolitik can influence the racial status of a nation. Whether considered in the international or in the specific context of the British Empire, the Anglo-Japanese alliance was an anomaly equal to that of having a modern 'coloured' nation. By the end of the nineteenth century, the British Dominions of New Zealand, Australia and Canada had all promulgated exclusionary laws aimed at Asians and were deeply concerned with keeping their territory free of non-Whites: as Cornelis Heere wrote, 'By 1914' – that is at a time the alliance was still active – 'every dominion (even tiny Newfoundland) had enacted some combination of law and policy to bar Asian migrants from its shores'.[46] The decision of the British government to enter into an alliance with a non-White people, despite its old policy of 'splendid isolation', was therefore in direct contradiction to the global imperialist trends of the time, as well as with the racial policies of its own dominions. Some observers did criticise the British government for its 'treason': Wilhelm II (1859–1941), the German Kaiser, accused the British in an interview from 1908 of being 'a traitor to the White man's cause'.[47] By others, Great Britain was accused of 'standing behind' Japan,[48] and at some later point the Australians feared that the British would abandon their support for a 'White Australia' in favour of the alliance.[49]

Despite the accusations of race treachery, it would be a mistake to read signs of racial tolerance in the British decision. The *Kokumin shinbun* agreed that the alliance was 'marvellous' especially considering that 'a grave barrier exists between the two in the shape of racial and religious prejudice'.[50] However, the newspaper also warned that after some reflection, 'this marvel will disappear, for the trend of affairs in the Far East urged upon England the necessity of making an important departure in her diplomatic history'.[51] The alliance with a non-White race was above all a pragmatic decision, as for British diplomats Japan could prove, as Antony Best has aptly put it, 'a particularly useful piece in a global game of chess'.[52]

The question of incentive notwithstanding, proponents of the alliance needed to emphasise why Japan was different from the rest of the 'coloured' people. This was consistent with the working process of a racial middle ground, as it was this distinctiveness of Japan that justified the temporary repeal of the racial barrier in the first place. Hence, articles in the British press praising the 'specialness' of the Japanese were not hard to find: 'The awakening of Japan', as an article from *Blackwood's Edinburgh Magazine* stated,

> her easy attainment to a height of civilisation which has already caused more than one white nation to blush for its unsuspected inferiority . . . have been so startling, so dramatic, that they have forced themselves upon the notice of the least observant'.[53]

A new power was born in the East and 'Japan stands before the world to-day as the one Asiatic nation which has proved that she is capable of self-government'.[54] Interestingly, the article then went on to praise Japan's colonial accomplishments in Taiwan (without forgetting to mention its mentor Britain) and even put them above those of other European powers:

> Already she has tried an interesting experiment in oriental colonisation, having annexed Formosa, which she is now governing in no selfish spirit, and upon lines closely copied from those which Great Britain has worked out for the administration of an inferior people. Hitherto conquest in Asia by Asiatics has been synonymous with every kind of excess, and the subjugation of a weaker race has always resulted in ruthless tyranny. But in this, as in all else, Japan has revolutionised the traditions of the East, and to-day we have before us the remarkable spectacle of an Asiatic race ruling over a wild and turbulent brown people with a good sense and an altruism which does not always distinguish the colonial administrations of European nations.[55]

In just three sentences, *Blackwood's Edinburgh Magazine* had acknowledged the superiority of Japan over the rest of the Asian people, put it on par with European powers, and even went as far as deeming it more apt to colonial rule than other European nations. The British publicist Wemyss Reid, publishing in the *Nineteenth Century and After*, agreed with this assessment:

> Never in the known history of mankind has any nation undergone so complete and astounding a transformation within a limited period as that which Japan has undergone within the last forty years . . . It is, in many respects, more modern than any European country, including England.[56]

Reid's view on the alliance with Japan was that it should not 'be regarded as placing us on a lower plane than an alliance with any European state would have done'.[57]

Elevating Japan over other 'coloured' nations was not only a matter of words but also of acts. Antony Best gave a fascinating account of how the British government used royal honours, such as decorations, on Japanese statesmen in order to foster the signing of the Anglo-Japanese Alliance.[58] This also worked to make the difference between the Japanese and other non-White nations visible: invited to the coronation of Edward VII, the Japanese delegate Prince Komatsu was granted a state carriage for the journey to Westminster Abbey, while delegates from Persia, China, Korea, Egypt, Ethiopia and Zanzibar were not.[59]

The recent victory against China and the alliance with Great Britain had highlighted that Japan was now a great power worthy to join the ranks of White nations. It also highlighted the fact, however, that the nation possessed a substantial military force and an increasing influence in East Asia. The implications of this realisation also had a negative effect on Japan's image, as the spectre of the infamous 'yellow peril' came to haunt the nation's relations with the West. The catchphrase refers to the idea that members of the 'yellow' race pose a threat to the White nations. This threat can take several forms: an economic one, in the form of cheap Asiatic labour flooding Western markets; a military one, as an Asian military alliance (usually under Japanese guidance) invading the West; and a cultural threat, with Asian customs 'sullying' Western cultural standards.[60]

Retracing the origin of the idea is difficult,[61] but the end of the First Sino-Japanese War and especially the Tripartite Intervention at the end of the war contributed to popularising it on a global level. The terms of the Peace Treaty of Shimonoseki signed on 17 April 1895 guaranteed the cession of Taiwan, the Pescadores, and the Liaodong Peninsula to Japan. Alarmed by these developments, Russia, Germany and France decided to intervene and gave 'friendly advice' to Japan to retrocede the Liaodong Peninsula in the interest of peace in Asia.[62] While race was not the decisive factor in the decision of the three powers to intervene, it was not entirely absent from it. One month before the actual intervention, the German Foreign Minister Adolf Marschall von Bieberstein (1842–1912) met with a Russian diplomat and warned him that an alliance between members of the 'yellow race' would be dangerous:

> The Japanese are, like the Chinese, members of the 'yellow' race. They have already earned a great deal of prestige in the eyes of the Chinese. If they manage to build a protectorate in China, this will not only go against the interests of the European powers, but also lead the 'yellow' race to think that they have common interests.[63]

The person who was notorious for his phobia of the 'yellow peril' is the already mentioned German Kaiser Wilhelm II. The lasting contribution of the Kaiser in this regard was his commission of the infamous painting *Völker Europas wahrt eure heiligsten Güter* (Ye Mighty Nations of Europe, Protect Your Most Holy Goods, 1895). The painting metaphorically represents a military alliance between Japan and China against the European nations. In the background, a Buddha (Japan) is riding a fiery dragon (China), while in the foreground several female warriors, each representing a European nation, are guided by the archangel Michael. A cross floats above the head of the European warriors, symbolising their common denomination as Christian nations. The Kaiser had copies of the painting sent to the European rulers and displayed in German ships.[64] The painting also quickly became well known in Japan, where a reproduction was published in early 1896, with the emperor seeing it the same year.[65]

It is hard to say to what extent the Western nations – beyond a few individuals – took the spectre of the 'yellow peril' seriously. The Kaiser's painting quickly became the object of ridicule after it became public, with satirical papers all over Europe reprinting their own version of it. On the other hand, the ascendancy of Japan did occur during a time when a struggle between the different races of the world was thematised by numerous writers on race.[66]

The abundant publications about the declining influence of Western civilisation bear witness to how acute the subject seems to have been.[67] The British-born historian Charles H. Pearson (1830–94) for example, warned in his *National Life and Character* (1893) that the Black and 'yellow' races had been educated by the White race but might very likely turn against their former teachers. Fleets of non-Western countries would sail the world seas, non-Whites would fill European conference rooms and salons, and intermarriage would destroy Western society.[68] Following its military and political developments, it was natural that Japan became the main suspect, as it was the only non-White power that had the potential to resist European and American imperialism.[69] The excuse of race could therefore prove especially convenient to counter Japanese ambitions. Whatever the importance of the 'yellow peril' in the West, then, the Japanese took the idea very seriously. The army surgeon and writer Mori (Rintarō) Ōgai (1862–1922) recognised this early on. In a lecture given at Waseda University in November 1903,[70] that is, a few months before the start of the Russo-Japanese War, Ōgai warned his audience about the implications of the idea:

> People from the White race usually lump our [Japanese] people together with the other 'yellow' races. I feel nothing but contempt and a feeling of distrust for this. Because of that, even if it pains me, I came to the realisation that it is my fate to oppose myself to the White race . . . The study of the so-called 'yellow peril' is the study of the enemy's feelings. . . .[71]

Considering this, it seems natural that when the country was inevitably drifting towards war with Russia, race became, along land and naval warfare, a component that needed strategic planning. On 30 December 1903, the Japanese cabinet ministers met in a small council and discussed the course to take if Russo-Japanese relations were to escalate into an open war. One of the issues that had to be taken care of was the resurgence of the 'yellow peril' idea. The instructions read as follows:

> Prevent the renewed outbreak of the cry of 'yellow peril'
>
> Lately, the cry for the 'yellow peril', namely the fear of the White race that the 'yellow' race emancipates itself, is not to be heard. However, as before it is hidden deep inside Western people and if we decide to move [wage war against Russia] this fear will break out, with the risk of them uniting under this delusion. Therefore, should Japan and China unite and fight against Russia, this could possibly become the reason for a renewed cry for the 'yellow peril' and as a result lead countries such as France and Germany to intervene.[72]

The ministers were thus concerned with two factors: the first was that with regards to Japan fighting Russia, Whites would think in binary terms of 'White' versus 'yellow'. The second was that race could become a problematic factor. Accordingly, the Japanese had to prove that there was neither a problem with race nor with a potential alliance with China. This is where the racial middle ground was necessary: when the expected war finally came in 1904, those who reinforced the middle ground had to reassure the parties not directly involved in the conflict that Japan had no hidden agenda that could threaten nations of European descent. This in turn implied downplaying the importance of race in the conflict and avoiding at all costs the idea of an alliance of the 'yellow' races.

Agents of the racial middle ground

The agents from Japan who helped to maintain the racial middle ground were acting on behalf of the state. The Western side was composed of a more heterogeneous group: some were working for the Japanese state, while others were defending the interests of their own government. The common factor for both sides was that they focused their efforts on framing Japanese actions in terms acceptable to the West by insisting that Japan was behaving in the interest of Western civilisation.

Kaneko Kentarō, who we already know from his correspondence with Herbert Spencer, was one of the agents hired by the Japanese government 'to enlighten public opinion' (*yoron no keihatsu no tame*)[73] in the United States. Before leaving for America, he was given precise instructions by Prime Minister Katsura Tarō (1848–1913) and Foreign Minister Komura Jutarō (1855–1911) that can be summarised as follows: Kaneko was to make explicit that the war had started because of Russia. Furthermore, Russia was nurturing the fear of the 'yellow peril' and Kaneko was to prevent any further outbreak. He also had to emphasise that the Japanese government was doing everything possible to restrict the sphere of conflict. Finally, as the Japanese government's efforts to educate the Chinese were interpreted by some Western observers as a concrete manifestation of the 'yellow peril', Kaneko needed to explain that civilising the Chinese was in the interest of the world as a whole.[74]

Kaneko was an obvious choice. He had studied law at Harvard University, where he was enrolled alongside the later President Theodore Roosevelt. It was he who Kaneko met shortly after his arrival in the United States in mid-March 1904. According to a secret telegram (dated 29 March 1904), sent by the Minister to Washington Takahira Kogorō (1854–1926) to Foreign Minister Komura, Kaneko met Roosevelt on 26 March.[75] The meeting seems to have been more than pleasing: 'The president expressed his highest admiration for the marvellous progress Japan has made', and confidentially remarked that he believed in a Japanese victory.[76] This victory would prove to be

> a great blessing to the rest of world, by finding a new factor in the Empire as the centre of Western civilization in Asia, and she [Japan] would ultimately be able to establish herself as the great civilizing force in the East.[77]

Regarding the 'yellow peril', the president dismissed it as a 'cunning fabrication'. The German emperor did not know what he was talking about and 'to prove that so-called yellow peril was entirely a myth so long as it referred to the Japanese, the President emphasized the fact that it was Japan which alone bravely and successfully resisted Ghingiskhan [*sic*] in his invasion'.[78]

Quite a satisfactory meeting indeed: in his first discussion with Roosevelt on his mission, Kaneko had secured the middle ground for the Japanese, as the president not only defined Japan as a Western proxy in East Asia but also refuted the idea of a 'yellow peril'.

Kaneko continued his campaign by publishing articles in the American press and giving lectures in strategic places. On 28 April 1904 he gave a speech at his alma mater.[79] He began by clarifying that Japan had engaged in fighting moved 'by the same aspirations towards the progress of the race as those which characterize Anglo-Saxon civilization the world over'.[80] Tackling the issue of religion, Kaneko lamented that

> it is a matter of regret to me, even of sorrow, to hear any such views, for we the Japanese are not fighting for religion, we are battling against one of the greatest world powers for the peace of Asia, as well as for the national existence of Japan.[81]

Nevertheless, he rhetorically asked his audience which of Japan and Russia, considering their respective behaviour on and off the battlefield, could be praised for its Christian behaviour. Referring to the benevolent treatment of Russian POWs by the Japanese military and contrasting it to that of Japanese civilians by Russian authorities, he concluded that,

> A moment's examination of the facts will suffice to show that in this war it is we who have acted like Christians, and the Russians who have behaved like pagans.[82]

Kaneko then went on to try to persuade his audience of Japan's usefulness for the West. Probably inspired by his meeting with Roosevelt a month earlier, he used the rather far-fetched argument of the thirteenth-century Mongolian invasions to prove that the Japanese had already saved the West once by repelling the Mongol army:

> When, therefore, we hear people talk about the 'yellow peril' in the East, with obvious reference to Japan, we are bound to reply by asking who it was that, by the gallantry of its people, crushed back the tide of Mongolian invasion, and saved Europe from the fiendish wickedness of the only 'yellow peril' the world has ever known?[83]

Japan had once been 'the savior of Europe when Europe did not even know who saved her'.[84] For Kaneko, there was no 'yellow peril'. It was a manoeuvre designed by cunning diplomats who tried to alienate the Japanese from their Western allies.[85]

While it would be difficult to attribute all the blame for the resurgence of the 'yellow peril' to Russian diplomats, Kaneko was not entirely wrong. Russia did try to enlist the sympathy of the Western nations and also to unite its own people under a common banner by fuelling the fear of a race war. By pretending to fight a holy war against a terrible racial foe, the Russian Empire could distract its people from national problems, and at the same time gather support from eventual allies amongst the European or American nations.[86] The Russian minister to the US, Count Arthur Pavlovich Cassini (1836–1919), for example, was known for his constant portrayal of the Japanese as 'yellow monkeys'.[87] He too tried to gain American public opinion for his country, by pretending that Russia was acting as a White vanguard against a united army of the 'yellow' race. In an article for the *North American Review*, a publication outlet Kaneko was also using for his campaign, he warned his readers that,

> It is not a thoughtless statement that were Japan to obtain supreme control in Manchuria, the dominant military spirit of the Japanese would lead them to organize the Chinese into a modern army of such proportions that Europe and America would stand aghast at this menace to their peace and well-being. That is a phase of what has been called the 'Yellow Peril' that it would be well for the thoughtful and intelligent classes to consider carefully.[88]

Cassini asked readers to imagine such a 'union of the two great Mongol races', one of these ambitious and dreaming of domination 'not only in the Far East, but in the councils of the Powers'.[89] Directly addressing the readers, he warned: 'You of America, as well as we of Europe, have this to confront. It is not Russia alone that the danger threatens, but the whole family of Caucasian nations.'[90]

The Russian diplomat was trying to prevent the maintenance of the middle ground by emphasising the racial otherness and potential threat of the Japanese. If we contrast his approach to Kaneko's speech above, it becomes quite noticeable that the Japanese envoy tried on the contrary to emphasise the likeness of Japan to White nations: according to him, Japan was on a mission and 'simply seeks to . . . conserve the influence of Anglo-American civilization in the East'.[91] It was the duty of Japan to 'extend these blessings to other oriental nations whom we could influence'.[92] Emphasising the role of Japan as a proxy, Kaneko assured that 'Japan is really acting as the pioneer of Anglo-American civilization in the East. It is for this which we are fighting, and only this which is the meaning of the war.'[93]

The constant reminder that Japan was only acting on behalf of the Western powers might rightly seem redundant. But it is also revealing of how strong the need for justification for the Japanese was, and how dangerous the idea of the 'yellow peril' could be. Hence the emphasis on Japan's true aims, which Kaneko also stressed elsewhere: 'Such then, is the ultimate aspiration . . . of the Japanese race . . . Japan hopes to introduce Western culture and science into the continent of Asia.'[94]

Across the Atlantic, the Japanese Minister to Austria Makino Nobuaki (1861–1949) decided to hire the services of a scholar from the University of Budapest, Hermann Vámbéry (1832–1913) to act as an agent for the Japanese government. Makino explained his motivations in a telegram to Komura as follows:

> In view of growing mischief done on the Continent by [*sic*] absurd cry of yellow peril paganism etc. I asked Vambery to write [*sic*] pamphlet on the subject with a view to dissipate the notions and he is willing to do so.[95]

According to Makino, about 10,000 copies in German and French could be distributed throughout Europe.[96]

It is not quite clear why Vámbéry accepted, and one can only speculate that he did it either for the financial aspect or out of sympathy towards the Japanese. Whatever the reasons, he wrote a small booklet of thirty-six pages entitled *Die Gelbe Gefahr: eine Kulturstudie* (1904).[97] Vámbéry criticised the Europeans for being hypocritical, for while they warned of a 'yellow peril', Germany and Russia were carving their way into China. Japan, he claimed, was only moving because its existence was being threatened.[98] Setting the Japanese apart from other Asians, Vámbéry claimed that Japan had left Asianism (*Asiatismus*) and could not possibly want to jeopardise its efforts now.[99] The Japanese were enlightened and many of the persons in high positions were Christians. Such people, he stated, could not become a threat to Europe.[100] Vámbéry dismissed any idea of an alliance with China because he saw the Japanese and the Chinese as two different people:

> One will never have to speak of a fraternisation between the two people under the leadership of Japan because of this [their differences]. How fundamentally different these two people are, can best be demonstrated by emphasising that while China has been in contact with the West for centuries without having learned anything from it, Japan has completely Europeanised itself in a few decades.[101]

Turning to Russia, Vámbéry stated that it was in no position to complain as in matters of political culture, Russia was more Asian than Japan:

> It is hard to understand why it belongs to Russia to accuse the Japanese of being dangerous and a peril to our culture. This Russia should put its own house in order in matters of Asiatic condition, as its gruesome absolutism and tyranny do not find their equals even in Asia. The Mongolian strain in Russia is much stronger than in Japan.[102]

Vámbéry's attempt to switch the roles by presenting Russia as the Asian nation and Japan as the European one was a cunning move. It should be remembered that the aim of a racial middle ground is to 'elevate' the racial status of the race in the middle. Vámbéry did so using Russia as 'the race at the bottom' and by arguing that it was not skin colour but political or societal behaviour that mattered. This enabled him to argue that the Russians were more 'Mongolian' than the Japanese. He was not alone in using this argument. We have seen earlier that Kaneko had tried to convince his audience that Japan was more Christian in its behaviour than Russia. He went further in one article by stating that a Japanese victory would mean the 'occidentalizing' of the East, while Russia was standing for an 'absolutism that is Oriental'.[103] A Russian victory would lead to 'the perpetuation of ignorance and the reign of force'.[104]

Theodore Roosevelt himself believed that it was the Russians who were the descendants of the Mongol Empire and as such the real 'yellow peril'.[105] He even went as far as claiming that despite not being Christians, the Japanese were closer to the Whites than the Slavs.[106] The 'Slavic' argument was also used by American observers of the war, who divided the Caucasian race into the superior Anglo-Saxon branch and the inferior Slavic one. Hence, even if Russians were Whites, they remained an inferior type of Whites.[107]

Some people went so far as to question whether the Russians were even White to begin with. One article from the *North American Review* asked in its title if Russia did represent Aryan civilisation.[108] According to the author, Russia was trying to stir up fears of the 'yellow peril' and attempting 'to enlist sympathy by assuming the part of "Champion of the Aryan Race"', while in truth, there was 'much Mongolism in Russia herself'.[109] He explained that historically speaking the Russians were more 'Mongolian' than Slav, and with the thirteenth-century Mongol invasions had become 'doubly Mongolized'.[110] When the Mongol Empire fell apart, Czardom emerged on its ruins 'as a continuation, so to say, of the despotic rule of the Khans'.[111] Great parts of Russia were made up of a mixed or non-Aryan population, and even a world-famous Russian painter had 'Tatar blood' in him.[112] 'All I wished to show', the author claimed 'is that, with such facts before us, the Russian Government has the least claim to the part of Defender of the Aryan Race and of European Culture.'[113]

The animosity towards Russia displayed in the article was no isolated case. Western politicians, missionaries and journalists did not fail to criticise the tsarist regime and the Russian Orthodox Church as the remnants of a stagnant and backward system. For this, the Western-trained Japanese and their recent commitment to religious freedom proved to be a convenient tool.[114] This leads us to an interesting understanding: the fact that Japan's opponent in the war was Russia significantly influenced the racial middle ground between Japan and Western powers. One can only speculate on the outcome of such negotiations if the opponents of Japan had been Great Britain or the United States. What is certain is the fact that the strategic comparison between an 'Oriental' Russia, with its backwardness and conservatism, and a modern, 'European'

Japan questioned, if only temporarily, the very fabric of racial identities. To fully comprehend the momentousness of such theoretical acrobatics, it is useful to position the Russo-Japanese War into the wider racial context of the time.

Despite all the evidence presented above, the preservation of the racial middle ground during the Russo-Japanese War remains a perplexing case. Viewed inside the basic framework of international relations, it was a pragmatic, almost superficial act: Japan and Russia were fighting each other; the nations of European descent outside of the conflict were inclined to dislike Russia and hence supported Japan. For this, race did not really matter in the decision to side with Japan. However, the picture is altered if we view the war in the context of the global race relations of the time. While the result remains the same – a negotiation zone was created out of pragmatism and race became temporarily irrelevant – the reasoning that leads to this conclusion is reversed: race was not absent from the story because it was unimportant. It was because race was a crucial and ubiquitous factor that it was necessary to put it in the background.

The Russo-Japanese War had been a global conflict, in the sense that its repercussions were felt beyond the borders of the two nations actively engaged in it.[115] It also coincided with global trends towards racial expansion, separation and exclusion, and occurred at a time when discussions on race shifted their focus from the inequality between the races to the international struggle of existence between them.[116] The struggle was on several fronts – domestic and international – and fought through different means – imperialism and immigration. Commentors chose to frame it with social Darwinism, which provided scientific legitimation for racial laws and imperialism as natural developments.[117] The events unfolding everywhere on the globe seemed to confirm that the winner of this struggle would be the White race.[118]

Yet, despite these developments, another theme emerged parallel to the discussions of White supremacy: that of the impeding defeat of the White race. The most famous iteration of this idea was made by the already mentioned Charles H. Pearson in his *National Life and Character*.[119] Pearson's work is infused with pessimism and the sense that Whites could not escape their annihilation at the hand of 'coloured' races: 'If we cannot change manifest destiny, we may at least adapt ourselves to it, and make it endurable.'[120] He was, however, not equally afraid of all 'coloured' races. Pacific Islanders for example were, according to him, harmless, since doomed to vanish.[121] Those who were to be feared, Pearson warned, were the 'coloured' races who had been trained in Western ways, such as the Japanese.[122] The future that Pearson was envisioning for the White race was grim:

> The day will come, and perhaps is not far distant, when the European observer will look round to see that globe girdled with a continuous zone of the black and yellow races, no longer too weak for aggression or under tutelage, but independent, or practically so, in government, monopolising the trade of their own regions, and circumscribing the industry of the European.[123]

Whites who believed that the world belonged to those of the Aryan race and Christian faith,

> shall wake to find ourselves elbowed and hustled, and perhaps even thrust aside by peoples whom we looked down upon as servile, and thought of as bound always to minister to our needs. The solitary consolation will be, that the changes have been inevitable.[124]

Pearson died in 1894, the year Japan embarked on its civilisational test. Nevertheless, his work on the future of race relations made a sensation even before the First Sino-Japanese War.[125] The Australian Prime Minister Edmund Barton (1849–1920) used the above quote in in support of the Immigration Restriction Bill which aimed at excluding 'coloured' races from Australia.[126] On the American side, Roosevelt wrote to Pearson to express his personal admiration for the work.[127] And while the book earned Pearson the label of a 'race traitor', its most significant legacy, as Lake and Reynolds argue, was to 'shape the discursive and psychic frameworks in which much subsequent discussion of changing world forces would take place, in particular coming rivalry between East and West'.[128]

After the First Sino-Japanese War, Pearson's vison was not an abstract prophecy anymore. In his outlook for the twentieth century, American naval officer and confidant of Roosevelt's Alfred Thayer Mahan (1840–1914) warned his readers that,

> We stand at the opening of a period when the question is to be settled decisively, though the issue may not be long delayed, whether Eastern or Western civilization is to dominate throughout the earth and control its future.[129]

It was in this climate that the Russo-Japanese War unfolded: an intellectual and ideological framework that gave uttermost importance to race; a schizophrenic understanding of White supremacy, divided between the belief in the hegemony of the White race and its impending doom; a certainty regarding a future great race conflict; an awareness that this conflict would unfold in the East; and then, finally, an actual war that opposed 'White' Russians against 'yellow' Japanese.[130]

And yet, despite this 'end of an era' mood, no nation bothered to intervene on the side of the Russians. Where one would expect to find hysteria due to the Japanese deeds of war, one finds on the contrary the willingness to grant the Japanese a special racial status amongst White powers. This peculiar fact was not overlooked by French historian René Pinon (1870–1958), who, as a witness to the events, was surprised by the overwhelming sympathy shown by the Western nations towards Japan. In an essay from 1904, he reflected on the situation and wrote:

> One would believe, at first, that apart from some interested parties, the sympathy of European nations would naturally go to the European against the Asiatic, to the

white against the yellow, to the Christian against the non-Christian. But that is not the case.[131]

Pragmatism, which is probably the main driving force behind any racial middle ground, is not sufficient as an explanation in the case of the Russo-Japanese War. Roosevelt for example, called the two nations to the negotiation table in Portsmouth because he wanted a swift end to the war and balance in the Far East. As he explained to one of his senators, it was 'best' that Russia 'be left face to face with Japan so that each may have a moderative action on the other'.[132] Upsetting the racial status quo solely for this aim seems excessive.

Besides the animosity aimed at Russia mentioned earlier, there is another factor that could be considered: genuine sympathy towards Japan. This probably stemmed from several factors. It is plausible to think that sympathy was felt towards Japan because, as it was the case a decade earlier, it was in the position of an underdog, and because the nation had made astonishing progress in only a few decades. Also not negligible as a factor was the popularity that Japan, especially its art, enjoyed in the West at the time. *Japonaiserie* (Japanese-inspired creations) had taken over artistic circles. Susan J. Napier writes of a 'cult of Japan' that swept intellectuals and bohemians alike and led Western upper-class women to wear 'the latest kimono-inspired fashion' and the middle class to 'decorate their parlors with Japanese curios and fans'.[133] It is not irrational to think that this early form of involuntary 'soft power' helped to attract the sympathy of the West. The reasons behind the upholding of the negotiation zone during the Russo-Japanese War therefore must be seen as a combination of several factors, with maybe a healthy dose of historical mystery. Much more concrete, however, are the results that were obtained.

The successes of the racial middle ground can best be measured based on what did not occur. The first obvious achievement was that, unlike at the wake of the war against China ten years earlier, no foreign power intervened during or after the conflict. Roosevelt's role in negotiating the Treaty of Portsmouth (5 September 1905) can hardly be compared to the Tripartite Intervention of 1895: it did not rob Japan of any war gains, nor did it happen against Japan's will. On the contrary, Japanese cooperation in the negotiations was motivated by the understanding that Japan would lose the conflict in the long run. In this sense, Roosevelt's intervention may be seen as beneficial, not punitive for the Japanese.[134]

A second indicator of the success of the racial middle ground was that the issue of race did not have any influence during the war. Despite Russia's attempt to stir up fears of the 'yellow peril', Western public opinion tended to sympathise with Japan and not with Russia. So much so that after the war, a Russia-friendly American journalist complained that Americans had celebrated the Japanese victories during the conflict as if they had been their own.[135] This does not mean that race did not matter. If it didn't, Kaneko would not have gone to the United States, Vámbéry would not have written on behalf of the Japanese government, and other writers would not have questioned the racial identity of the Russians. However, through the racial middle ground, notions of fixed racial identities, and the factors that were supposed to constitute these, were put into question. Therefore, in the time of conflict, a space was created in which Japan was not handicapped by its racial belonging. In this sense, the middle ground of the Russo-Japanese War reached the 'purest' form of the idea: it suspended the divisive function of race.

Notes

1. For details on the First Sino-Japanese War, see for example Sarah C. M. Paine, *The Sino-Japanese War of 1894–1895: Perceptions, Power, and Primacy* (Cambridge: Cambridge University Press, 2002).
2. Jean sans Terre, 'La Chine ouverte', *Le Petit Journal*, 28 November 1894.
3. Ibid.
4. Ibid.
5. Ibid.
6. Thomas L. Hardin, 'American Press and Public Opinion in the First Sino-Japanese War', *Journalism Quarterly* 50, no. 1 (1973): 54–5.
7. Douglas Howland, 'Japan's Civilized War: International Law as Diplomacy in the Sino-Japanese War (1894–1895)', *Journal of the History of International Law* 9, no. 2 (January 2007): 179–201.
8. Rolf-Harald Wippich, ed., *'Haut Sie, dass die Lappen fliegen!': Briefe von Deutschen an das japanische Kriegsministerium während des Chinesich-Japanischen Krieges 1894/1895*, vol. 067, OAG Taschenbuch (München: Iudicium, 1997), 2.
9. Ibid., 50.
10. Howland, 'Japan's Civilized War', 180.
11. 'Capture of Port Arthur', *Chicago Daily Tribune*, 27 November 1894.
12. 'How It Was Done', *Chicago Daily Tribune*, 5 December 1894.
13. 'Awful if True', *Los Angeles Times*, 29 November 1894.
14. Donald Keene, *Emperor of Japan: Meiji and his World, 1852–1912* (New York: Columbia University Press, 2002), 492–3.
15. Jeffery M. Dorwart sees Creelman as laying the basis for sensationalist reporting in American newspapers. For this and details on Creelman's work, see Jeffery M. Dorwart, 'James Creelman, the New York World and the Port Arthur Massacre', *Journalism Quarterly* 50, no. 4 (1973): 697–701.
16. Ibid., 699.
17. James Creelman, 'A Japanese Massacre', *New York World*, 12 December 1894.
18. Dorwart, 'James Creelman, the New York World and the Port Arthur Massacre', 699.
19. Paine, *The Sino-Japanese War of 1894–1895*, 209.
20. 'How the Japs Did It', *The Atlanta Constitution*, 30 November 1894.
21. See for example: 'Some of Them Crucified', *The Atlanta Consitution*, 18 December

1894; 'Japan on Its Behavior', *The New York Times*, 18 December 1894; 'Japs on the Cross', *Los Angeles Times*, 18 December 1894.

22. 'Tortured by Chinese', *The Washington Post*, 18 December 1894.
23. 'Japan and China', *Los Angeles Times*, 19 December 1894.
24. Ibid.
25. As cited in Hardin, 'American Press and Public Opinion in the First Sino-Japanese War', 55.
26. As cited in ibid., 55.
27. S. Kurino, 'The Oriental War', *The North American Review* 159, no. 456 (November 1894): 536.
28. 'The Other Side of the Story', *The Washington Post*, 1 December 1894.
29. Ibid.
30. As cited in *The New York Times*, 'Japanese Accused Unjustly', 20 December 1894.
31. Ibid.
32. Ibid.
33. Mills, *The Racial Contract*, 56.
34. Ibid.
35. 'The Port Arthur Massacre', *The Atlanta Constitution*, 14 December 1894.
36. 'Horrors of Oriental Barbarity', *The Washington Post*, 8 January 1895.
37. Ibid.
38. 'The Truth about Port Arthur', *The Atlanta Constitution*, 10 January 1895.
39. Henning, *Outposts of Civilization*, 143.
40. Iriye, *Pacific Estrangement*, 46–7.
41. S. Kurino, 'The Future of Japan', *The North American Review* 160, no. 462 (May 1895): 631.
42. The origin and effects of the alliance have been scrutinised by numerous historians, amongst them Ian Nish. See Ian Nish, *The Anglo-Japanese Alliance: The Diplomacy of Two Island Empires, 1894–1907* (London: Bloomsbury, 2012).
43. Moriyama Tokō, 'Nichi-Ei no dōmei', Taiyō 8, no. 3 (March 1902): 59.
44. 'Nichi-Ei dōmei no happyō', *Asahi shinbun*, 13 February 1902.
45. Mori Toyokichi, *Nichi-Ei dōmei* (Tokyo: Kōbunsha, 1902), 49. For additional sources on the reaction of the Japanese public to the Anglo-Japanese alliance, see Yoshitake Oka, 'The First Anglo-Japanese Alliance in Japanese Public Opinion', in *Themes and Theories in Modern Japanese History: Essays in Memory of Richard Storry*, ed. Susan Henny and Jean-Pierre Lehmann (London: Bloomsbury; reprint, 2012), 185–93.
46. Cornelis Heere, '"That Racial Chasm That Yawns Eternally in our Midst": The British Empire and the Politics of Asian Migration, 1900–14', *Historical Research* 90, no. 249 (2017): 591. For more details on the role of race inside the Anglo-Japanese alliance in, see Heere's recent study: Cees Heere, *Empire Ascendant: The British World, Race, and the Rise of Japan, 1894–1914* (Oxford: Oxford University Press, 2020).
47. Iikura Akira, 'The Anglo-Japanese Alliance and the Question of Race', in *The*

Anglo-Japanese Alliance, 1902–1922, ed. Phillips Payson O'Brien (London: Routledge, 2004), 159–60.

48. Ibid., 160.
49. Heere, '"That Racial Chasm That Yawns Eternally in our Midst"', 595.
50. As cited in 'The Press on the Anglo-Japanese Alliance', *The Japan Times*, 14 Februrary 1902.
51. Ibid.
52. Antony Best, 'Race, Monarchy, and the Anglo-Japanese Alliance, 1902–1922', *Social Science Japan Journal* 9, no. 2 (October 2006): 173.
53. 'Problems of the Pacific', *Blackwood's Edinburgh Magazine* 171, no. 1040 (June 1902): 852.
54. Ibid., 852.
55. Ibid., 852–3.
56. Wemyss Reid, 'Last Month', *The Nineteenth Century and After* 51 (March 1902): 508. Also found in Best, 'Race, Monarchy, and the Anglo-Japanese Alliance, 1902–1922', 174.
57. Reid, 'Last Month', 509.
58. Best, 'Race, Monarchy, and the Anglo-Japanese Alliance, 1902–1922', 177–81.
59. Ibid., 177–8.
60. The classic study on the 'yellow peril' remains Heinz Gollwitzer, *Die Gelbe Gefahr: Geschichte eines Schlagwortes. Studien zum imperialistischen Denken* (Göttingen: Vandenhoeck & Ruprecht, 1962). Also see Ute Mehnert, *Deutschland, Amerika und die 'Gelbe Gefahr': zur Karriere eines Schlagworts in der grossen Politik, 1905–1917* (Stuttgart: Steiner, 1995). For a more recent study in Japanese, see Iikura Akira, *Ierō periru no shinwa: Teikoku Nihon to kōka no gyakusetsu* [The Myth of the Yellow Peril: Imperial Japan and the Paradox of the Yellow Peril] (Tokyo: Sairyūsha, 2004).
61. Iikura elaborated on the problem in Iikura, *Ierō periru no shinwa*, 48–51.
62. For details, see Zachmann, *China and Japan in the Late Meiji Period*, 31–9.
63. Iikura, *Ierō periru no shinwa*, 56.
64. Ibid., 77–83. Gollwitzer, *Die Gelbe Gefahr*, 211–13.
65. The painting was reproduced in the *Kokumin shinbun*. See Zachmann, *China and Japan in the Late Meiji Period*, 46. For the Japanese emperor being introduced to the painting, see Iikura, *Ierō periru no shinwa*, 95.
66. Lauren, *Power and Prejudice*, 50.
67. See Iriye, *Pacific Estrangement*, 27–32.
68. See ibid., 29–30.
69. Lauren describes the situation of other non-White nations as follows: 'China, with its strength withering and its national integrity emasculated, could only plead for indulgence. India, under the nearly total control of the British, could come with only a beggar's bowl in hand'. Lauren, *Power and Prejudice*, 63.
70. This lecture was later published as Mori Rintarō, *Kōkaron kōgai* (Tokyo: Shun'yōdō, 1904). The quotes in the present work are taken from this published version.

71. Ibid., 2–3. It is interesting to note that it was the association of the Japanese with the Chinese that Ōgai saw as problematic, not the idea of a dangerous Japan per se.
72. Nihon gaikō monjo, 'Kakugi kettei: tai-Ro kōshō ketsuretsu no sai Nihon no toru beki tai-Shin-Kan hōshin', Man-Kan ni kansuru Nichi-Ro kōshō ikken (30 December 1903), 44.
73. This was not the first attempt of the Japanese government at manipulating Western public opinion. During the Boxer War (1899–1901) the government managed to have Western newspapers publish Japan-friendly articles. Also, Kaneko had a counterpart who was sent to Europe to the same end, Suematsu Kenchō (1855–1920). For details, see Robert B. Valliant, 'The Selling of Japan: Japanese Manipulation of Western Opinion, 1900–1905', *Monumenta Nipponica* 29, no. 4 (1974). For additional details on the Japanese attempt to influence Western public opinion during the Russo-Japanese War, also see Rotem Kowner, 'Becoming an Honorary Civilized Nation: Remaking Japan's Military Image during the Russo-Japanese War, 1904–1905', *The Historian* 64, no. 1 (Fall 2001): 19–38.
74. Valliant, 'The Selling of Japan', 422–3.
75. Diplomatic Archives of the Ministry of Foreign Affairs, Takahira to Komura (29 March 1904), *Kaneko Kentarō*, call number of holding: 5-2-18-0-33.
76. Ibid.
77. Ibid.
78. Ibid.
79. The speech was so well-received that it appeared in printed form the same year as: Kentaro Kaneko, *The Situation in the Far East* (Cambridge: The Japan Club of Harvard University, 1904). The following analysis is based on this version.
80. Ibid., 1.
81. Ibid., 17.
82. Ibid., 18–20. Quote on 20.
83. Ibid., 24.
84. Ibid.
85. Ibid., 24–5.
86. Iikura, *Ierō periru no shinwa*, 194–5.
87. Valliant, 'The Selling of Japan', 424.
88. Comte Cassini, 'Russia in the Far East', *The North American Review* 178, no. 570 (1904): 686–7.
89. Ibid., 687.
90. Ibid.
91. Kaneko, *The Situation in the Far East*, 25.
92. Ibid., 28.
93. Ibid.
94. Kentaro Kaneko, 'The Yellow Peril Is the Golden Opportunity for Japan', *The North American Review* 179, no. 576 (1904): 648.
95. Diplomatic Archives of the Ministry of Foreign Affairs, Makino to Komura (30 May 1904), *Hikōkaron henjutsu hakkō no gi ni kanshi ōkoku kōshi yori hinshin ikken*, call number of holding: 7-2-2-16.

96. Ibid.
97. In this work, Vámbéry explains that the fear of the 'yellow peril' was irrational and 'a sign of intellectual waywardness and I see it as a duty, as much as possible, to stand against the groundless assumptions of a "yellow peril"'. H. Vámbéry, *Die Gelbe Gefahr: Eine Kulturstudie* (Budapest: Königliche Universitäts-Buchhandlung, 1904).
98. Ibid., 3–5.
99. Ibid., 7–8.
100. Ibid., 10–16.
101. Ibid., 20.
102. Ibid., 33.
103. As cited in Henning, *Outposts of Civilization*, 144.
104. Ibid.
105. Ibid., 145.
106. George Sinkler, *The Racial Attitudes of American Presidents: From Abraham Lincoln to Theodore Roosevelt* (New York: Doubleday, 1971), 393.
107. Joseph M. Henning, 'White Mongols? The War and American Discourses on Race and Religion', in *The Impact of the Russo-Japanese War*, ed. Rotem Kowner (London: Routledge, 2006), 166.
108. Karl Blind, 'Does Russia Represent Aryan Civilization?', *The North American Review* 178, no. 571 (June 1904): 801–11.
109. Ibid., 802.
110. Ibid., 804.
111. Ibid.
112. Ibid., 805.
113. Ibid.
114. For details on the role of missionaries and the importance of religion in shaping the image of Japan at the turn of the century, see Henning, 'White Mongols? The War and American Discourses on Race and Religion'; Henning, *Outposts of Civilization*.
115. Some of these repercussions, such as the 'enlightenment' of the Western public opinion, have already been discussed. For more examples, see amongst others Maik Hendrik Sprotte, Wolfgang Seifert and Heinz-Dietrich Löwe, eds, *Der Russisch-Japanische Krieg 1904/05: Anbruch einer neuen Zeit?* (Wiesbaden: Harrassowitz Verlag, 2007); John Steinberg et al., eds, *The Russo-Japanese War in Global Perspective: World War Zero, Volume II* (Brill, 2006); Rotem Kowner, ed., *The Impact of the Russo-Japanese War* (New York: Routledge, 2007).
116. Lauren, *Power and Prejudice*, 50.
117. Ibid., 51.
118. For additional details, see ibid., 42–3, 64–6. Also see Lake and Reynolds, *Drawing the Global Colour Line*.
119. Charles H. Pearson, *National Life and Character: A Forecast* (London: Macmillan and Co., 1893). For additional details on Pearson's work and its impact, see Lake and Reynolds, *Drawing the Global Colour Line*, 75–94.
120. Pearson, *National Life and Character: A Forecast*, 13.

121. Ibid., 32.
122. Ibid., 32–3.
123. Ibid., 84.
124. Ibid., 85.
125. Lake and Reynolds, *Drawing the Global Colour Line*, 87.
126. Lake and Reynolds mention the speech. See ibid., 137. The speech, given on 7 August 1901, is available online under: *Parliamentary Debates, House of Representatives*, Edmund Barton Speech, Wednesday August 7, 1901: http://parlinfo.aph.gov.au/parlInfo/search/display/display.w3p;query=Id%3A%22hansard80%2Fhansardr80%2F1901-08-07%2F0037%22
127. Lake and Reynolds, *Drawing the Global Colour Line*, 87.
128. Ibid., 92–3.
129. Alfred T. Mahan, 'A Twentieth Century Outlook', *Harper's New Monthly Magazine* 95 (June 1897): 527.
130. Lauren retells an anecdote that is exemplary of the war's importance from a racial perspective: after the naval battle of Tsushima in 1905, a lecturer at Oxford University, Alfred Zimmern, put his class on Greek history aside, 'because I feel I must speak to you about the most important event which has happened, or is likely to happen, in our lifetime: the victory of a nonwhite people over a white people'. As cited in Lauren, *Power and Prejudice*, 73.
131. René Pinon, 'La guerre russo-japonaise et l'opinion européenne', *Revue des Deux Mondes* 21 (May 1904): 199.
132. As cited in LaFeber, *The Clash*, 32.
133. Susan Jolliffe Napier, *From Impressionism to Anime: Japan as Fantasy and Fan Cult in the Mind of the West* (New York: Palgrave Macmillan, 2007), 23–4.
134. For a detailed account of the negotiations, incentives and results of the peace negotiations, see Raymond A. Esthus, *Double Eagle and Rising Sun: The Russians and Japanese at Portsmouth in 1905* (Durham, NC: Duke University Press, 1988).
135. Manfred Berg, '"A Great Civilized Power of a Formidable Type": Theodore Roosevelt, die USA und der Russisch-Japanische Krieg', in *Der Russisch-Japanische Krieg 1904/05: Anbruch einer neuen Zeit* (Wiesbaden: Harrassowitz Verlag, 2007), 253.

Chapter 5

Further Successes and the Limits of the Racial Middle Ground – The California Crisis

There is a notion of continuity in the negotiation zone from its inception up to its current state in this study. While the reasons for its maintenance and the actors involved varied, the feeling that Japan was an exception among 'coloured' races and had to be treated differently remained constant. During the First Sino-Japanese War, granting a special racial status to Japan was made easier by the fact that its enemy was China. Widespread contempt for the alleged backwardness and weaknesses of the Chinese helped to build the image of Japan as a Western proxy in the East. The context of the Russo-Japanese War was far more complex. Fear was added to the equation, and both the Japanese and the Russian side actively tried to influence the effectiveness of the middle ground.

One point, however, needs to be emphasised: the middle ground described up to this point was only relevant for international relations. It had nothing exceptional, if anything at all, to say about interpersonal relations and it is important not to be misguided in believing that the preferential treatment of the Japanese nation automatically extended to Japanese individuals. Statesmen often have different perspectives and agendas than their citizen. In the West, politicians were at first concerned with what meaning Japan would have for future relations in the Far East. On the societal level, the concern was more with what influence the Japanese, as individuals, would have on the daily lives of people. People chose to view the Japanese in the frameworks of economic competition, social norms, morality and racial purity. In some cases, the frameworks used by state and civil society actors could overlap. However, the latter tended to disregard the potential threat of Japan as a nation in favour of the one posed by Japan as a race. State actors, on the other hand, kept in mind that the existence of Japanese individuals implied the presence of a Japanese state in the background. This discrepancy in priorities was nowhere more obvious than in the interactions between Japan and the United States.

Becoming visible: Japanese immigration to the United States

American sympathetic feelings towards Japan started to fade away once the Russo-Japanese War ended, leaving the Japanese confused about their status in the world. Much of this can be attributed to a change in the visibility of Japan and its people. For the Western observers of the two wars, the battlefields had been in distant lands. The Japanese soldiers who fought and died there were, apart from the few famous military officers whose names appeared in Western newspapers, anonymous, faceless people who would eventually fade away. Japan and its people, therefore, were more of an abstract concept confined to this moment in time. And if Japan the nation had all the qualities of a modern White Western nation, it was also separated by an ocean and dissociated from the everyday lives of American citizen.[1]

However, this changed after the war. The Japanese nation had gained enough confidence to shift its focus from military to peaceful economic and human expansion. With this, the meaning of Japan changed as well: as opposed to Japan as a nation, the Japanese individual was no abstract concept. He was a very real existence who was now settling on American soil. Emigration from Japan had existed before, but the end of the war gave new impetus and opportunities for the movement of capital and people.[2] Hawaii witnessed a peak of Japanese immigration in the years after the war: 30,393 passports (the highest number in history) were issued for Hawaii in 1906.[3] Many of the Japanese leaving for Hawaii did not settle there but decided to move on to the American continent instead.

Japanese entries to the United States doubled between 1906 and 1907, from 14,243 to 30,842.[4] These numbers might seem impressive, yet Japanese immigration remained weak when compared to the total number of immigrants that entered the country: while more substantial than in its early days (the population census of 1870 recorded fifty-five Japanese), it is estimated that 275,000 Japanese entered the country between 1861 and 1924, compared to thirty million immigrants from Europe alone. At the time of their highest number, the Japanese population accounted for 0.001 per cent of the total American population.[5] Small numbers notwithstanding, the Japanese went from anonymous soldiers during the Russo-Japanese War to real individuals 'flooding' the West Coast of the United States and entering a direct competition with the White population on the labour market. This negative trend paralleled evolutions in the geopolitical realm: both the United States and Japan wanted to expand in the Pacific and were therefore bound to clash with one another. The Americans did not lose any time in recognising this: War Plan ORANGE, designed by Roosevelt and his military advisers in 1906, concluded that Japan was a probable enemy in the Pacific and contained plans for a potential war.[6]

Both realms – immigration and geopolitics – were part of a Japanese policy of expansion; both had consequences for the racial middle ground: because Japan was able to expand, it was feared and respected as a nation; but because expansion meant human interaction, and therefore confrontation, Japanese individuals became targets of discrimination.[7]

This led to questions regarding Japan's newly gained status as a first-rate nation. According to Iriye, after the war the Japanese sensed the 'more complex issue of race, culture and national purpose'. He adds that 'it was as if all of a sudden the Japanese were reminded that they were an Asian nation' and needed to define their 'existence in a world of racial and cultural diversity and tension'.[8] Iriye acknowledges that these were but feelings, and that in reality racial issues had already been as serious before the war.[9] It is doubtful, however, whether the Japanese did at any point forget that they could be considered an Asian nation. The efforts to prevent the spread of the 'yellow peril' idea during the Russo-Japanese War were proof enough of this. And when serious problems started in California, Japan soon had to acknowledge that the respect earned as a nation would not extend to its people.

The Japanese who came to California became victims not only of a long tradition of American racism but also of a racism peculiar to the West Coast. Before their arrival, the Pacific Coast had been the theatre of racial conflicts between White settlers and, respectively, Native Americans, Mexicans and Chinese.[10] Japanese immigrants inherited much of the prejudice that was directed towards other non-Whites. Despite the very limited scale of Japanese immigration described above, opposition to the arrival of Japanese labourers grew louder until the Japanese and Korean Exclusion League (later renamed the Asiatic Exclusion League) was organised on 7 May 1905. The League's demands can be outlined as follows: (1) laws excluding Chinese had to be extended to Japanese and Koreans; (2) League members should not employ or patronise Japanese, nor persons employing Japanese, and should boycott products coming from firms employing Japanese; (3) a campaign to get the attention of the president and Congress had to be launched; and (4) the cause should be supported by all labour and civic organisations.[11]

The situation escalated in 1906. On 18 April, a devastating earthquake damaged the city of San Francisco. Out of solidarity, the Japanese Red Cross sent a quarter of a million dollars of relief to the victims. Despite this benevolent act, on 11 October of the same year, the San Francisco Board of Education singlehandedly ordered all Japanese, Chinese and Korean children to attend a separate Oriental Public School, effectively instituting school segregation for Japanese pupils. What followed was a diplomatic feud between three parties – the Japanese government, President Roosevelt and the State of California – in which the racial middle ground would be the main component.

The School Board's decision to separate Japanese children from White schools deeply upset Theodore Roosevelt. His outrage came from a curious blend of geopolitical realism, aversion, but also genuine respect for the Japanese, which in the end led him to intervene on their behalf. Thereby, the president became not only an agent of the middle ground; he also became a personification of the idea: as a firm believer in the validity of race as an objective human taxonomy, he saw Whites as representing the pinnacle of a racial hierarchy. Yet, the achievements of Japan as well as his pragmatism forced him to relativise his views on certain non-Whites.

Theodore Roosevelt and the Japanese racial identity

In matters of race, Roosevelt was undeniably a product of his time. He lived during the 'efflorescence of laws and policies built upon racism and with the accompanying explosion of formal racial theories'.[12] Through his elite education and intellectual exchange with numerous scholars and friends, Roosevelt became an ardent believer in the validity and significance of race, which led him to see most of the issues of his days through a racial lens.[13] He had no doubt that 'English-speaking' Whites were superior. At the same time, he was obsessed with the idea of 'race suicide' – the fear that the White race would not reproduce itself rapidly enough and therefore would vanish.[14]

Yet while Roosevelt was clearly prejudiced in line with his contemporary racial thinkers, it would be hasty to rank him amongst the convinced racists of his time. The president was indeed able to show a certain (ambivalent) tolerance towards non-White people. The widely publicised dinner with the African American leader Booker T. Washington (1856–1915) at the White House, which led to the foreseeable alienation of Southern voters, is but one testimony of this ambivalence.[15] Roosevelt was, according to Gerstle, a 'civic nationalist', who did not argue for the complete exclusion of non-Whites from the political community because they were non-Whites per se, but because he believed that non-Whites at their current state – except for individuals that proved him wrong – did not meet the requirements necessary to become part of the American citizenry.[16] He seems to have seen the presence of non-Whites on American soil (immigrants now settling in the United States were a different problem) as a *fait accompli* and as a matter that all Americans had to cope with in a just and fair way:

> I have not been able to think out any solution of the terrible problem offered by the presence of the Negro on this continent, but of one thing I am sure, and that is that inasmuch as he is here and can neither be killed nor driven away, the only wise and honorable and Christian thing to do is to treat each black man and each white man strictly on his merits as a man, giving him no more and no less than he shows himself worthy to have.[17]

This cannot eclipse the fact that Roosevelt could be harsh in his opinion about non-Whites: Native Americans, for example, he saw as a doomed race whose fate it was to disappear under the White advance in America. We have seen earlier that the murder of the American indigenous population was justifiable for him, as the standard of civilisation that was applied to Western societies could not be upheld in dealing with the 'red man'.[18]

The Japanese, however, presented him with a dilemma. His personal letters and notes offer us a window into what can be interpreted as his sincere feelings. In a letter written during the Russo-Japanese War, Roosevelt reported to his close friend (and best man for his second marriage), the British diplomat

Cecil Spring-Rice (1859–1918), that two Japanese envoys, Kaneko Kentarō and Takahira Kogorō, had visited him.[19] During his discussion with the two envoys, he had advised the Japanese not to get 'the big head' and avoid entering 'a general career of insolence and aggression'.[20] This, however, he did not envision because he was a 'firm believer in the Japanese people', and

> most earnestly hoped as well as believed that Japan would simply take her place from now on among the great civilized nations, with, like each of these nations, something to teach others as well as something to learn from them.[21]

For Roosevelt, race was not a relevant factor in the relationship between the United States and Japan: 'I am not much affected by the statement that the Japanese are of an utterly different race from ourselves and that the Russian are of the same race', concluding that 'I see nothing ruinous to civilization in the advent of the Japanese to power among the great nations'.[22] These are quite tolerant statements, especially when considering Roosevelt's racial education as well as his well-known disdain for the Chinese.[23] In fact, he was swift to point out that the Chinese and the Japanese could not be considered the same: 'What nonsense it is to speak of the Chinese and Japanese as of the same race? They are of the same race only in the sense that the Levantine Greek is of the same race with Lord Milner.'[24]

In hindsight, Roosevelt's positive inclination towards the Japanese is not surprising. An advocate of manly and militaristic virtues, he could but approve the martial image of Japan as well as its recent military victories. After the naval Battle of Tsushima (May 1905), he wrote in excitement that 'even the battle of Trafalgar could not match this', and 'I grew so excited that I myself became almost like a Japanese, and I could not attend to official duties.'[25] There was a time when he would wrestle three times a week with Japanese wrestlers.[26] He also read Nitobe Inazō's *Bushido*: in a letter to Kaneko in which he thanked his Japanese acquaintance for the gift of several books, he wrote that,

> Perhaps I was most impressed by this little volume on Bushido . . . It seems to me, my dear Baron, that Japan has much to teach to the nations of the Occident, just as she has something to learn from them. I have long felt that Japan's entrance into the circle of the great civilized powers was of good omen for all of the world.[27]

'Certainly I myself', the letter went on, 'hope that I have learned not a little from what I have read of the fine Samurai spirit, and from the way in which that spirit has been and is being transformed to meet the needs of modern life.'[28]

When the San Francisco School Board of Education ordered the segregation of Japanese schoolchildren, however, it was not Roosevelt's admiration for Japan that forced him to intervene. Too rational to overlook that having its children segregated from White schools was bound to be perceived as an insult by Japan, he was ready to put racial concerns at the state level aside for the interests of diplomacy. Two weeks after the segregation order, he wrote to his son Kermit that: 'The infernal fools in California, especially in San Francisco, insult the Japanese recklessly and in the event of war it will be the Nation as a whole which will pay the consequences.'[29] He would be ready to fight, but 'I would loathe to see it [the American nation] forced into a war in which it was wrong.'[30]

Roosevelt was not alone in his concerns. On the same day he wrote his letter, Secretary of State Elihu Root (1845–1937) gave the following warning:

> Owing to their recent admission to recognized equality with the other civilized nations, they [the Japanese] are particularly sensitive about everything which questions that equality; one-tenth of the insults which have been visited upon Chinese by the people of the United States would lead to immediate war.[31]

This was the reason why the federal government was worried, and why it became necessary to maintain a racial middle ground and grant Japan a special racial status: Japan actually had the power to fight back. The situation was perfectly summarised in an article by the *Boston Daily Globe*:

> That the Japanese should officially take note of the color prejudices of the Caucasian is another interesting phase of the mild crisis now existing in the relations of Japan and the United States. We have drawn the color line with impunity on the Indian and the African; they have no governments to resent any indignity put upon them. We have drawn it sharply on the Chinaman, and his government has had neither the spirit nor the physical power to make us feel its displeasure. But a man of color with the laurels of Mukden and the sea of Japan on his dusky brow, who refuses to be made a jim crow [*sic*] of, gives us pause. Since the bronzed Saracen . . . there has been no one until now to challenge the white man's scorn.[32]

In a move that was interpreted by the Californians as an attack on their state, Roosevelt intervened on behalf of the Japanese to avoid an open conflict. In his yearly address before Congress,[33] the president virulently criticised the segregation order: while in the greater part of the United States the Japanese were treated in the same way as 'the stranger from any part of civilized Europe', some parts of the country showed unnecessary hostility towards them.[34] Excluding the Japanese from public schools was a 'wicked absurdity' and the Americans had as much to learn from Japan as Japan had to learn from the United States. The president then asked for 'fair treatment for the Japanese as I would ask fair treatment for Germans or Englishmen, Frenchmen, Russians and Italians'.[35] Roosevelt went even further: 'I recommend to Congress that an act be passed specifically providing for the naturalization of Japanese who come here intending to become American citizen.' He also assured that he would use every force available, 'military and civil', to protect the rights of the Japanese.[36]

Roosevelt's address deserves more than a passing comment. While the president did use some strong language, the true violence of his words lies in their implications for the legal framework in which American race relations were defined at the time. The decision to segregate Japanese children from White schools was certainly immoral. Yet, it was also legal. The groundwork for racially separated schools in California had already been laid in the 1850s. The School Law of 1860 specifically ordered the segregation of children of Black, Chinese and Indian descent.[37] After a certain span of time in which children of 'Mongolian' descent were barred even from segregated public schools, the 'Separate but Equal' doctrine customised in the South was fixed by law for the West Coast in the 1880s. The amended school laws read:

> Trustees shall have the power to exclude children of filthy and vicious habits, or children suffering from contagious or infectious diseases . . . and also to establish separate schools for children of Mongolian or Chinese descent. When such separate schools are established, Chinese or Mongolian children must not be admitted into any other school.[38]

The school laws did not specifically mention children of Japanese descent. But in light of the increasing number of Japanese attending White schools, in 1906 the San Francisco School Board rebranded the Chinese Primary School into the Oriental Public School, which Japanese children were now forced by law to attend.[39]

While at the state level the issue of the legality of the segregation order seems straightforward, it becomes intricate when considered at the federal level. The State of California had its own law regarding the education of non-White children – yet the United States had also signed a treaty with Japan. This treaty, the Treaty of Commerce and Navigation between the United States and Japan (signed on 22 November 1894), had guaranteed the Japanese in the United States the same rights as American citizens.[40] What it did not explicitly state, however, was whether public education was one of these rights, and whether the facilities which offered public education had to be the same for everyone. This is where the notion of 'most-favoured nation' comes into play. If the treaty signed between Japan and the United States was understood to include such a clause, then the United States was obliged to accord access to the same schools as it did to children of European descent. The interpretation of the treaty signed between Japan and the United States thus became a quest for those concerned with the legal aspect of the whole matter.

Numerous legal scholars of the time tried to tackle the issue and published their results in academic journals.[41] The majority seemed to agree that the treaty did not contain an all-encompassing most-favoured nation clause: privileges concerning residence, travel and property were indeed to be granted according to the most-favoured nation principle, as well as those regarding commerce and navigation. Public schooling, however, was nowhere explicitly mentioned in the treaty, and hence providing one for Japanese children was not binding.[42] Thomas Bailey dedicated some pages to the legal problem in his exhaustive study of the

California Crisis.[43] He described how Secretary of Commerce Victor H. Metcalf (1853–1936), who had been dispatched to California by President Roosevelt to investigate the crisis, did look for a most-favoured-nation clause in the treaty, but found it limited only to the rights mentioned above.[44] Secretary of State Root did believe that rights of residence implied rights of schooling. But even then, Root doubted that separated schools were a violation of this principle.[45]

The question was never answered, as on 24 February 1907 Foreign Minister Hayashi wrote a note laying the basis for what would be known as the Gentlemen's Agreement: Japanese schoolchildren could return to White schools, and in return the Japanese government would limit emigration to non-labourers who were relatives of people already living in the United States as well as labourers who owned property there.[46] The question of the legality of the segregation order thus became irrelevant. The final verdict on the matter must be left to legal experts. What can be said, however, is that if the Supreme Court of the United States did not deem the segregation order as contrary to the treaty signed between the United States and Japan, and therefore did not rule against it, the order was not against the law. This means that President Roosevelt was threatening the School Board of San Francisco with legal and military force to defend foreigners of another race, while the city was in fact acting in concordance with federal law.

Without condoning the nature of exclusionary legislation, it is worth noting that Roosevelt's actions on behalf of the Japanese went against not only the legal framework of the country but also against the organisation of the American societal order of the time. A brief look at the situation of African Americans suffices as proof. The California Crisis occurred during the period historians have dubbed 'the nadir of Black American history': from the end of the nineteenth century, Blacks from the Southern states saw the rights they had gradually acquired in the wake the Civil War (1861–5) vanish. The disfranchisement of Black voters had been the first step in relegating African Americans to a caste of second-class citizens.[47] Once Black citizens were prevented from voting, the Southern states began promulgating the infamous 'Jim Crow laws', thereby enforcing a legal separation of Blacks and Whites inside American society. African Americans were not allowed to go to hotels, restaurants and theatres reserved for Whites. Schools as well as public transportation were segregated. In 1896, the Supreme Court of the United States handed down its 'Separate but Equal' judgment in the *Plessy* v. *Fergusson Case*, thus officially giving federal sanction to segregation.[48]

This explains why Roosevelt's attitude was so puzzling to the opponents of the Japanese: they were acting in accordance with the usual treatment of other non-White minorities. As a San Francisco newspaper asked: 'If the Southern States can segregate the races in its schools, why may not the Californians do so?'[49]

Roosevelt's stance does not make much sense when explained in terms of the usual dichotomy between White and non-White races. Reasoning in terms of the Racial Middle Ground helps obtain a clearer picture of the situation: the proponents – agents – of the middle ground were Roosevelt and his government, while the opponents were the State of California and the anti-Japanese movement. The reason why both were opposed was the problem of granting a special racial status to the Japanese that would enable them to escape the customary treatment of American non-Whites (in this particular case racial segregation).

This conflict of opinions came from the fact that both sides were addressing the issue from two different perspectives, both attributing a different measure of importance to race for their immediate agenda: the proponents of the middle ground were concerned with geopolitical matters and tried to push the issue of race in the background, while their opponents were plagued by racial concerns. Accordingly, both parties envisioned Japan differently: for those wanting to provide a special racial status for Japan, the problem was Japan as a nation and as a military power; their detractors feared Japan as a race. And while even the opponents of Japanese immigration acknowledged that Japan was a modern military power, they did not see this as a sufficient reason for allowing Japanese individuals to enter and settle in the United States. In a speech to Congress on 13 March 1906,[50] California Senator Hayes made this point unequivocally:

> The valorous achievements of any nation have in all ages challenged the admiration of the world. And when a nation, making up for its lack of number by its energy, courage, and discipline, emerges from a contest with a nation numerically much stronger with the triumphant success which has recently attended the arms of Japan in its contest with Russia we, in common with the rest of the world, shout our out bravos to the plucky little island nation . . . Their achievements, which are not small, are the common heritage of mankind, and for that reason I glory in them.[51]

However, what mattered, the Senator went on, was whether

> it was better for this nation [the United States] that the Japanese people should be allowed to come and settle among us as we allow aliens of the Caucasian race to come, or is it better for the whole people of our country that they should be wholly or partly excluded?[52]

This question could not 'be wisely answered by simply pointing to the great achievements of the Japanese people in war'.[53] Or as another senator, this time from Oregon, put it without the cover of praise:

> It must be admitted that, while the Japanese in the aggregate, as a nation, are admired for their wonderful pluck, energy and marvellous progress of late years, the individual Japanese, as we see and know him on the Pacific Coast, is not a favorite with our people.[54]

The anti-Japanese movement made the distinction between Japan as a nation and Japan as a race obvious. In its beginnings, the bulk of the movement was made of the working class, while the upper middle class seems to have accepted the immigration of 'good' elements (that is, educated non-labourers). With time, however, moral issues such as the threat of racial purity caused by the arrival of Japanese immigrants united all classes against them.[55] A resolution unanimously passed by the California legislature in March 1905 indicated what the matter with the Japanese was: 'Japanese laborers, by reason of race habits, mode of living, disposition and general characteristics, are undesirable.'[56] It is noteworthy that the alleged racial characteristics of the Japanese individuals which the resolution and the anti-Japanese movement as a whole were condemning were the exact opposite of those the proponents of the middle ground lavished on Japan as a Western proxy.

Two years after the Gentlemen's Agreement was brokered, the *Annals of the American Academy of Political and Social Science* ran a special issue on the topic of Asian exclusion, giving a voice to both opponents and proponents of the Japanese.[57] This issue is a mine of information on the anti-Japanese movement, since it conveniently summarises the reasons why Californians had supported the segregation order and why they continued to oppose immigration from Japan. In hindsight, the problem with the Japanese could be summarised quite simply: they refused to remain where the American racial system wanted them to stay, that is, amongst other non-White minorities. One contributor to the issue acknowledged that White Americans indeed preferred a certain type of non-Whites and pointed out that:

> It must always be remembered that the white American's standard of judging strange peoples is personal and unobjective. The average southern white man, for instance, is most favorably disposed toward a type of Negro objectively inferior, – the type, namely, which best fits the inferior status which the white man prefers the black man to occupy.[58]

This is why, despite calling for their exclusion, the Americans had preferred the Chinese: 'We find the Chinese fitting much better than the Japanese into the status which the white American prefers them both to occupy', that of 'biped domestic animal in the white man's service'.[59] The Japanese were different, they were quicker and brighter than the Chinese, but not as reliable because they were not afraid to break a contract.[60] Worse, they could even coerce White people into accepting their own terms: another contributor lamented that 'the Japanese have learned their power and use it unmercifully', for they were striking for higher wages.[61]

For opponents of the Japanese, the very fact that they refused to subscribe to the American racial status quo was proof of their incapacity to assimilate into American society. Where other racial minorities allegedly accepted their situation, the Japanese had complained about their discrimination: 'Hoodlums make assault upon other foreigners. But nothing is heard of them, but the Japanese insist upon converting every difficulty in which they become involved into an international affair.'[62] The Japanese were making their appeals because 'they considered themselves as subjects of the Mikado', whom they believed 'exercises as much influence on this side of the Pacific as he does in his own empire'.[63] The capacity of the Japanese to retaliate was something that seemed to particularly upset the proponents of their exclusion. A justice from California lamented that the city of San Francisco had established a school for Chinese children for many years, and that no complains had been heard by Chinese parents. Yet, 'when a proposition is made to have Japanese attend so-called Oriental schools a storm is raised which causes extreme agitation in Tokyo and in Washington', as well as 'column upon column of denunciation in the press of both countries'.[64]

It has been explained earlier in this work that the resentment felt towards Japanese immigrants needed to be understood in the wider context of American racial thought. The ire of the anti-Japanese movement was not necessarily aimed at the Japanese per se, but at what was seen as another race problem. The exclusionists saw the cohabitation between the two races as impossible, not because the immigrants were Japanese, but because they saw the cohabitation of the White race with a non-White race as neither desirable nor even possible: 'History teaches us that it is impossible to make a homogeneous people by the juxtaposition upon the same soil of races differing in color', warned Nevada Senator Francis G. Newlands, and 'race tolerance, under such conditions, means race amalgamation, and this is undesirable'.[65] The only solution to prevent this problem was exclusion:

> The time has come . . . when the United States, as a matter of self-protection and self-preservation, must declare by statutory enactment that it will not tolerate further race complications upon our soil. Our country, by law to take effect upon the expiration of existing treaties, should prevent the immigration of all peoples other than those of the white race, except under restricted conditions relating to international commerce, travel, and education.[66]

Newlands also added that the government should take measures regarding 'the people of the black race now within our boundaries, which . . . will minimize the danger which they constitute to our institutions and our civilization'.[67]

As an agent of the racial middle ground, Theodore Roosevelt had separated Japanese immigration from the domestic 'race problem'. The opponents of the racial middle ground did not and tried to remind him and his followers that the United States already had one race problem – African Americans. In this sense, the Black minority and Japanese immigrants were two faces of the same coin, and it would therefore be inaccurate to see the San Francisco segregation order as an instance of peculiar anti-Japanese racism. The hostility directed towards the Japanese was fundamentally speaking the same type of hostility that was already well anchored inside American society. That Japanese were Japanese or 'Mongolians' did in the end not matter as much as the fact that they were not White.

The opinions of those championing a 'White America' illustrate this point well: the already mentioned Senator Newlands was summoned by Roosevelt to exert his influence in calming anti-Japanese agitation in his state. Newlands, however, was an ardent proponent of Japanese exclusion and saw in the presence of non-Whites the gravest threat to the United States. In a letter reproduced in numerous newspapers and which most probably formed the basis for the article he wrote for the *Annals of the American Academy of Political and Social Science* quoted above, Newlands admonished the readers that diplomacy had no place in issues of race homogeneity: 'The race question is now the most important question confronting the nation.'[68] Blacks were 'the great problem and peril of the future', and he urged 'the inauguration of a national policy which . . . shall recognize that blacks are a race of children, requiring guidance'.[69] The Pacific Coast was facing Asia with 'nearly a billion people of the brown race' endangering White properties. According to Newlands, history had told the Americans that racial miscegenation would not lead to the creation of a homogeneous people on American soil. He then again warned against race mixing and called for exclusionary laws against non-Whites.

It was no accident that Newlands brandished race amalgamation as a threat. The mixing between races was a highly emotional issue and attitudes towards it were another indicator of how deeply imbedded the Japanese issue was within the greater framework of the American race problem. Historian Peggy Pascoe explains that between the 1860s and the 1960s, 'Americans saw their opposition to interracial marriage as a product of nature rather than a product of politics'.[70] As such, it served 'as the bottom line of white supremacy and the most commonsense justification for all other forms of race discrimination'.[71] At first promulgated to prevent interracial marriage between Whites and 'Negroes' or 'mulattoes', the Californian anti-miscegenation laws were amended in 1880 to prohibit marriage with 'Mongolians'.[72] The association of Asians with people of African descent thus became stronger until both were seen as equally undesirable.[73]

The history of the contempt towards both Black and White and as well as Japanese and White unions in the United States is full of anecdotes that only confirm the linkage between the two issues. Missionary Sidney Lewis Gulick (1860–1945) was asked during his investigation of the Japanese problem in the United States if he would let his daughter marry a 'Jap'.[74] Likewise, a Californian notoriously stated:

> Near my home is an eighty-acre tract of as fine land as there is in California. On that land lives a Japanese. With that Japanese lives a white woman. On that woman's arm is a baby. What is that baby? It isn't Japanese. It isn't white. I'll tell you what it is. It is a germ of the mightiest problem ever faced in this state; a problem that will make the black problem of the South look white.[75]

As a final example, a district court judge of Nevada refused to allow the marriage between a Japanese man and a White woman, despite the state only prohibiting marriage between Whites and Chinese. As a justification, he proclaimed that if the category 'Chinese' did not apply to the Japanese, 'I would say a Jap was a black in the interests of morality and charity'.[76]

The strong association of the Japanese with African Americans within the minds of the opponents of Japanese immigration naturally leads to the question of the African American opinion on the subject. What did Black Americans think about the Japanese and the racial middle ground that the federal government granted to them. So far, this study has mostly been concerned with two actors: Japan in the middle, which tried to escape its racial status, and the race at the top, the White race, which decided the scope of the negotiation zone. Yet, a middle ground can only properly function – in fact, can only exist – if a third actor is involved: the 'race at the bottom'. The treatment of this race serves as a reference point to assess the effects of the middle ground: the more the 'race in the middle' is treated differently from the race at the bottom, the greater the effects of the negotiation zone. Evidently, the 'race at the bottom' witnesses the differential treatment of the 'race in the middle', and its reaction to that privileged treatment can serve as a measure of the success of the racial middle ground. Blacks were, despite domestic laws effectively telling the contrary, citizens of the United States. For them, the preferential treatment of the Japanese must have left a particularly sour taste.

Notes

1. This point can also act as an explanation for the support Japan gained, especially from the socialists, in Europe during the Russo-Japanese War. It is questionable whether the situation of Japanese workers of the time was significantly better than that of Russian ones. The Japan as seen – or maybe it would be more fitting to say 'used' – by its supporters was not really Japan as it truly was, in a vein similar to how China was envisioned during the Tokugawa era. It was now Japan's turn to become a metaphor. The already quoted René Pinon's critic of Japan's supporters during the Russo-Japanese War seems quite on point here: 'Inside the hopes of the socialist leaders, Japan is a fabulous battering ram . . . which starts to shake the fortress in which all the prejudice that chains humanity and paralyzed its upsurge, desperately resists the assault of new ideas . . . The torpedoes and shells of Admiral Togo are revolutionary ideas.' See Pinon, 'La guerre russo-japonaise et l'opinion européenne', 196.
2. Iriye, *Pacific Estrangement*, 126–30.
3. Ibid., 132–3.
4. Roger Daniels, *The Politics of Prejudice: The Anti-Japanese Movement in California and the Struggle for Japanese Exclusion*, 2nd ed. (Berkeley: University of California Press, 1977), 111.
5. Ibid., 1.
6. LaFeber, *The Clash*, 90. Also see Gomi Toshiki, 'Anguro-sakusonizumu to sen kyūhyaku nijūyo nen iminhō', in *Nichi-Bei kiki no kigen to hai-Nichi iminhō*, ed. Kimitada Miwa (Tokyo: Ronsōsha, 1997), 198.

7. Regarding the influence of Japan's geopolitical expansion on the image of the Japanese people as individuals, Daniels rightly observes that 'the hostility generated by Japan's imperialistic foreign policy was transferred to her nationals and their descendants'. Daniels, 'Japanese Immigrants on a Western Frontier', 82. For a succinct analysis of the worsening of US–Japan relations, see Akira Iriye, 'Kyōsō aite Nihon: Sen happyaku kyūjūgo nen kara sen kyūhyaku jūnana nen', 145–80.
8. Akira Iriye, *Across the Pacific: An Inner History of American-East Asian Relations*, rev. ed. (Chicago: Imprint Publications, 1992), 113.
9. Ibid.
10. Daniels, 'Japanese Immigrants on a Western Frontier', 83.
11. Motoko Tsuchida, 'A History of Japanese Emigration from the 1860s to the 1990s', in *Temporary Workers or Future Citizens?: Japanese and U.S. Migration Policies*, ed. Myron Weiner and Tadashi Hanami (London: Palgrave Macmillan, 1998), 93.
12. Dyer, *Theodore Roosevelt and the Idea of Race*, 1.
13. Gary Gerstle wrote that: 'If for Karl Marx history was the history of class conflict, for Roosevelt history was the history of race conflict: of the world's various races struggling against each other for supremacy and power.' Gerstle, *American Crucible*, 17.
14. Dyer, *Theodore Roosevelt and the Idea of Race*, 11–12, 16–17. See the same book for details on Roosevelt's racial education.
15. On 16 October 1901, Theodore Roosevelt invited African American leader and educator Booker T. Washington (1856–1915) to the White House for a dinner. The decision to invite a Black man to the White House provoked strong criticism from White conservatives. For details, see Deborah Davis, *Guest of Honor: Booker T. Washington, Theodore Roosevelt, and the White House Dinner that Shocked a Nation* (New York: Atria Books, 2012).
16. Gerstle, *American Crucible*, 45–6.
17. *Letter from Theodore Roosevelt to Albion W. Tourgée, 8 November 1901*, Theodore Roosevelt Digital Library, Dickinson State University: http://www.theodoreroosevelt center.org/Research/Digital-Library/Record?libID=o180529 (accessed 28 May 2022).
18. Dyer, *Theodore Roosevelt and the Idea of Race*, 69–88.
19. *Letter from Theodore Roosevelt to Cecil Spring Rice, June 13, 1904*, Theodore Roosevelt Papers, Library of Congress Manuscript Division: https://www.theodorerooseveltcenter.org/Research/Digital-Library/Record?libID=o267973 (accessed 28 May 2022). Roosevelt was probably referring to the meeting described by Takahira in his telegram to the Japanese Foreign Ministry mentioned earlier in this work.
20. Ibid.
21. Ibid.
22. Ibid.
23. For Roosevelt on the Chinese, see Gerstle, *American Crucible*, 59.
24. *Letter from Theodore Roosevelt to John Hay, September 2, 1904*, Theodore Roosevelt Papers, Library of Congress Manuscript Division: http://www.theodoreroosevelt

center.org/Research/Digital-Library/Record?libID=o189070 (accessed 28 May 2022).

25. As cited in LaFeber, *The Clash*, 82.
26. For Roosevelt and Japanese martial arts, see Christopher Benfey, *The Great Wave: Gilded Age Misfits, Japanese Eccentrics, and the Opening of Old Japan* (New York: Random House, 2003), 239–64.
27. *Letter from Theodore Roosevelt to Kaneko Kentarō, April 23, 1904*, Theodore Roosevelt Papers, Library of Congress Manuscript Division: https://www.theodorerooseveltcenter.org/Research/Digital-Library/Record/ImageViewer?libID=o187994&imageNo=1 (accessed 28 May 2022).
28. Ibid. Benfey relativised Roosevelt's enthusiasm for *Bushido*, stating that: 'Roosevelt read *Bushido*, but he did not like it.' Indeed, he asked a friend 'whether that is really studied in Japan, and represents home Japanese philosophy, and not Japanese philosophy for export'. See Benfey, *The Great Wave*, 246. Roosevelt's (justified) doubts about the nature of Nitobe's work could be seen as a proof of his interest in things genuinely Japanese.
29. *Letter from Theodore Roosevelt to Kermit Roosevelt, October 27, 1906*, Theodore Roosevelt Papers, Library of Congress Manuscript Division: http://www.theodorerooseveltcenter.org/Research/Digital-Library/Record?libID=o280819 (accessed 28 May 2022).
30. Ibid.
31. Iriye, *Pacific Estrangement*, 157.
32. 'Japan and the Color Line', *The Boston Daily Globe*, 28 October 1906.
33. The full text of Roosevelt December speech was reproduced in several newspapers. The one published by *The New York Times* was used here. See 'President Demands Citizenship for Japanese', *New York Times*, 5 December 1906. The Japanese government knew of the content of Roosevelt's address long before it was held. On 1 November 1906, Aoki wrote to Hayashi that 'when I . . . had an interview with the President, at which Mr. Root was present, he confidentially showed me some draft page of his message which is being prepared for presentation to Congress . . . In those passages he refers eloquently to the achievements of Japan which entitle her people to the same treatment as the subjects of first class European Power [*sic*] and he earnestly recommends appropriate action of Congrss [*sic*] to permit acquisition of U.S. citizenship by Japanese through naturalization. This he authorized to telegraph to Imperial government secretly. The above is strictly confidential until presentation to Congress.' Nihon gaikō monjo, Aoki to Hayashi (1 November 1906), *Nihon ni oite honbō imin tokō seigen narabi Sōkō hai-Nichi undō no ken*, 455.
34. Ibid.
35. Ibid.
36. Ibid.
37. Joyce Kuo, 'Excluded, Segregated and Forgotten: A Historical View of the Discrimination of Chinese Americans in Public Schools', *Asian American Law Journal* 5 (January 1998): 190.
38. As cited in ibid., 198.

39. Ibid., 206.
40. 'Treaty of Commerce and Navigation between the United States and Japan, 1894, Article I', reproduced in 'Treaty of Commerce and Navigation between the United States and Japan', *The American Journal of International Law* 5, no. 2 (April 1911): 106–16.
41. Dozens of papers were published on the subject. Interested readers will find a good starting point in the following publications: 'Rights of the Japanese in California Schools', *Harvard Law Review* 20, no. 4 (February 1907): 337–40; 'Japanese Situation', *The American Journal of International Law* 1, no. 2 (April 1907): 449–52; Lewis Wm. Draper, 'Can the United States by Treaty Confer on Japanese Residents in California the Right to Attend the Public Schools?', *The American Law Register (1898–1907)* 55, no. 2 (February 1907): 73–90.
42. For the relevant articles of the treaty and their non-applicability to the California Crisis, see for example Amos S. Hershey, 'The Japanese School Question and the Treaty-Making Power', *The American Political Science Review* 1, no. 3 (1907): 393–409.
43. See Thomas Andrew Bailey, *Theodore Roosevelt and the Japanese-American Crises: An Account of the International Complications Arising from the Race Problem on the Pacific Coast* (Stanford, CA: Stanford University Press, 1934).
44. Ibid., 188.
45. Ibid., 189.
46. For further details on the process that culminated in the Gentlemen's Agreement and the agreement itself, see for example Daniels, *The Politics of Prejudice*; LaFeber, *The Clash*.
47. For details about the process of disenfranchisement of Black voters during the Reconstruction period, see for example John Hope Franklin and Evelyn Brooks Higginbotham, *From Slavery to Freedom: A History of African Americans*, 10th ed. (New York: McGraw Hill, 2021).
48. In the case, the Supreme Court decided that state laws requiring segregation in public places did not go against the Constitution of the United States as these did not endanger the guarantee of equal protection under the law. For the text of the decision, see *Plessy* v. *Fergusson*: http://www.law.cornell.edu/supremecourt/text/163/537 (accessed 28 May 2022).
49. As cited in Daniels, *The Politics of Prejudice*, 31.
50. The consulate sent a copy of the speech to the Japanese government. See Nihon gaikō monjo, Hioki to Saionji (30 March 1906), *Nihon ni oite honbō imin tokō seigen narabi Sōkō hai-Nichi undō no ken*, 377–94.
51. Ibid., 378.
52. Ibid.
53. Ibid.
54. C. W. Fulton, 'American Schools and Japanese Pupils', *The North American Review* 183, no. 605 (December 1906): 1225.
55. See Bailey, *Theodore Roosevelt and the Japanese-American Crises*, 12; Daniels, *The Politics of Prejudice*, 19.

56. As cited in Daniels, *The Politics of Prejudice*, 27.
57. 'Chinese and Japanese in America', *The Annals of the American Academy of Political and Social Science* 34, no. 2 (September 1909).
58. Chester H. Rowell, 'Chinese and Japanese Immigrants: A Comparison', in ibid., 3.
59. Ibid., 3–4.
60. Ibid., 5.
61. A. E. Yoell, 'Oriental vs. American Labor', in ibid., 29.
62. John P. Young, 'The Support of the Anti-Oriental Movement', in ibid., 17.
63. Ibid., 18.
64. Albert G. Burnett, 'Misunderstanding of Eastern and Western States regarding Oriental Immigration', in ibid., 41.
65. Francis G. Newlands, 'A Western View of the Race Question', in ibid., 50.
66. Ibid., 51.
67. Ibid.
68. Extracts from the letter have been reproduced in 'White Schools Shut to Japs; Roosevelt Mad', *The Atlanta Constitution*, 5 February 1909; 'Race Question Great Problem before the Nation', *The Atlanta Constitution*, 8 February 1909. Interestingly, the same paper reacted to the letter. While it did not question the fact that race amalgamation was a problem, it criticised Senator Rowlands for putting Japanese and Blacks on the same level. The only flaw in Rowlands's statement, according to the paper, was that 'it coupled with an effort to commit the nation to a policy that puts the negro and the Jap on the same plane'. The Blacks were without any doubt children, the paper claimed, but the Japanese were by far superior to them. See 'The Jap and the Negro', *The Atlanta Consitution*, 9 February 1909.
69. 'Race Question Great Problem before the Nation', *The Atlanta Constitution*, 8 February 1909.
70. Peggy Pascoe, *What Comes Naturally: Miscegenation Law and the Making of Race in America* (Oxford: Oxford University Press, 2009), 1.
71. Ibid.
72. Ibid., 84.
73. Ibid., 85.
74. Sidney L. Gulick, *The American Japanese Problem: A Study of the Racial Relations of the East and the West* (New York: Charles Scribner's Sons, 1914), 118.
75. As cited in Lake and Reynolds, *Drawing the Global Colour Line*, 267.
76. As cited in Pascoe, *What Comes Naturally*, 89.

Chapter 6

African Americans and the Racial Middle Ground

The African American reaction to the events in California was a complicated one. The similar situation in which Black Americans were stranded without doubt led to feelings of sympathy towards the Japanese. However, sharing the White animosity directed towards the Japanese may have given African Americans the opportunity to improve their position inside the American racial system, that is, being granted a racial middle ground of their own.

The race at the bottom (I): the Black press and the California Crisis

The ambivalent position of Black Americans hinders us from giving a uniform account of their reaction to the California Crisis. This is reflected in the Black American press[1] of the time: commentators from outside the Pacific Coast area tended to be more objective in their assessment of US–Japan relations, while those from the West Coast were prone to denounce the privileged position of the Japanese.[2]

The intellectual W. E. B du Bois (1868–1963) promptly recognised the torn feelings of his community. According to him, the educated African Americans on the West Coast understood the implications of anti-Japanese feelings, but Black labourers shared the animosity of their White counterparts.[3] The question was what would matter most: racial solidarity or economic competition? Du Bois was unequivocal: school segregation was 'a mark of contempt, an institution of inferiority, where it is imposed on the man who has to attend it against his free choice'.[4] In his understanding, the hostile feelings directed towards both the Japanese and Blacks were the same race bigotry based on the belief that the White race was 'the natural and divine guardian of all other races'.[5]

Du Bois was not isolated in his criticism. *The Colored American Magazine*, for example, assured that African Americans 'do not subscribe to race prejudice'.[6] Adding a pinch of salt to its solidarity, it asserted that the Japanese hated Chinese people and were 'in haste to show their contempt for the Negroes'.[7] Nervetheless, 'race hatred was wrong per se'.[8] The *Voice of the Negro* used the unclear stipulations of the treaty between the Unites States and Japan to assure that the segregation order was illegal. Recognising the parallels between the

Japanese exclusion from White schools and the segregation of Black children in the South, the magazine assured its readers that 'we are watching this controversy with great interest. On its final culmination hangs a movement for the righting of another kindred wrong which we forbear to mention now.'[9]

Some observers envisioned this final culmination in the form of a war. Contrary to the government, however, some American Blacks yearned for it to come. *The Colored American Magazine* asked its readership:

> Wouldn't it be a good idea to the Californians and the Southern States that sanction her Jim Crow laws for Japanese children in the schools pool issues and turn loose the dogs of war on Japan?[10]

The Nashville Globe warned that the Japanese were not like Southern Blacks and would not submit to segregation; a conflict would surely come.[11] Another publication reported that the opposition party in Japan was becoming increasingly dissatisfied with the how the government was handling the California Crisis. A Japanese statesman is reported to have warned: 'Should diplomacy fail to bring about a satisfactory solution, the only way open to us is to appeal to arms.'[12] The journalist left no doubt regarding on which side his sympathy rested: 'At any rate in the Japanese the United States is going to find a colored race that must be respected. It will be a novel in this country.'[13]

The question that naturally arose from such discussions was which side African Americans ought to take in the case of a war. Some inside the Black press (re)pledged their allegiance to the United States and assured that they would fight for their country.[14] Others, however, envisioned war as a potential tool for destroying the American racial system and hence saw Japan as an ally in the fight against White supremacy. A contributor to the African American newspaper *The Broad Ax* warned its readers that if Black Americans continued to be mistreated, nobody could blame them for siding with Japan in the event of a war.[15] He also warned: 'Japan is a nation not to be lightly dealt with. She could . . . give San Francisco more than an earthquake.' Britain, as an ally of Japan, would join the war and 'arm southern Negroes. . . . Who can doubt which side the Negroes would take, and who could blame them?'[16] A few years later, the newspaper reproduced a letter by the same person, in which he saw an 'excellent opportunity' for Blacks to 'impress the U.S. government of their importance'.[17] If 'our 9 million Negroes should bid goodbye to this country and become Japanese, Teddy or his descendants might regret the outrage he perpetrated on the Brownsville Negro soldiers'.[18]

As we now know, the war came much later than anticipated and the school controversy ended in an agreement. Concerning this, too, the African American community was divided. Some cheered for Roosevelt's engagement, some were perplexed; and even in Black newspapers that were decidedly pro-Japanese one can sense a note of jealousy. After all, at the time of Roosevelt's presidency, children of African descent had been barred from White schools for decades.

It is also noteworthy that African Americans were American citizens, while the Japanese were 'aliens ineligible for citizenship'. Roosevelt thus intervened on behalf of people destined to remain foreigners, while he kept silent on the abuse of his own citizens. It is no surprise, then, that the racial middle ground was hard to fathom for the African American community.

The Black press became a vehicle for criticising Roosevelt's preferential treatment of the Japanese. One contributor disapproved of the president's intervention in California by contrasting it to his conspicuous silence after a race riot in Atlanta:

> Why has President Roosevelt kept his mouth hermetically sealed in the face of this outrage? When a few Japanese children in San Francisco were removed from the white's children school and placed in one of their own and Japan protested against the indignity, President Roosevelt was ready to act and sent Secretary Metcalf to California to adjust the matter at once. Why does he turn a deaf ear to our Colored citizen when their rights are evicted and they brutally murdered?[19]

Roosevelt was indeed applying a double standard: he did not intervene when the Supreme Court decided that the State of Kentucky was within its right to uphold segregation, something Black commentators immediately compared with the president's anger at the Californians:

> In a dozen states, under specific laws, 1,000,000 Negro children are today educated in schools separated from whites. Mr Roosevelt is silent. In one state a few Japanese are to be excluded from white schools. Mr Roosevelt is horrified. Mr. Roosevelt friend of Japan, is notably more emotive than Mr. Roosevelt, friend of the Negro.[20]

More virulent language could sometimes be used: one newspaper lamented that 'the wishes of yellow aliens from . . . Japan [are] of more consequences to this nation than [those of] its loyal Negro citizen'.[21]

The reactions expressed in the Black press illustrate that, in the end, neither race nor citizenship mattered in front of political pragmatism. Where the US government accepted the discrimination of African Americans because of their race, it protected the Japanese due to their geopolitical significance. For this analysis to be complete, we now need to turn to the importance of African Americans for the Japanese. This will exemplify how the 'race in the middle' can use the 'race at the bottom' to underscore its claim to preferential treatment.

The race at the bottom (II): the meaning of African Americans for Japan

Black Americans have been a part of US–Japanese relations from the very beginning.[22] It is only natural, then, that the Japanese concerned with the United States would take a closer look at their situation. The existing scholarship on

African American and Japanese interactions, however, tends to be too optimistic in its assessment of the meaning of Blacks for the Meiji Japanese. Koshiro Yukiko for example, writes that Japanese leaders tended to see African American people (as westernised 'coloured') as models for Japan in its aspirations to modernise itself.[23] Similarly, Atsushi Tajima and Michael Thornton, based on Koshiro, assert that African Americans were a 'special case' that enabled the Japanese to 'decipher the West' and became a 'possible role model' for Japan since they were 'of color and Western, and came closer to any other group of color to being what the Japanese desired'.[24]

Before going into details, these assertions can be safely doubted solely by pointing to the geopolitical evolutions described throughout these pages. The legitimacy of White supremacy in Japanese eyes as well as the paranoia-inducing popularity of social Darwinism certainly did not contribute to interpreting other 'coloured' races as models. Furthermore, as will be explained in further detail below, Japanese observers almost exclusively witnessed Black Americans in a position of political, economic and social subordination. The modernisation efforts of Japan were precisely about not ending up in the same situation they were witnessing. The same was true for the position of African Americans inside the United States: the Japanese were fighting against being relegated to the margins of society. If African Americans were an example to follow for the Japanese, then it was probably as an indication of what to avoid. This does not mean that the Japanese showed no interest in the plight of African Americans. But it implies that Blacks in America, marginalised socially, politically and economically, were a materialisation of the worst fears of the young Japanese nation. Hence, at least in the Meiji period, any interest of the Japanese in Black Americans should be seen as reflecting a concern for their own survival. As the 'race at the bottom', African Americans represented the subordinate racial status that the Japanese were determined to escape. Hence, to racially 'elevate' themselves to the status of 'race in the middle', the Japanese had to consciously distance themselves from African Americans.

Early Japanese views of African Americans

In 1860, an official Japanese embassy to the United States was sent to ratify the Treaty of Amity and Commerce concluded between the two countries in 1858.[25] This became the first opportunity for Japanese envoys to witness African Americans in their country. Arriving a few months before the beginning of the Civil War, that is, as slavery had not yet been abolished, the Japanese envoys were bound to witness the racial problem of the United States. And this they did: one delegate compared the situation of Blacks to that of the Japanese outcasts:

> The laws of the land separate the Blacks. They are just like our *eta* caste. But they [the Whites] employ the Blacks as their servants. The Whites are of course intelligent, and

> the Blacks stupid. Thus the seed[s] of intelligence and unintelligence are not allowed to mix together.[26]

Another claimed that Blacks 'are inferior as human beings and extremely stupid'.[27]

White Americans sometimes fostered these assessments: on his way to a reception at the White House, the fourth-highest-ranking member of the embassy, Morita Moriyuki, shared a carriage with the US Minister to Spain, William Preston. Morita recorded the small journey as follows:

> Preston was a big man, around thirty-eight or thirty-nine years of age. He was proud as he pointed out the flags of the Rising Sun to me, saying 'very good'. As he singled out Black women, he said they were the same color as the black wool suit he had on, and sneered at them, calling them ugly. He seemed very pleased with the White people and, whenever he saw White women, said 'very good', and pointed them out to me.[28]

The first official encounter between Japanese and African Americans in the United States evidently did not occur on neutral ground. The Japanese envoys saw that it was the Whites who were at the top of the American social hierarchy. Neither did they miss the fact that African Americans were in a subordinate position.

The statements above do not hint at any criticism, which presupposes that the Japanese envoys took the alleged inferiority of Blacks for granted. However, it is necessary to emphasise that any prejudice the Japanese might have possessed towards people with dark skin colour originated in the circumstances in which they actually met them. In this particular instance, it was a racial system that had reduced Blacks to social outcasts, similar to those existing in Japan. That Japanese envoys would compare – and dislike – both is therefore not surprising. Some scholars tried to envision the interactions between Japanese and Africans Americans as doomed from the beginning because of the negative association of the colour black inside Japanese culture. Wagatsuma Hiroshi writes that before any contact with foreigners, Japanese people valued white skin for its beauty and disliked black skin for its ugliness. Hence, the Japanese response to White people was spontaneously a positive one, while that to people with dark skin was negative.[29]

This assumption is problematic on several levels. Historically speaking, the spontaneous reaction to the white skin of Europeans was far from positive: during the Tokugawa period for example, Europeans were not considered particularly beautiful, but on the contrary were seen as hairy barbarians or feared as long-nosed demons (*tengu*).[30] Recent scholarship has also demonstrated that early images of people of African descent were not unanimously negative, and sometimes were even quite positive.[31]

One might also point out that the negative connotation of the colour black is not peculiar to Japanese culture, but also has a long history of association with sin, despair and death within European thinking. Yet, this too did not necessarily influence European views of dark skin colour. Fredrickson rightly reminds us that medieval European depictions of Black people 'range from the monstruous and horrifying to the saintly and heroic'.[32] Furthermore, he also warns not to exaggerate the significance of the negative conations of the colour black for the actual meeting with dark-skinned people.[33] Leaving aside cultural views of colours, it is more fruitful to look at what the Japanese actually wrote about African Americans.

Tajima and Thornton claim that it was at the time of the Paris Peace Conference that 'the Japanese media introduced to their readers the plight of African Americans'.[34] However, a search through Japanese newspapers from the 1880s reveals that readers had fairly regular access to information about Black Americans and were thus able to understand the race problem of the United States. Two topics stand out in the articles: the status of Black citizens as a political issue, and racial antagonism. The *Yomiuri shinbun*, for example, published a series of interviews with an exchange student named Nakamura Tadao.[35] Nakamura had just returned from his studies in the United States and was questioned on a variety of topics, ranging from American law and politics to societal issues. Asked about the problems faced by American politicians, Nakamura replied 'the racial conflict' (*jinshu no arasoi*).[36] He explained that Blacks, especially numerous in the South, gained their freedom after the Civil War but were not considered equal. They were comparable to Japan's former *eta* and *hinin* outcastes, albeit with more rights.[37] A few years earlier, the *Yomiuri* had already reported that Southern Blacks feared the revival of slavery after the election of President Grover Cleveland (1837–1908). Cleveland, however, issued a statement reassuring them that their rights would be protected.[38]

The Japanese media were astute in grasping the political constellation of the United States, recognising that the status of African Americans was a critical issue capable of influencing voting patterns. The magazine *Gaikō jihō* covered the already mentioned dinner between Roosevelt and Washington and correctly commented that the Southerners could not fathom the president's decision to invite a Black person to the White House.[39] Two years later, in 1903, it reported that the president was attributing key public office positions to Blacks despite having public opinion against him.[40] The newspaper *Asahi shinbun* was more specific and pointed out the nomination of a Black man to the post of collector of customs in Charleston as a source of discontent in the South.[41] It also reported that Roosevelt's handling of the 'Black problem' was cause for growing discontent in the United States.[42]

The second topic – racial antagonism – was illustrated with articles about lynching, race riots and segregation, through which the Japanese received an overall picture of the racial situation in the United States. A short commentary on terminology is necessary before going further. The interpretation of Japanese articles written at the time is made challenging by the use of two words in reference to Black people: *kuronbō* and *kokudo*. The origins of the words are unknown, but both possess an obvious pejorative connotation and are usually translated as the racial epithet 'nigger'.[43] These terms were used despite the neutral alternative *kokujin* (Black person) being available in the Meiji period. This makes the tone of some articles about racial antagonism in the United States sound rather ambiguous.

The following example about a lynching from 1886 is telling: the *Yomiuri* reported that a Black man named Alexander Reed had been lynched for murdering a White girl in Alabama on 28 December 1886.[44] The article emphasised the victim's beauty and youth, describing her as: 'sixteen years old pretty girl with a beautiful face'.[45] She was allegedly attacked by the armed Reed (for his first appearance labelled as *kokujin*) on her way back from a friend's house. The girl managed to escape Reed's grip but 'the nigger (*kokudo*) loaded a bullet in his rifle and shot. After he saw the girl fall, he put his rifle against her head and shot again.'[46] The corpse was discovered, and after Reed was found a mob of some five hundred people gathered. They spat on him and after building up a stake slowly burned him until 'the nigger's (*kokudo*) body was carbonized, and he died'.[47]

The article did not explicitly condone the lynching. Yet, even if one assumes that the terms used to refer to Black people are not racial epithets, the tone can be deemed ambivalent at best.[48] This holds true for most of the articles on the topic: even in the publications that dismiss lynching as barbaric, it seems that the true aim of the writers was less to condemn the treatment of Blacks, and more to point out the hypocritical behaviour of Whites who were engaging in such a practice while at the same time preaching ideals of democracy, virtue and justice. This impression is reinforced by the fact that most writings maintain that African Americans were inferior to Whites. And without going as far as saying that Blacks deserved their treatment, one can discern a hint of understanding for the behaviour of White Americans.

The following article from the magazine *Kyōkai hyōron* from 1896 illustrates this pattern. The text starts with an impressive amount of detail on African American history and the condemning (almost pathetic) tone is undeniable:

> Their [Black Americans'] history goes hand in hand with the dark one of the slave trade. The merchants of North America, without humanity, without morality, started very early to land on the African coast . . . They stole the able-bodied Blacks and went back to their ships, where they threw them in the dark . . . Without caring for crying mothers and weeping wives, the Whites and their ships would return to their homeland with hundreds of unfortunate abducted persons.[49]

The article then described in graphic terms the journey and the human trade once on the American continent. 'This', the author writes, 'is the origin of the arrival of Blacks in North America, and the reasons for it are proper cause for sadness and grief.'[50]After an explanation of the Civil War and the difficulties the emancipated slaves encountered, the author of the article clarified his position on lynching: it was an 'immense stain on the civilisation of North America' and a practice that should not be found in a civilised country in the nineteenth century. Lynching as a practice was comparable to the treatment of former *eta* after they had committed an offence against warriors or commoners.[51]

However, this righteous condemnation of lynching was only one aspect. At the same time, the article questioned the capacity of Black Americans to live as free citizens: '[Their] sense of responsibility is weak and following the rules of society as well as fulfilling their duties as citizen is an utterly difficult task for Blacks.'[52] This was the reason why the criminality rate amongst them was so high. Moreover, since they were irresponsible and uneducated, the article claimed, it was simple to buy their vote and 'one can even hear that a Black will sell his vote for a cup of coffee'.[53] In the end, the author did acknowledge that African Americans were 'devoted and jolly', but 'what to do with Blacks is one of the biggest problems that Americans have to consider in the present and for the future'.[54]

While never condoning violence against Blacks outright, the peculiar tendency of Japanese authors to feel empathy for both sides remained consistent. So is the characterisation of the Black presence as a problem inside American society. The years after the Russo-Japanese War saw the publication of numerous works about the United States, a trend that is not surprising considering the development of Japanese immigration, and the ensuing problems, described earlier. Equally predictable, a great number of these mentioned the so-called *Kokujin mondai* (Black problem). Now that both Japanese and African Americans were the targets of abuse, any information on why Blacks were on the margins of the American society could help to improve the status of the Japanese.

The 'Black problem' or how to sell Japanese immigrants

The expression *Kokujin mondai* demands caution as it can be misleading. When reading Japanese works which mention the 'Black problem' and which were written after the Russo-Japanese war, one rapidly realises that what the writers meant was not the problems African Americans were encountering in the United States, but, on the contrary, the problems the United States were facing with Blacks. As before, African Americans were described as immature, prone to crime and, above all, generally unfit to assume their responsibilities as American citizens. The context in which they came to be envisioned after the Russo-Japanese War, however, also drastically altered their meaning for the Japanese. Roosevelt had managed to maintain the racial middle ground, but the price had been high: the Gentlemen's Agreement was in essence brandmarking the Japanese as undesirable on American soil. Even the retraction of the school segregation order could not hide this fact. As privileged as the Japanese status was compared to other non-Whites, it remained extremely precarious. The

'Black problem' became a convenient tool to criticise this situation, by pointing to the discriminating behaviour of White Americans but also at the same time elevating the Japanese over other 'coloured' races.

Such a critique can be read in *Hokubei sezokukan* (1909) by the author Tamura Shōgyo (1874–1948). Tamura had spent six years as a student in the United States (from 1903–9) and described a broad range of topics in his book. Several chapters are dedicated to the race problem and Tamura strongly criticised lynching as contradictory to the Christian way.[55] However, he also then claimed:

> The race one has to pity the most on this earth is the Black race. What kind of divine punishment has fallen on them I do not know, but from their birth on they are completely black. The ugliness of their skin is painted on their whole body, and it is now impossible for them to escape the worst deficiency a human being can have.[56]

And while he acknowledged that Blacks had made some progress since their emancipation from slavery, he turned to the well-known trope of Black males raping White women to describe them further: 'Because Blacks are very weak in restraining their sexual desires, they lose their ability to distinguish between good and evil as soon as they gaze upon a White female silhouette. Therefore, they rape her.'[57] This, according to Tamura, was the reason why Whites would hunt them down, and once they find a Black criminal, 'they hang him from a tree . . . pile up firewood under him and burn him to death'.[58] The police were complicit in this, and if no criminal was to be found, the mob killed random strangers. 'This', wrote Tamura, 'is called lynching and is the unique custom of White people killing Blacks.'[59] The author left no doubts concerning his feelings:

> The Americans, who pride themselves with being the representatives of civilisation but engage without remorse in such an inhumane and illegal act, are so hideous that they cannot be seen as people of a civilized nation. I cannot help to be outraged at the Americans who are drunk with the luxury they got from this world and step on humanity with their feet.[60]

Tamura, who published his work only three years after the San Francisco school controversy, seemed more interested in pointing out the lack of Christian behaviour and the brutality of White Americans than in defending Blacks. At the same time, he asserted the inferiority of Blacks, describing them as cursed and driven by sexual desire. Some authors went a step further: while they did not only assert the inferiority of African Americans, they also speculated about the reasons for it. Furthermore, they used Blacks as a scapegoat for the American race problem and thereby tried to divert White animosity from Japanese immigrants.

One author for example, a certain Suzuki Hanzaburō, claimed that Blacks were 'obedient, naïve as children . . . lewd, lazy, without ambition and they do only mimic as they have no creative abilities'.[61] There was no consensus among writers regarding the reasons of this alleged inferiority, but some chose to trace it back to Africa. The countries from which African Americans came were seen as inferior, 'even by African standards'.[62] Their capture and enslavement had for the first time brought African natives in contact with civilisation and therefore slavery had been beneficial.[63] Regarding slavery, Yokoyama Matajirō, a natural scientist from Tokyo Imperial University, commented that the stories about the mistreatment of slaves were highly exaggerated: they had been cruel masters, but the truth was that most of them treated their slaves well.[64]

The crucial issue in the works quoted above was the emancipation of slaves, as the authors agreed that something was wrong with the freeing of Blacks: 'People from outside the United States believe that the "Black problem" was solved with emancipation', Suzuki explained, 'but in reality, the American "Black problem" originated because of the emancipation order'.[65] One interpretation for this was that Blacks were inferior in spirit and could therefore not possibly take part in a democratic society:

> Like cattle . . . that becomes a tool for civilisation, Blacks live inside civilisation without noticing it. The virtue they learned through slavery is obedience. There is no doubt that the spirit of Blacks lacks the independence necessary in a civilised country and especially in a democratic state.[66]

According to Yokoyama, the Americans had made 'a grave mistake by trying, under the name of equity, to make free citizen out of them. And they now badly regret it.'[67]

Yokoyama was keen on telling what the 'truth' about emancipation was: after the Civil War, 'all state governments granted . . . every Black family tax-free land and even gave them funds, tools, and cattle'.[68] He lamented that Blacks only had to use these gifts in order to enter White society. Yet, 'within a few years, they proved themselves to be good for nothing except to be slaves. Not one single plot of land they were granted has been farmed.'[69] Moreover, although the government had given books and pencils to Black children, school attendance was low so that 'the number of illiterate Blacks is now three times as high as during the slavery era'.[70] Suffrage was another issue: White criminals were buying the votes of Blacks with alcohol and other methods, so that the states had to restrict their voting rights.[71]

It was no accident that Yokoyama chose precisely those examples to condemn the alleged inferiority of Black Americans. His book was written in 1915, that is, two years after the passing of the Alien Land Law that banned Japanese immigrants from owning land.[72] Considering the context, the story of African Americans receiving tax-free land and leaving it unfarmed must have been painful to the Japanese readership. The same is true for the alleged low school attendance, in view of the San Francisco segregation order. Regarding suffrage rights, the Japanese immigrants were still 'aliens ineligible for citizenship' and as such unable to vote. Yokoyama, therefore, gave the impression that African

Americans were unjustly receiving opportunities that Japanese were barred from.

The allegations he made were of course not without motive: his downplaying of the cruelty of slavery as well as his emphasis of the alleged inability of African Americans to become citizens were all aimed at promoting Japanese at the expense of Blacks. For him, Blacks were 'obviously an inferior race compared to us'.[73] They were unable to assimilate, nor could they learn proper English.[74] They were a burden, 'a tumour in the otherwise healthy body of the Americans'.[75] 'That is why', Yokohama exclaimed, 'there is something I must say: You Americans, welcome a lot of Japanese! The Japanese are as learned as Americans. We are assiduous, honest, and cheap labour. There is no one that is more lucrative than we are.'[76] It was highly illogical, he concluded, that Americans were excluding 'good people' like the Japanese but at the same time suffering with Blacks.[77]

At a time when both were facing similar problems in the United States, Yokoyama decided to promote Japanese immigrants at the expense of Blacks, thereby defining the racial identity of the Japanese as opposite to that of African Americans. Due to his authority as a scholar from the Tokyo Imperial University, his influence in shaping the Japanese view of African Americans should not be underestimated. With the memories of the California Crisis and Alien Land Law still vivid, his text certainly did not help to promote a positive image of Black America. It did also confirm what a certain number of Japanese intellectuals of the time were already thinking, namely that Blacks were inferior to Japanese. Yoshino argued that the solution to the 'Black problem' was the betterment of the race, which could only happen through education, as miscegenation was out of question for Whites. But he also cautioned that education was not a satisfactory option: to see the results, one would have to wait for several centuries.[78] Suzuki repeatedly emphasised that the 'Black problem' was caused by the emancipation of slaves:

> American intellectuals, whose education was influenced by the concepts of religion, freedom, equality, and humanism do not want to hold people as slaves. Yet, Blacks in the South remain unconscious of their situation and live like wild animals. They do not want to live independently or with the help of someone else, but want to be raised by someone else, and that is why this serious problem exists.[79]

The point that stands out the most, however, is that for all of the authors quoted above, the 'Black problem' was presented as a case study for a failed democratic experiment, in which civil rights (and privileges) had been given to people unable to enjoy them.

In hindsight, the sources presented above tell us more about how precarious the position of the Japanese was as an elusive 'race in the middle', than about the Japanese view of African Americans. 'White' according to a standard that should have made them 'coloured' but could not make them equal, the Japanese were never fully accepted either as a 'great nation' or a 'great race'. African Americans were at all times an uncomfortable reminder of this, as well as a convenient tool to criticise those very circumstances. Early reports on the American race problem in Japanese printed media were rather neutral, emphasising the political and societal importance of race inside American society. The tone began to change as Japanese immigrants increased in number on American soil. With the 'Black problem', the Japanese could conveniently criticise a system that excluded them, and at the same time elevate themselves above Blacks.

The analysis of the California Crisis in the framework of the Racial Middle Ground showed that, in truth, the whole crisis that unfolded after the decision of the School Board of San Francisco was created by the racial middle ground itself. Acting on behalf of the Japanese, Roosevelt created a fundamental dissonance between how non-White people were supposed to be handled in the United States and how the Japanese were actually treated. More than considerations of character, literacy, work ethic or capability for assimilation, it is the national situation which differentiated the Japanese from other non-Whites immigrants. In contrast to African Americans, Native Americans or the Chinese, the Japanese had a government to back them up. And this government had the military capacity to defend its immigrants.

The opponents of Roosevelt, however, could not fathom the implications of his behaviour; for them, these went well beyond accepting a few Japanese children into White schools, and were a threat to the very foundations of White supremacy in the United States. If the Japanese were first, the Chinese could come next, followed maybe even by African Americans. The latter were well aware of the racial middle ground and their reaction to it was an undecided one: between jealousy and the hope that this negotiation zone would one day extend to them. Their hopes were in vain, as it would take only a few more years, with a little more provocation, for the racial middle ground to collapse.

Before moving to its end, however, there is one additional aspect of the middle ground that is worth mentioning briefly. Chapter 5 explained that until the Russo-Japanese War, the Japanese were but a faceless abstraction in the American mind. While this is true for the majority of the American people, there were in fact a number of Japanese individuals who went to the United States long before substantial emigration from Japan started. Amongst them were students who, sometimes on behalf of their government, went to the United States to study the ways of the West and whose experiences were to become an asset for the future of Japan. While their numbers were low, the experiences of some of them, which are thankfully available to us through the writings they left behind, are a rare window into what could be called the human aspect of the racial middle ground. What did it mean for an individual to be in the middle?

The human aspect of the racial middle ground

With regard to the human aspect of the middle ground, Frantz Fanon's classic work on the plight of the Black French from the Antilles comes naturally to mind: 'It is another fact: some Blacks want to demonstrate to Whites, whatever the cost, the richness of their thoughts, the equal power of their spirit.'[80] Replace 'Blacks' with 'Japanese' and the essence of the Japanese rise to modernity in terms of the racial middle ground is summarised in one sentence. If one delves deeper into Fanon's work, the similarities between the Meiji Japanese and the '*noir*' become palpable. It was when in contact with the White man, Fanon wrote, that he was made aware of his actual Blackness: by 'taking an objective look at myself, [I] discovered my blackness, my ethnic characteristics'.[81] Here, it is the famous novelist Natsume Sōseki's (1867–1916) traumatic realisation of his 'ugliness' in front of the British people that comes to mind:

> We are yellow . . . completely yellow. When I was in Japan, while not completely White, I at least saw myself as having a colour close to something human. But in this country, I came to the realisation that I was of a colour that had nothing human to it.[82]

The later Governor of the Bank of Japan and member of the House of Peers Mishima Yatarō (1867–1919) had a similar experience while studying in the United States, albeit almost twenty years earlier than Sōseki. In a letter to his parents, he wrote that:

> While I was in the country [Japan] I never thought of my facial colour as being 'dead'. But since I came here [the United States] and look at myself in the mirror next to a Westerner, my face has a miserable colour. That my face has a bad shape can be traced back to the fact that I am Japanese and cannot be changed. But the colour of my face, compared to that of a Westerner, is like that of a cadaver; dark-blue.[83]

Mishima also half-heartedly joked that he had managed to become a polished (white) handsome man at the beginning of his stay. But due to his outdoor activities, his hands and face had turned black and he had returned to his original state of 'yellow Japanese'.[84]

Fanon's study, however, focuses on a dichotomy: 'The Black has two dimensions: one with his peer, the other one with the White. A Black behaves differently with a White than with another Black.'[85] The situation was more complicated for Japanese students in the United States. As the examples above show, the students could develop an inferiority complex. Unlike Fanon's Black men from the Antilles, however, most of the Japanese students remained convinced nationalists and as such kept a certain notion of pride. What Eiichiro Azuma has written about the Japanese elite's view of emigration is also true for the exchange students from earlier times: going abroad was above all a patriotic act, which was designed to support the nation and the imperial institution.[86] Similar to the distinction between the Japanese as a nation and the Japanese as a race discussed earlier, the inferiority complex of the exchange students to the United States therefore did not stem from belonging to the Japanese nation. It came from being part of the 'Asian race', which included, amongst others, the much-hated Chinese.[87]

This takes us back to the three levels of the racial middle ground, this time with the Chinese as the 'race at the bottom': in the early phase, the urgent task for the Japanese elite that went to the United States was less the suppression of any alleged Japanese characteristics (becoming a modern Japanese was in par with becoming westernised anyway), and more the dissociation from the Chinese. Or, as Majima aptly puts it, they needed to 'differentiate to assimilate'.[88] Unsurprisingly, then, the Japanese students developed a contempt for the Chinese that rivalled that of American bigots.

Besides this racial component, there also was a definite class aspect to it. The concerns of the Japanese students mirrored those of the government as well as those of the Japanese immigrant elite. In their minds, China was synonymous with backwardness and lack of civilisation, a stark contrast to the image of modernity the Japanese were trying to display. As Azuma pointed out, the Japanese immigrant elite possessed their own Orientalist views of Chinese immigrants and were striving for the recognition of White America, despite the anti-Asian feelings that saw both groups as equally undesirable.[89] But Orientalist views were not the only thing the Japanese elite shared with White Americans. In a peculiar blend of race and class prejudice, the elite agreed that the Japanese labourers and prostitutes that came to the United States were of the same kind as the Chinese. This 'fabricated the dual cultural affinities between the elite Japanese and the white American middle-class, and between the lowly *gumin* [ignorant masses] and the excluded Chinese'.[90] The implications for the middle ground were evident: for it to work, it was necessary to remove the Chinese characteristics of the 'lowly' immigrants.

For the Japanese students, the contempt for the Chinese flourished even before they reached American shores. Describing the conditions aboard the ship bound to the United States, Mishima wrote that the Japanese travelling second class (he travelled first class) were excluded from most areas of the ship. Furthermore, 'their room was close to that of the Chinese therefore the smell was terrible'.[91] His disdain was shared by many, including the Christian educator Uchimura Kanzō (1861–1930) and the Prime Minister Takahashi Korekiyo (1854–1936).[92] The situation did not improve once in America as the students were constantly mistaken for Chinese. Uchimura was asked where his laundry shop or 'queue' were.[93] Mishima complained that a great deal of people in New York did not know Japan 'and when they see us, they mock us as Chinese. It is pitiful.'[94] The White Americans would mistake them for Chinese and mock them when he and his friends would wear traditional attire. This led Mishima to buy a Western suit.[95] In his case, the anxiety of being mistaken for a Chinese man turned to hatred:

> As always, the Chinese are being despised. During this summer too, workers from Colorado formed a mob of a hundred and fifty people, hunted the Chinese down, and

> shot twenty-one of them. In this country, the Chinese are being treated like dogs. Confucius and Mencius have spent their time writing complicated things, but these are meaningless. It is laughable to think that the Chinese there [in China] spend years learning thousands of complicated characters and therefore neglect other studies. I too am praying that Chinese characters will be abolished in our country [Japan].[96]

Mishima's contempt reflected both the Japanese government's policy of modernisation and of 'leaving Asia behind' as famously advocated by Fukuzawa Yukichi.[97]

As mentioned earlier, the Japanese government was appalled by the 'Chinese characteristics' of the Japanese labourers that settled in the United States. It therefore showed great interest in the living conditions of its citizens and sought to remedy what Azuma has called their 'Sinification'. This occurred in cooperation with the immigrant elite, and both actors were engaged in a 'partnership . . . for the transformation of ordinary *Issei* (first generation immigrants) from the "Sinified" Japanese to the "truly" Japanese fit for modern life'.[98] And indeed, 'acting Western' could pay off, and in true middle ground fashion, the Japanese could be praised for their 'un-Chinese' behaviour. The already mentioned Takahashi was told by an American girl that the Chinese and Japanese differed greatly, and gave the example of one Japanese student who bought a dictionary with his first pay packet to learn English properly while the Chinese were saving their money for their return.[99] Mishima told his parents that when he was called Chinese he would get angry and scream that he was Japanese so that 'I can finally be treated as a human being.'[100]

At other times, however, even looking Western was not sufficient. Henry 'Yoshitaka' Kiyama (1885–1951) was one of the youths who decided to try their luck in the United States. At the age of nineteen, in 1904, he left for San Francisco to study fine arts. In addition to conventional works of art, Kiyama also created a documentary comic-book about his experience in America.[101] The book gives us a rare visual insight into the life of Japanese immigrants in the United States. Episode 11 of the comic starts with a Japanese student quitting his job as a 'schoolboy'.[102] His angry former employee, an American lady, vows to find a better 'boy'. She first addresses two Chinese men, mistaking them for Japanese. Finally, she addresses a finely dressed Japanese gentlemen and offers him a job as a houseworker. The Japanese man, who in truth is a consul, is visibly offended and replies: 'I am not such a domestic labor. But I am consul of Empire [*sic*].' To what the lady responds: 'But your looks [*sic*] like my laundry boy.'

Notes

1. I chose to give only the most representative examples in this chapter. For an exhaustive study of Japan's meaning as reflected in the Black press, see Kearney, *African American Views of the Japanese*.
2. Ibid., 49.

3. Arnold Shankman, '"Asiatic Ogre" or "Desirable Citizen"? The Image of Japanese Americans in the Afro-American Press, 1867–1933', *Pacific Historical Review* 46, no. 4 (November 1977): 587.
4. As cited in David J. Hellwig, 'Afro-American Reactions to the Japanese and the Anti-Japanese Movement, 1906–1924', *Phylon* 38, no. 1 (1977): 94.
5. Ibid.
6. 'Japan and San Francisco Discrimination', *The Colored American Magazine* 11, no. 5 (November 1906): 285.
7. Ibid.
8. Ibid.
9. 'The Controversy with Japan', *The Voice of the Negro* 4, no. 2 (March 1907): 93.
10. 'The California Muddle', *The Colored American Magazine* 12, no. 3 (March 1907): 168.
11. Kearney, *African American Views of the Japanese*, 43.
12. 'The Japanese Question', *The Voice of the Negro* 4, no. 7 (July 1907): 287.
13. Ibid.
14. Kearney, *African American Views of the Japanese*, 44.
15. John T. Campbell, 'What May Result if the Persecution of the Negro Continues', *The Broad Ax*, 19 January 1907.
16. Ibid.
17. John T. Campbell, 'Chance for the Afro-Americans to Join Hands with the Japanese and Bring on a Bloody War in this Country', *The Broad Ax*, 15 April 1911.
18. Ibid. The Brownsville Affair was an incident that occurred in Brownsville, Texas in August 1906. Black soldiers from the 25th Infantry Regiment stationed there were falsely accused of shooting a local bartender. Fabricated evidence led to the dishonorable discharge of 167 soldiers thus barring them from military pension and the right to work in civil jobs. The discharge was ordered by President Roosevelt, despite obvious lack of evidence and substantial public protest. Thomas C. Holt, *Children of Fire: A History of African Americans* (New York: Hill and Wang, 2010), 235–6.
19. 'Rev. J. M. Foster in the Christian Nation, New York', *The Broad Ax*, 5 January 1907. On 22 September 1906 the alleged rapes of White women led to three days of racial violence in the city of Atlanta and resulted in at least twenty-five deaths and 120 wounded. For details, see Holt, *Children of Fire*, 237–40.
20. 'Negro and Japanese Pupils', *The Broad Ax*, 13 February 1909. The readers were nevertheless encouraged to join Japan in its efforts to have segregation abolished.
21. Shankman, '"Asiatic Ogre" or "Desirable Citizen"?', 576.
22. For the sake of historical accuracy, it is necessary to point out that the Perry expedition was not the first recorded encounter between Japanese and Black Americans. According to the available sources, the first African American to arrive on Japanese shores was a sailor named Pyrrhus Concer, a former slave turned whaler from Southampton. In April 1845, that is eight years before Perry's arrival, Concer arrived in Japan onboard the *Manhattan*. For details about his journey and the lack of information available in Japanese about him, see Matsumura Masayoshi,

'Nihon ni kita saisho no Amerika kokujin', *Gaikō Jihō* 1185 (July 1981): 18–26. The meaning of Concer's story inside US–Japan relations has been overstated by several scholars. Koshiro, for example, wrote that 'Concer . . . played a substantial role in U.S.-Japanese relations since their earliest phases', while Furukawa Hiromi goes as far as stating that the event 'layed the foundation for opening the country when Commodore Perry came to this shore eight years later in 1853'. The aim here is not to downplay the importance of Pyrrhus Concer's actions. But it is noteworthy that the crew of *Manhattan* was not allowed on shore and nothing indicates that the arrival of the ship led to deeper exchange between the United States and Japan. For Koshiro's assumption, see Koshiro, 'Beyond an Alliance of Color', 183. For Furukawa, see Furukawa Hiromi, 'Black Presence in Japan-U.S. Relations', *Kokujin kenkyū* 64 (1994): 10.

23. Koshiro, 'Beyond an Alliance of Color', 185.
24. Atsushi Tajima and Michael Thornton, 'Strategic solidarity: Japanese Imaginings of Blacks and Race in Popular Media', *Inter-Asia Cultural Studies* 13, no. 3 (2012): 354.
25. This embassy was the first of its kind. For an extensive analysis of it, see Masao Miyoshi, *As We Saw Them: The First Japanese Embassy to the United States (1860)* (Berkeley: University of California Press, 1979). The Treaty of Amity and Commerce was signed in Shimoda on 29 July 1858. It guaranteed the opening of five Japanese ports to American commerce and granted extraterritoriality to American citizens.
26. Ibid., 61.
27. Ibid.
28. Ibid., 62.
29. Hiroshi Wagatsuma, 'The Social Perception of Skin Color in Japan', *Daedalus* 96, no. 2 (Spring 1967): 407. Kowner and Demel, based on Wagatsuma, assert that in premodern Japan 'negative attitudes towards dark skin were common well before the first encounter with Black people'; Rotem Kowner and Walter Demel, 'Modern East Asia and the Rise of Racial Thought: Possible Links, Unique Features and Unsettled Issues', in *Race and Racism in Modern East Asia: Western and Eastern Constructions*, ed. Rotem Kowner and Walter Demel (Leiden: Brill, 2013), 20.
30. John G. Russel, 'The Other Other', 89.
31. For details about the Japanese reaction to dark-skinned people in early modern Japan, see Fujita Midori, *Afurika hakken: Nihon ni okeru Afurika-zō no hensen* (Tokyo: Iwanami shoten, 2005).
32. Fredrickson, *Racism*, 26.
33. Fredrickson fittingly asks: 'If black always had unfavorable connotations, why did many orders of priests and nuns wear black instead of some other color?'; ibid., 26.
34. Tajima and Thornton, 'Strategic solidarity', 356.
35. The series of interviews was published under the title 'Beikoku-dan' from 7–15 September 1887. For details about Nakamura, his studies and his return to Japan, see 'Nakamura Tadao-shi', *Yomiuri shinbun*, 3 September 1887.

36. 'Beikoku-dan', *Yomiuri shinbun*, 9 September 1887.
37. Ibid.
38. 'Gasshūkoku shindaitōryō no ronkoku', *Yomiuri shinbun*, 1 January 1885.
39. 'Gasshūkoku daitōryō kokujin o shōtai shite nanbō no jinbō o ushinau', *Gaikō jihō* 47 (December 1901): 48.
40. 'Beikoku daitōryō no kokujin tōyō', *Gaikō jihō* 63 (April 1903): 72.
41. 'Beikokujin no ijinshu ken'o', *Asahi shinbun*, 2 December 1902.
42. 'Kokujin mondai to Beikoku daitōryō', *Asahi shinbun*, 10 January 1903.
43. Russel, 'The Other Other', 89.
44. 'Shōjo no ōshi', *Yomiuri shinbun*, 27 January 1886.
45. Ibid.
46. Ibid.
47. Ibid.
48. For another example of an article on lynching, see 'Zangyaku naru shikei', *Yomiuri shinbun*, 8 January 1900.
49. 'Beikoku no kokujin', *Kyōkai hyōron* 48 (January 1896): 25.
50. Ibid.
51. Ibid., 27.
52. Ibid.
53. Ibid.
54. Ibid., 28.
55. Tamura Shōgyo, *Hokubei sezokukan* (Tokyo: Hakubunkan, 1909), 44.
56. Ibid., 45.
57. Ibid., 46–7.
58. Ibid., 47.
59. Ibid., 48.
60. Ibid., 49.
61. Suzuki Hanzaburō, *Beikoku kokuminsei no shinkenkyū* (Tokyo: Rakuyōdō, 1916), 386. From the introduction of the book we learn that Suzuki spent several years in the United States and that he used a multitude of sources to write his work.
62. See for example Yoshino Sakuzō, ed., *Gendai Beikoku* (Tokyo: Min'yūsha, 1916), 80–1.
63. Ibid., 81; Yokoyama Matajirō, *Sekai ni okeru shizen no kikan* (Tokyo: Kōbun shoten, 1915), 345.
64. Yokoyama, *Sekai ni okeru shizen no kikan*, 345.
65. Suzuki, *Beikoku kokuminsei no shinkenkyū*, 387.
66. Yoshino, *Gendai Beikoku*, 81–2.
67. Yokoyama, *Sekai ni okeru shizen no kikan*, 358.
68. Ibid., 352. Yokoyama is probably referring to the Special Field Order No. 15: on 16 January 1865, General Sherman of the Union Army issued an order for the requisition of a coastal area stretching from South Carolina to Florida for the exclusive use of freed slaves. Each household head was to receive forty acres of land (to which was later added one army mule, hence the alternative designation 'forty acres and a mule' for the field order). One year after the order, however, the Black settlers were

chased from their plots and the land was given back to its former owners. See Holt, *Children of Fire*, 168–9.

69. Yokoyama, *Sekai ni okeru shizen no kikan*, 352.
70. Ibid., 353. Yokoyama's information on illiteracy amongst African Americans is wrong. The percentage of Blacks and other non-Whites unable to read or write was 70 per cent in 1870 but had dropped to 23 per cent in 1920. National Center for Education Statistics, '120 Years of American Education: A Statistical Portrait' (1993): https://nces.ed.gov/naal/lit_history.asp#illiteracy (accessed 28 May 2022).
71. Yokoyama, *Sekai ni okeru shizen no kikan*, 353.
72. The Alien Land Law is further discussed in Chapter 7 of this work.
73. Yokoyama, *Sekai ni okeru shizen no kikan*, 358.
74. Ibid., 356.
75. Ibid.
76. Ibid., 358–9.
77. Ibid., 359.
78. Yoshino, *Gendai Beikoku*, 91–2.
79. Suzuki, *Beikoku kokuminsei no shinkenkyū*, 400.
80. Fanon, *Peau noire, masques blancs*, 7.
81. Ibid., 90.
82. As cited in Majima Ayu, *Hadairo no yūutsu: Kindai Nihon no jinshu taiken* (Tokyo: Chūō kōron shinsha, 2014), 87.
83. Mishima Yatarō, *Mishima Yatarō no tegami: Amerika e watatta Meiji shoki no ryūgakusei*, ed. Mishima Yoshiyasu (Tokyo: Gakuseisha, 1994), 128. The letter is dated from November 1885.
84. Ibid., 172. Letter dated from May 1886.
85. Fanon, *Peau noire, masques blancs*, 13.
86. Azuma, *Between Two Empires*, 19–20.
87. Majima Ayu provided us with an exhaustive study of the psychological component of race for Japanese intellectuals. See Majima, *Hadairo no yūutsu*. A summary of her work is available in English: Majima Ayu, 'Skin Color Melancholy in Modern Japan: Male Elites' Racial Experiences Abroad, 1880s–1950s', in *Race and Racism in Modern East Asia: Western and Eastern Constructions*, ed. Rotem Kowner and Walter Demel (Leiden: Brill, 2013), 391–410.
88. Majima, 'Skin Color Melancholy in Modern Japan', 393.
89. Azuma, *Between Two Empires*, 38.
90. Ibid.
91. Mishima, *Mishima Yatarō no tegami*, 29. Letter dated from October 1884.
92. For Uchimura, see Majima, *Hadairo no yūutsu*, 43. For Takahashi, see Korekiyo Takahashi, *Takahashi Korekiyo jiden (jō)*, ed. Uetsuka Tsukasa (Tokyo: Chūō kōron shinsha, 2013), 40–2. Takahashi's experience with the Chinese onboard his America-bound ship seems to have been so traumatic for him that when he bought his return ticket one year later, he specifically asked to be in a room without Chinese. See ibid., 70.

93. Majima, *Hadairo no yūutsu*, 93.
94. Mishima, *Mishima Yatarō no tegami*, 43. Letter dated from October 1884.
95. Ibid., 45. Letter dated from December 1884.
96. Ibid., 127. Letter dated from November 1885. The combination of modernisation policies and rising nationalism did actually influence the status of Chinese characters in Japan, and some linguists did advocate for the suppression of classical Chinese (*kanbun*) in Japan. See Kazuki Sato, '"Same Language, Same Race": The Dilemma of *Kanbun* in Modern Japan', in *The Construction of Racial Identities in China and Japan*, ed. Frank Dikötter (Hong Kong: Hong Kong University Press, 1997), 127.
97. In his famous text 'Datsu-A ron' (On Leaving Asia Behind, 1885) Fukuzawa admonished the Japanese to separate themselves from China and Korea and to commit to Western civilisation. The text was originally published as an editorial in Fukuzawa's newspaper *Jiji shinpō*.
98. Azuma, *Between Two Empires*, 38.
99. Takahashi, *Takahashi Korekiyo jiden*, 55.
100. Mishima, *Mishima Yatarō no tegami*, 76. Letter dated from March 1885.
101. A complete translation of the comic (which was originally published bilingually in English and Japanese) can been found in: Henry (Yoshitaka) Kiyama, *The Four Immigrants Manga: A Japanese Experience in San Francisco, 1904–1924*, trans. Frederik L. Schodt (Berkeley, CA: Stone Bridge Press, 1999). The episode presented here is taken from the original: Kiyama Henry (Yoshitaka), *Yonin shosei manga* (San Francisco, CA: The Yoshitaka Kiyama Studio, 1931), 28–9. The original is available in the Japanese American Research Project collection (Box 362) of the University of California, Los Angeles.
102. The Japanese students who did not get governmental support had to finance their studies by other means. A great number of them became so-called 'schoolboys', studying during the day and performing household chores for an American family. For details about the lives and experience of these schoolboys, see: Yamamoto Hidemasa, 'Shoki nihonjin tobeishi ni okeru gakusei kanai rōdōsha', *Eigakushi kenkyū* 19 (1987): 141–56.

Chapter 7

The End of the Racial Middle Ground

Despite the successes of the racial middle ground, the reasons that led to its creation also led to its demise. Lashes of school segregations and Gentlemen's Agreements were bound to leave some scars on the Japanese image of the United States. More than anything else, the California Crisis exposed the hypocrisy of the American racial system and Japanese observers of the events slowly began to call into question the legitimacy of the American model.

The end of the negotiation zone between Japan and the United States was neither abrupt nor unexpected, but was a process that culminated into one event, the Paris Peace Conference of 1919. Signs of discontent were, of course, already visible years prior to the peace settlement. First, the California Crisis was far from over. The Gentlemen's Agreement had temporarily calmed minds about the immigration issue in the United States, but it did not solve the problem of the Japanese presence on American soil. Second, there was a growing feeling of irritation on part of the Japanese for being continuously relegated to the rank of a second-rate nation. Third, the loss of prestige of the American model in Japanese eyes was part of the global collapse of the Eurocentric model as a whole: the First World War as well as ravenous Western imperialism led individuals in non-European nations to reconsider the legitimacy of Eurocentrism. This occurred in Japan too, where thinkers began to explore alternative world views. The combination of these factors eventually led to the collapse of the racial middle ground.

The crisis goes on: the Alien Land Law of 1913

Two aspects of the middle ground have been emphasised throughout this work: human agency and cooperation. Two parties agree that a negotiation zone is mutually beneficial, and agents act in a framework that is acceptable for both to produce such a zone. 'Beneficial' and 'acceptable' are key. Since the inception of the middle ground described in these pages, the Japanese government had been accepting the Western framework because it proved beneficial for the nation: the preservation of national sovereignty, the possible acceptance as a great power, and, theoretically, avoiding the shame of being branded as an unwanted race –

all these expectations were somewhat realistic after Japan had reached the standard of civilisation.

Yet the task of creating and maintaining the middle ground was an arduous and long process that spanned several decades. This not only led to timely reappraisals of the goals of the negotiation zone, but also naturally to a change in its agents. The retraction of the school segregation order was for the most part achieved through Theodore Roosevelt's intervention. And while the agreement cannot be deemed a prodigious outcome, it had at least limited the damages and secured an acceptable status quo. The end of his presidency in 1909, however, also meant the loss of Japan's most influential agent. Roosevelt was willing to foster the United States' relation with the country. His successors, however, were not.

The decade after Roosevelt's presidency began on a grim note for the Japanese in California. The year 1911 saw the proposal of twenty-seven anti-Japanese law proposals in the state legislature.[1] A change in the Californian political constellation promoted this negative atmosphere: a bellicose anti-Japanese and pro-White campaign one year earlier had led the Democrats to win 44 per cent of the seats in the assembly, thereby ending the Republican hold on the state. Republicans, in turn, realised that anti-Japanese feelings were convenient for winning votes and both sides became competitors in their antagonism towards the Japanese.[2] The 1912 presidential election saw the victory of the Democrat Woodrow Wilson. Wilson, who had consciously based his campaign in California on the memory of the San Francisco debacle and the frustrated anti-Japanese movement, emphasised two points: Japanese exclusion and the respect of state rights.[3] Unsurprisingly, when the Californian State Legislature opened its first session in 1913 (the year Wilson was sworn in), thirty-three out of the fifty-seven law proposals were anti-Japanese.[4]

These developments had drastic consequences for the racial middle ground. The negotiation partner for the Japanese was now an individual who had openly campaigned against them. The chances of winning him or anyone in his entourage as an agent were slim to say the least. The Japanese government in fact did not entertain any illusions about its American counterpart: one month before Wilson was even sworn in, the Japanese Consul to the United States Chinda Sutemi (1857–1929) warned Foreign Minister Katō Takaaki (1860–1926) that it was vain to expect sincere help from Washington.[5] This pessimism was justified, for only five months into 1913, the middle ground failed gravely for the first time: on 19 May, the Californian State Legislature passed an anti-Japanese bill which, on 10 August, came into effect as the California Alien Land Law of 1913. The law limited leases of agricultural land to 'aliens ineligible for citizenship' to a maximum of three years and banned the further purchase of land by said aliens. Those who already owned land could not sell or transfer it to fellow immigrants. The text of the law did not explicitly mention the Japanese. In fact, it did not even mention race. Yet naturalisation had been limited to free White persons and persons of African descent since the Nationality Act of 1870, and Japanese immigrants were therefore unable to become American citizens. The designation 'aliens ineligible for citizenship' became a convenient way to circumvent any critique that the law was specifically aimed at Japanese immigrants.[6]

Wilson and his administration were the most obvious culprits for the failure of the middle ground. Even if the president did try to prevent the passing of the Alien Land Law with belated and lacklustre efforts,[7] his laconic responses to the Japanese representatives he negotiated with betray his lack of motivation: the then Foreign Minister Makino Nobuaki (1861–1949) recalled in his memoirs that Wilson had denied him any explanation except that the law was based on economic reasons, not racial ones.[8] According to the Japanese observers, the second group that was responsible for the collapse of the negotiation zone was the segment of the American society that formed the bulk of the anti-Japanese movement. The magazine *Taiyō* explained that there were two types of people in the United States: the true Americans, that is those who saw the dawn of the American nation and of which only a few were left. The other type was recent immigrants from poor European states. The new immigrants wanted to exclude the Japanese because of economic and racial reasons. Since the vast majority of people in California were not real Americans but children of foreigners, the magazine explained, anti-Japanese sentiments were particularly strong there.[9] Terashima Seiichirō (1870–1929), a member of the House of Peers who had studied in the United States and in France, confirmed this view in an essay[10] about the Californian situation: 'The recent immigrants are quite different from the old ones, not in their mental and moral character alone, but also in their physical constitution.'[11] It was those newer immigrants who disliked the Japanese:

> If all the Americans of to-day were the same in type and ideals as the original Americans, as the founders of the great Republic, their spirit of freedom and equality, as well as their democratism, would never have allowed them to undertake such a thing as the exclusion of the Japanese.[12]

Whoever the culprit, the Alien Land Law led to the re-evaluation of the Japanese image of America. Critics vigorously denounced the American hypocrisy of making great claims about freedom and equality while at the same time discriminating against others on the account of race. *The Japan Times* summarised the situation best:

> The California episode was, in a sense, a disillusionment to the Japanese. The Japanese newspapers said, *ad nauseam*, they would rely upon the American spirit of justice and humanity. They did not know until quite recently that the American national policy could be moved so determinedly by the dictates of the 'interests', either political or economic. They had built a castle of idealism in America, and it collapsed.[13]

Indeed, the disillusionment, even if not entirely unpredictable, must have been hard: Tokutomi Sohō (1863–1957), the former editor of the magazine *Kokumin no tomo*, condemned the 'White snobbery' and lamented that appeals to the American ideals had been fruitless, that the Christian universal brotherhood did not exist and that the only remaining thing was racial discrimination.[14]

Criticism also came from inside governmental circles. The Christian educator and member of the House of Peers Ebara Soroku (1842–1922), whom the government had sent to the United States to study the California Crisis, was pessimistic regarding a solution to the problem: 'When it comes to racial prejudice, there is no easy solution. Especially inside American people, the feelings of enmity towards Oriental people are deeply rooted and very strong.'[15] This was the reason why restrictions against immigrants coming from European countries were applied without much conviction, while those against immigrants from the East were very strict. According to Ebara, this was 'unreasonable and goes against the spirit of universal morality (*sekai jindō*), and it is not possible to solve this problem by insisting on reason'.[16]

The racial middle ground had temporarily solved the problem of the differential treatment Ebara mentioned. However, the Alien Land Law of 1913 brought this issue back to the forefront and, once again, a now familiar question came back to haunt US–Japan relations: were the Japanese mere Asians or 'better'? Two Western commentators famously fought over that question in the London *Times*: the already mentioned American naval officer Alfred T. Mahan and the British diplomat Sir Ignatius Valentine Chirol (1852–1929).[17]

For Chirol, the problem was not that of Japanese residency in the United States, but of Japan's standing in the world:

> The ultimate issue involved is, in fact, whether Japan, who has made good her title to be treated on a footing of complete equality as one of the Great Powers of the world, is not also entitled to rank among the civilised nations . . . or whether her people are to be individually subjected to the disabilities imposed upon Asiatics collectively, whose lower plane of civilisation is held to justify their exclusion from the enjoyment of rights freely accorded to all those who come with European credentials.[18]

He seemed to be troubled by the fact that the 'ignorant and squalid mass of Slovaks, Ruthenians, Russian and Polish Jews' could become American citizens while the Japanese could not. According to him, religion and education were no serious factors: the number of Japanese Christians was increasing, and the Japanese people were highly educated. 'The bar of race would therefore seem to be the only one which could be plausibly maintained', he guessed, since the Japanese, as Asians, could not become American citizens.[19] Chirol perfectly understood the dilemma caused by Japan: 'A nation which is neither Occidental, nor White, nor Christian has for the first time taken its place alongside the nations who pride themselves on being Occidental and White and Christian.'[20] Not only that, but Japan had also 'shaken the fatalistic acquiescence of other races in the White man's claim to pre-eminent dominion'.[21]

The *Times*, acting as a commentator and a referee at the same time, judged that how to classify the Japanese was indeed a question of global importance. The paper acknowledged that Japan had fought hard to establish itself as a great power and was now seeking 'from the powerful white races which have long dominated every continent recognition upon terms of equality'.[22] It also cautioned, however, that Japan was acting in a self-serving manner: 'She [Japan] does not ask for a general relief from the disabilities which many white communities impose upon Asiatics, but she claims exemption for herself.'[23] Moreover, Japan 'roundly challenges the disposition to classify her progressive people with the rest of the Asiatic races'.[24]

At the other end of the spectrum, Admiral Mahan was far from convinced that the Japanese citizen deserved special treatment. For him, there was no correlation between great power status and naturalisation or immigrant rights. The decisive matter was neither descent, nor the belonging to a certain state. What made assimilation possible to him was 'prolonged common experience', as in the case of Europe and the United States.[25] Mahan did acknowledge Japan as a great nation, but did not extend his admiration to its people:

> We who do think – I am one – cordially recognize the great progresses of Japan and admire her achievements of the past half-century, both civil and military; but we do not perceive in them the promise of ready adaptability to the spirit or our own institutions which would render naturalization expedient; and immigration, as I have said, with us implies naturalization.[26]

Echoing the proponents of 'one race problem is enough', the American officer conceded that the Japanese were 'by far' superior to African Americans, but still relegated them to the rank of a different, problematic race:

> It appears to me that a great number of my fellow-citizens, knowing the problem we have in the coloured race among us, should dread the introduction of what they believe will constitute another race problem; and one much more difficult.[27]

Mahan's arguments were not surprising. The alleged inability of the Japanese to assimilate into American society was a key issue for the proponents of Japanese exclusion. More noteworthy in Mahan's case is that a decade prior to his above-cited article, the officer held a more lenient position, something the *Times* did not fail to point out:

> There was a time when Admiral Mahan was disposed to admit the validity of Japanese claims. More than ten years ago he wrote: – 'In the European family are evidently to be included the people of the United States, as direct inheritors therefrom by blood and by accepted position, and also, more significantly still, Japan, if her claim be admitted as I think it should be.' If we read Admiral Mahan's letter aright, his views must have undergone considerable modification during the last decade.[28]

Thinking in terms of what has been described throughout this work, Mahan's opinion did not change but was in fact quite consistent with anti-Japanese attitudes in the United States. As did the proponents of Japanese exclusion during the San Francisco school controversy, Mahan was willing to grant the status of great nation to Japan, but not to threaten the racial integrity of the United States.

For the Japanese, the exclusion from the ranks of American citizenship per se was not the issue. The true problem was that other foreign people were given rights, while the Japanese were singled out as undesirable. As Minohara pointed out, 'Tokyo was quite content if the law prevented all aliens from possessing land, but targeting the Japanese and relegating them to the status of second-class citizen was unbearable.'[29] Even the most cautious politicians who continued to believe in the possibility of cooperation between the United States and Japan began to lose patience. Ōkuma Shigenobu still insisted that it was 'Japan's mission to harmonize Eastern and Western civilizations in order to help bring about the unification of the world.'[30] However, he insisted that 'to brand us Japanese as inferior because we are a colored race is a bigotry that we must fight and eliminate through the fulfilment of our national mission'.[31] Some went further and prophesised a race war: a contributor to *Taiyō* made the gloomy prediction that 'this century' will see 'a great race war between the White and the "yellow" races. The anti-Japanese movement in California is a part of it.'[32]

Whereas the Meiji period efforts for the revision of the unequal treaties were undertaken by Japan to be accepted, the opposition to anti-Japanese legislations was primarily aimed at having the Japanese respected. For the Japanese side, maintaining the racial middle ground was becoming a matter of prestige. The years after the promulgation of the Alien Land Law saw a further decline in the legitimacy of the American model. This, however, was not solely due to anti-Japanese legislation in the United States but was part of a global loss in legitimacy of the Western civilisational model, that was quite literally shell-shocked in the trenches of the First World War.

Losing appeal: the West, Japan and alternative visions of world orders

From a civilisational point of view, the First World War was, as Lauren aptly put it, a 'profound embarrassment' for Europeans and Americans.[33] The rhetoric of White superiority, higher civilisation and duty to civilise others sounded hollow, as European nations, joined later by the Americans, slaughtered each other on the battlefield. It did not help that numerous non-Whites participated in the conflict and witnessed the horrors of the war: Africans, Indians, Chinese, 'all were regarded equal when it came to fight and die, but not for protection under the law, or immigration'.[34] The conflict had far-reaching consequences in Japan too: proof of the decline of the West, the war gave birth to scepticism about modernity.[35] And for those already inclined towards anti-Westernism, it provided an opportunity to condemn a degenerated model and to assert the superiority of Japanese culture.

One of the detractors of the Western model was Endō Kichisaburō (1874–1921), an academic at the Hokkaidō Imperial University. Endō strongly criticised the blind worship of Western culture and warned the Japanese against taking the West as a model, especially when considering the ongoing conflict. Because of this worship, Endō complained that the Japanese were throwing away Japanese arts, literature as well as customs and morality (*ronri dōtoku*) that had been built throughout 2,500 years of history.[36] His point was that the West that Japan respected was already dead, and the First World War was only one element of proof of that: 'While the people of Japan were burning with respect for the West, the West dramatically degenerated.'[37] Endō was far from alone in seeing the First World War as a wake-up call for the Japanese. The already mentioned Tokutomi Sōhō suggested that the war arose because of the 'weaknesses and shortcomings of European civilisation'.[38] European civilisation had been blinding the eyes of the Japanese, but its true nature was finally revealed.[39]

This 'true nature' was explained by Wakanomiya Yūsuke (1872–1938), Keiō Gijuku professor for social sciences and notorious anti-Semite. In short, Wakanomiya denounced the Europeans for calling the Japanese brutal, 'but the truth is, the warlike people are not us the Japanese, but them, the Westerners'.[40] Proof was Western history itself, with its 'Hundred Years War', 'Seven Years War' and even 'Seven Weeks War'. Cruelty, according to him, was a characteristic of Western people.[41] Wakanomiya illustrated how he thought Europeans were corrupting things with the example of gunpowder: 'The Chinese have invented gunpowder. However, they used gunpowder to shoot fireworks, not to shoot guns.' When the Europeans got their hands on gunpowder, 'it became powder for guns'.[42]

The reassessment of Western civilisation occurred in parallel to geopolitical changes in the Far East. The main contesters of Japan in the region, Germany, France, Great Britain and Russia, were all distracted by the war raging in Europe. Only the United States remained to share in the Eastern treasure trove.[43] When Japanese guns went silent on the East Asian front, the conflict went into its diplomatic phase, except this time against its own allies.[44] As Yamamuro writes, for Japan, the First World War was in truth one military conflict against Germany as well as three different diplomatic ones against Great Britain, the United States and China.[45]

Great Britain and the United States were worried about Japan's advance in the Pacific region: the Japanese occupation of Micronesia could easily be used to disturb the liaison between Hawaii, the Philippines and the United States. During the war, according to Iriye, US–Japan relations sank to their lowest level up to that point.[46] Indeed the distrust was reciprocal: before the United States entered the conflict in 1917, Japan apprehended which side the Americans would take. That the Japanese would be on the other side seems to have been considered seriously, and the idea of an 'inevitable' war with the United States became a popular topic of discussions and of writing from that time on.[47]

Great Britain had also been wary about the Japanese entry into the war. Fearing that Japan would try to use the chaos to its advantage and undertake a military venture, the British envoy to Beijing even categorically opposed any Japanese intervention.[48] The British officially requested that Japan join their side on 7 August, but retracted their request two days later, asking the Japanese to stop any military action. The Japanese chain of command, however, had already readied its force for a military expedition and made plain its intention to enter the war – with or without British blessing. With no other choice, Great Britain accepted the Japanese entry into the war, on the condition that Japan did not undertake any unilateral action on German-occupied territories and that the Bay of Jiaozhou be returned to China. As a testimony of their distrust towards Japan, it sent its own troops to China and the German colony of Tsingtao was taken by a combination of Japanese and British forces.[49] As in the case of the United States, Great Britain feared that the Japanese advance in the Pacific could threaten its territories, especially the British Dominions of New Zealand and Australia.[50] Therefore, while the Japanese entry into the war was publicised as part of the Anglo-Japanese alliance, the true motive behind the British actions was distrust for Japan and the hope that military cooperation would be able to restrain Japanese actions in China.[51]

The caution on the part of the British was not unwarranted: in 1915, the Japanese government made, with the explicit request of secrecy, the Twenty-One Demands to China. The demands would have given Japan significant decisional power over Chinese domestic affairs and thus effectively put China under Japanese control.[52] China immediately leaked its content and asked Washington and London for support. The demands were a direct dismissal of the 'Open Door' policy in China cherished by the United States, and some were in opposition to British privileges on the continent. This duplicitous move increased distrust in the Japanese and hastened the later collapse of the Anglo-Japanese alliance.[53] Added to these geopolitical problems was that of immigration. The California Crisis was but one issue with one country: Australia, New Zealand, Canada and South Africa all had their variations of immigration restrictions that, amongst others, targeted the Japanese.[54]

Humiliation, duplicity, distrust and disillusionment were thus defining the relationship between Japan and the Great Powers during the First World War. It is therefore not surprising that some Japanese started to seriously consider alternatives to the Eurocentric world order and, as such, to the racial middle ground. They did not have to look far: alternatives were right in front of their eyes.

Embracing yellowness: the appeal of Pan-Asianism

The First World War had the curious side effect of raising Japanese self-esteem. The slaughter among the great powers had proven to them that Western civilisation, while having undeniable advantages, was also profoundly flawed. This led the Japanese to re-evaluate their place and their role in the world. A magazine published in 1917 could now proclaim to its readers:

> Nowadays, the great powers of the world are not isolated, but are bound by a close relationship. Just as in a nerve system, the great shaking [the war] has a profound influence on our diplomacy, politics, economy, and thoughts. The self-awareness, that our country is not just a great power of the Far East, but a great power of the world and that it rules over the fate of the whole mankind, is becoming increasingly stronger.[55]

Prime Minister Hara Takashi (1856–1921) would have agreed: reminiscing about the war, he concluded that the West had its chance, but now had to accept Japan as an equal power that could shape a global future.[56] He acknowledged that the White race had set the standard of civilisation. However, it was the flaws of this very civilisation that had caused the war and the task of maintaining peace now had to be the common commitment of the 'two civilizations, Oriental and Occidental'.[57] Hara was not especially impressed by the recent creation of the League of Nations, as, for him, its principles were already 'taught in Oriental civilisation thousands of years ago'.[58] The lofty ideals of the League, born out of a slaughter, were 'nothing other than the humanism fostered in the Orient for ages past'.[59]

It is worth noting that Hara, prime minister at the time, tied Japan's legitimacy as a leader to the authority of – and by extension to the belonging to – Oriental culture. This would have been a diplomatic disaster one decade prior: in 1907, for example, a conversation took place between Itō Hirobumi, then Resident General in Korea and Gotō Shinpei (1857–1929), President of the South Manchuria Railway Company. During the discussion, Gotō laid out his plan for the future of Japanese world policy. He believed that Japan had to help the Chinese in creating an Asia for Asians (*Tōyōjin no Tōyō*), which was the true form of Great Asianism (*Dai Ajiashugi*) and a way to secure peace in East Asia. Itō apparently interrupted Gotō and asked him to clarify what he meant by Great Asianism and warned him that using such expressions would lead the Westerners to associate Japan with the 'yellow peril'. No good could come from using that expression.[60] Gotō was not alone in being reprimanded for his promotion of Pan-Asianism: a few years earlier, in 1898, the President of the House of Peers Prince Konoe Atsumaro (1863–1904) was publicly disavowed by the Japanese government after writing an article about an alliance between the racially akin Japanese and Chinese against the West.[61]

The downfall of the West led to a more tangible expression of Pan-Asianism, which emphasised Oriental morality and tied it to the Japanese claim of leadership over Asia.[62] The negative connotations the idea of Asian solidarity may have had were lost on the battlefields of the Great War.[63] This, however, did not instantly reflect on official Japanese policy. As Weber writes, during the First World War, Pan-Asianist thought remained a theoretical enterprise, not a movement.[64] However, the very fact that the two last years of the war saw an 'outpouring of Pan-Asian writings'[65] shows that a growing number of Japanese intellectuals and politicians were ready to explore alternatives to the West.

Kodera Kenkichi (1877–1949) was certainly amongst them. The youngest person to be elected in the Lower House of the Imperial Diet, Kodera had already gained a solid knowledge of the West through his studies in the United States, Germany, Austria and Switzerland.[66] In 1916, Kodera wrote the first extensive treatise on Pan-Asianism, *Dai Ajiashugiron* (Treatise on Greater Asianism) in which he criticised the Western powers for spreading the idea of a 'yellow peril' while at the same time subduing most of Asia. Kodera also observed that 'the idea of racial unity is the main tendency in world politics'.[67] Various peoples of the West were uniting under 'pan' banners, such as Pan-Germanism or Pan-Slavism. The same thing would eventually happen in Asia: 'A powerful Pan-Mongolism is set to develop and this Pan-Mongolism will be an ideology of the union of the yellow race.' In this alliance, 'Japan, the pioneer of a new civilization, can profit from China economically', while China could gain from 'Japanese leadership in political matters'. This would be 'the first step toward the creation of a Greater Asianism'.[68]

Kodera was unequivocal on the purpose of a pan-Asian alliance:

> [Japan] must save East Asia from the threat of the White Race – this is our highest mission. To achieve this, we must become the leader of the Yellow race and guide [other nations], preserve the territorial integrity of China, and strengthen its people and culture . . . [We must] revive the whole of the Yellow race under this new ideology, attain political freedom and sovereignty, and unite the Yellow race all over the world.[69]

This is a long way from the 1903 instructions of the Japanese government to prevent the 'cry for the "yellow peril"'. Suddenly, being 'yellow' did not seem bad anymore. The popularisation of Pan-Asianist thoughts reflects a shift in the priorities that had previously been defined and secured by the racial middle ground. With Pan-Asianism, Japan was in reach of what the middle ground could apparently not grant: a place at the top of a hierarchy. And while Pan-Asianist thoughts had not yet been co-opted by the Japanese government as its official policy, the First World War had paved the way for alternative visions that seemed more attractive than a negotiation zone with the West.

The collapse of the racial middle ground: the Paris Peace Conference

The unspoken condition for the success of the middle ground has always been that both sides would deem its maintenance preferable to any alternative. There have been instances where the price was high and the Japanese side never ceased to protest the treatment of its citizens in the United States. However, examples such as the Gentlemen's Agreement indicate that the Japanese government, together with the American government, were ready to compromise on the issue of race. Both sides did not consider the mistreatment of Japanese immigrants sufficient reason for jeopardising diplomatic relations. That was until Wilson became president and the first cracks in the structure of the middle ground appeared. It is not surprising then, to find him at the head of the event that caused the collapse of the middle ground – the Paris Peace Conference of 1919. The outcome of the talks made any sort of compromise difficult for the Japanese and confirmed that, for both sides, a negation zone was not the most profitable course anymore.

Japan's fruitless efforts to have a racial equality clause inserted into the covenant of the League of Nations, which was created in the wake of the First World War, have already been well documented.[70] A brief reminder of the occurrences will therefore suffice here. When the negotiations to settle the peace and manage the post-war world started in January 1919, Japan found itself seated at the negotiation table as a great power. Its immediate negotiation partners were the United States, Great Britain, France and Italy, led by the 'Big Four' Woodrow Wilson, David Lloyd George (1863–1945), Georges Clemenceau (1841–1929) and Vittorio Emanuele Orlando (1860–1952). The Japanese delegation to the peace talks was composed of sixty-four members, among them former Prime Minister Saionji Kimmochi (1849–1940) as its head, Count Makino Nobuaki, the ambassador to the United Kingdom Chinda Sutemi, and the ambassador to France Matsui Keishirō (1868–1946). The Japanese delegates, quite oblivious to matters concerning the European continent, were focused on securing the Japanese spoils of war: the Shandong Peninsula in China and the Pacific islands north of the equator.

Wilson outlined his principles for the peace settlement in his Fourteen Points, which amongst other things contained the creation of the League of Nation and the right to self-determination for national minorities. Contrary to what the Japanese government expected, joining the League of Nations was a mandatory part in accepting Wilson's Fourteen Points and hence the post-war order. Understandably, the Japanese government began to worry about the position of their nation inside an alliance in which the major powers were excluding Japanese citizens on account of race. The government therefore instructed its delegates as follows:

> Nevertheless, if a League of Nations is to be established, the Japanese Government cannot remain isolated outside the League and should there appear any tendency

towards the establishment of a definite scheme, the Delegates will so far as the circumstances allow make efforts to secure suitable guarantees against the disadvantages to Japan which would arise as aforesaid out of racial prejudice.[71]

Hence the need to thematise the problem of racial equality at the Paris Peace Conference.

The above-quoted instructions were translated and became the basis of the racial equality proposal. The delegates submitted four drafts of it to Wilson's advisor Edward House (1858–1938) between 3–5 February. House subsequently talked with Wilson, who agreed to add the proposal as his own amendment to the article on religious freedom (Article 21) of the League Covenant.[72] However, this was opposed by the British delegates with the argument that racial equality was intrinsically tied to the issue of immigration – a sensitive topic for the British Dominions (Australia, Canada and New Zealand) present at the peace talks. Faced with Wilson's fruitless efforts to revise the proposal in a way that would please both the Japanese and the British, the Japanese delegates introduced the clause on their own to the League of Nations Commission on 13 February. The text read as follows:

The equality of nations beings a basic principle of the League of Nations, the High Contracting Parties agree to accord as soon as possible to all alien nationals of states, members of the League, equal and just treatment in every respect making no distinction, either in law or in fact, on account of their race or nationality.[73]

Brazil, Romania and Czechoslovakia were in favour of the proposal. The British delegates, however, deemed the amendment too dangerous (especially regarding its dominions) and argued for dropping Article 21 altogether. Wilson, who at first seemed to have been positively inclined towards the proposal, did not intervene to save it. The first attempt to have a racial equality proposal inserted in the Covenant of the League thus failed.

The Japanese delegates did not falter and when Wilson left Paris for almost one month (from 15 February to 13 March) they switched the focus of their efforts to the British delegation. Australia's Prime Minister William Morris Hughes (1862–1952) was the most vocal about rejecting the proposal and the Japanese hoped to rally the British representatives against him. As Hughes stayed adamant, the British became weary of the Japanese persistence and declared the problem an Australian, not a British, one. Without reliable allies, the Japanese had no other choice than to reintroduce a diluted proposal that, instead of an article, was to be inserted in the preamble of the Covenant. On 11 April, they presented the generic formula 'by the endorsement of the principle of equality of nations and just treatment of their nationals' for the preamble.[74] 'Race' had been replaced by 'nation'. But again, Great Britain and the Dominions refused the proposal. While Wilson remained silent, the Japanese persistence on the matter showed some results: France, Italy, China and Greece rallied behind

Japan and spoke in favour of the proposal. Confronted with this unexpected turn of events, Wilson declared that the matter should be discussed in a later point in time and not influence the creation of the League. His haste to push the issue into the background had been motivated by a note handed to him by his advisor House, warning him that the proposal 'would surely raise the race issue throughout the world'.[75]

Sensing that the winds were favourable, the Japanese plenipotentiaries called for a vote. Out of the seventeen members present at the meeting, eleven voted in favour of the proposal. Wilson, however, in his capacity as Chairman of the Commission, declared the proposal not accepted on the ground that the issue as such needed unanimity. This move was immediately criticised by the members who voted for the proposal, who pointed out that, in matters important to the United States, a simple majority had always been sufficient. The American president, however, claimed that the opposition against the proposal was too strong and that therefore it could not be accepted. Before the session closed, Makino asked for the transcripts of the meeting 'for the record'.[76] Japan had thus failed to secure a racial equality clause for the Covenant of the League of Nations.

The reasoning behind the racial equality proposal and its repercussions have been studied thoroughly by the scholars quoted in the above summary. Yet, there is one aspect of the proposal which has escaped scholarly scrutiny, but which is of crucial importance in the context of this work: the wording of the proposal itself.[77] For Japan, the whole point of the middle ground had been to challenge its identity as a 'coloured' race. The racial equality proposal introduced at the Paris Peace Conference, however, goes in the opposite direction. The original proposal submitted on 13 February was not a request for a special status close to that of Whites, but, on the contrary, an acknowledgement that the Japanese belonged to the unequally treated coloured races. The question of whether the proposal was supposed to have universal value or not, or whether the Japanese government was solely interested in having the Japanese protected from discrimination, is of secondary importance for the moment. Regardless of the eventual pragmatic aspect of the matter, the Japanese government had recognised that the racial middle ground and the honorary status of the Japanese had become obsolete. It specifically requested just treatment for all races, which implied a – genuine or not – identification with non-White people. In this sense, it can be said that the actual end of the racial middle ground for the Japanese side was the introduction of the racial equality proposal itself, not its refusal.

On the Western side, the definite end of the racial middle ground arose out of a problem of scope. Until the events at Paris, the status of Japan as a nation could be detached from the status of the Japanese as individuals. The racial equality proposal made this separation difficult: the two entities became intertwined as the Western delegates in Paris saw the proposal linked to the issue of Japanese immigration and therefore as restricting the rights of League members to prevent the entry of Japanese citizens into their countries. Second, the problem of true intention aside, the implications of the racial equality proposal went beyond granting a special status to Japan, hence beyond the scope of the middle ground. It could indeed be interpreted as equality for all. The meaning of such a thought is hard to overstate. As a horrified member of the British delegation reflected: 'Any statement about racial equality as proposed by the Japanese in the Covenant of the League implied the equality of the yellow man with the white man', which in turn 'might even imply the terrific theory of the equality of the white man with the black'. He added that 'no American Senate would ever dream of ratifying such a dangerous principle'.[78]

And, indeed, the argument that the proposal was dangerous due to its implications was immediately taken up by the proponents of Japanese exclusion in the United States. California Senator James D. Phelan (1861–1930) warned that the Japanese proposal required the United States to 'grant citizenship, the voting privilege, intermarriage, and the ownership of land' to them.[79] Phelan tried to show that the racial equality proposal was interfering with American domestic politics, and, at the same time, he presented the proposal as jeopardising the racial order of the country: 'The evil', he argued, 'consists in the nonassimiability [*sic*] of the Japanese, which, if tolerated, would produce a mongrel and degenerate population'.[80] Instead, Phelan argued for a White supremacist league, which would protect the interests of the race:

> This is the proper time to confirm the policy of the United States by a covenant among the nations, in which, doubtless, Great Britain and her colonies will join, because Canada and Australia have already protested, to put an end to the menace of our domestic peace, the prosperity of American institutions, and what is broadly known as Christian civilization. The same is expected to preserve and defend nationalities on racial lines and so prevent attempted conquests and avert war.[81]

The fear that the League and the Japanese proposal were a threat to White supremacy lingered on, even after the proposal had been defeated. During a debate on the topic in the American Senate, one senator from Missouri declared that 'the league would place the destinies of the white race in the hands of ignorant and superstitious nations of black and yellow population'.[82] The Covenant of the League would lead to an imbalance in votes, as 'a majority always could be brought together on any race question in opposition to white supremacy'.[83]

Were the fears about the universality of the racial equality proposal justified? The answer to that question is surprisingly difficult. Shimazu has convincingly argued that, since the proposal was 'so specifically geared towards securing Japan's own position . . . it could not have been intended to have the altruistic objective of seeking universal racial equality'.[84] There is proof, however, that the need to secure a guarantee against racial discrimination for the Japanese and for other non-White races was expressed early inside governmental circles. A secret memorandum from November 1918 warned that the League of Nations, as an international organisation, would limit state sovereignty and that therefore several points had to be considered in preparation for the Peace Conference. The first one had to do with race:

> The first thing that the Japanese must think about concerning the peace conference is if the organisation for the preservation of peace, that supposedly rests on liberty and equality, truly applies the principles of complete equality to different races and religion, without any regards to racial, religious, or historical differences. This precondition does not concern Japan alone but is a common problem that has implications for China and people from other races and religions too.[85]

Despite this apparent selflessness, doubts about the eventual altruism of the Japanese government can be safely dismissed when taking the colonial situation of the country into account. It is highly improbable that the government would willingly undertake steps that would jeopardise relations inside their own empire.

In fact, the irony of asking for equality and maintaining colonies at the same did not go unnoticed: the plenipotentiary envoy to China Obata Yūkichi (1873–1947) forwarded an article from the *Peking Daily News* to the Japanese Foreign Ministry, in which a contributor criticised the Japanese attempt to secure racial equality.[86] The core of his argument was that Japan was complaining about the treatment it endured at the hands of Whites, while at the same time using utmost cruelty to oppress the Taiwanese aborigines and Koreans:

> In view of the above facts, and in view of the attitude of Japan towards the races she has conquered by brute force and is set on exterminating with savage callousness, it is perhaps not surprising to read that the Japanese consider that 'Japan is peculiarly fitted to take up this question for ensuring equality and fairness of treatment of all races'.[87]

The contributor to the paper equalled Japan with Germany: 'There you have German lying and hypocrisy added to the results of a long course of German militarism and kultur [*sic*].'[88] Calling the Sino-Japanese War a war of defence was an 'imitation of the German lie regarding the war they deliberately prepared for forty years and then provoked against France'.[89] The conclusion was quite harsh:

> Japan has demanded the abolition of race-discrimination, while it is all the time practicing race-discrimination in its most diabolical form against the subject races it professes to love and cherish. Paradoxical though it may sound, I am convinced that the abolition of race-discrimination is permissible with regard to China, but not with regard to Japan.[90]

While the contributor to the *Peking Daily News* probably had a personal grudge against Japan, it must be remembered that at the same time that Japan was asking for racial equality, Koreans were petitioning the great powers assembled at Paris for the recognition of their human rights and for support for their self-determination.[91] Criticism in this regard also came from inside Japan: the politician Ishibashi Tanzan (1884–1973), for example, denounced the government for the hypocrisy of discriminating against Chinese, Koreans and Taiwanese.[92] As final proof of the highly pragmatic nature of the proposal, Foreign Minister Uchida himself said that the racial equality proposal was not aimed at achieving universal equality but was only aimed at members of the League of Nations.[93]

While there are no doubts left regarding the position of the Japanese government, the Japanese public's attitude, however, is a different matter. As far as the sources are concerned, a genuine idealism about racial equality – with a hint of racial chauvinism – came to the surface during the Paris Peace Conference. What the public had in common with the government, however, was the acceptance of the identity of Japan as a 'coloured' nation. They also shared the apprehension that the League would be an instrument to preserve the status quo.[94] For the public too, then, the abolition of racial discrimination became the prerequisite not only for joining the League but also for lasting world peace.

Already by November, just four days after the guns went silent in Europe, an interviewee for the *Asahi* claimed that the most important task in the coming peace conference was to require the end of racial prejudice, but also warned that 'the words of Wilson and his clique are magnificent indeed, but their actions seldom follow'.[95] The same newspaper published a series of articles by the Kyōto Imperial University economist Toda Kaiichi (1872–1924), in which he expressed his feelings about Japan's relationship with the West. Toda argued that countries such as the United States, Canada and Australia were excluding 'coloured' immigrants and trying to justify it by different means, but it in truth everything was leading back to racial prejudice. Japan, therefore, should submit a proposal for a system that abolishes the exclusion of immigrants.[96] The interesting point is what role Toda attributed to Japan for the future of race relations:

> We are the only country of the 'coloured' races that has an international influence. Therefore, if our country stands in for the abolition of the institutionalised exclusion at the peace conference, it would stand against the Whites as the representative of the coloured races as a whole and for the very right to existence of these races.[97]

Koda envisioned more for Japan: the Earth and its resources had not been created for the monopoly of Whites, he went on, and they had to acknowledge that the 'coloured' races had the same rights as them. The countries that Whites were exploiting for their resources were not their property, but that of natives who had been expelled or exterminated. Fighting for racial equality was not merely an altruistic move; by fighting for the suppression of racial discrimination and for equality in the world, 'the Japanese could realise their heavenly mission and undergo a moral transformation'.[98]

Shimazu argued that the racial equality proposal became a '*cause célèbre*' for the Japanese public because of its 'symbolic importance as a concrete manifestation of all of Japan's fears and expectations of the new government and international order'.[99] It is possible to go even further and argue that the enthusiasm of the Japanese public for the racial equality proposal was also a manifestation of Japan's boosted confidence and pride as a modern 'coloured' nation, as well as the reflection of the genuine belief that the country should act as a vanguard for all non-White races. Through this evolution in the appreciation of Japan's place in the world, the racial middle ground became obsolete because the acknowledgement of Western powers was not necessary anymore. With a new sense of national mission, the Japanese public could now set its own standard.

The establishment of the League for the Abolition of Racial Discrimination (*Jinshuteki sabetsu teppai kisei taikai*) is representative of this tendency. It emerged from a public movement led by military men and public officials. During their first mass meeting on 5 February 1919, which attracted some 300 people, the members of the organisation took the resolution that racial discrimination was fundamentally in contradiction with the principles of liberty and freedom, as well as the root for international competition. The abolition of racial discrimination was therefore necessary to ensure lasting peace. The members of the organisation then took the decision to telegraph its resolution to Clemenceau.[100]

A few days later, the Foreign Minister received a demand from them to telegraph their resolution to the Japanese plenipotentiaries. Foreign Minister Uchida, who had already warned Saionji of the creation of the *Jinshuteki sabetsu teppai kisei taikai*, informed Matsui in Paris of the demand and reproduced parts of speeches held by members of the organisation. Army Lieutenant General Satō Kōjirō (1862–1923) for example stated that the abolition of racial discrimination was obviously based on reason. He also attributed a special role to Japan for the future: 'It is a task of uttermost importance that we the Japanese, as the senior race (*senpai*) among the "coloured" races of the world, articulate this problem.'[101] The resolution of the organisation was ultimately translated in French by the theosophist Paul Richard and sent to Clemenceau.[102]

The discrepancy between the governmental pragmatism and the idealism of the public did not go unnoticed, even in the early stages of the peace negotiations. Kamikawa Hikomatsu (1899–1988), a professor of law at Tokyo Imperial University, complained that the government was not properly 'enlightening' the public on the issue of race discrimination and on Japan's mission in the world.[103] 'In view of the peace conference', he criticised, 'the motto of the Japanese people should be: "the abolition of racial prejudice, based on humanism"'.[104] Kamikawa's humanism was no empty rhetoric, as he was showing a notably tolerant stance for the time. He used brackets throughout to text to enclose the words 'Whites' and 'coloured' and his assertions testify to a genuine interest in equality. Kamikawa explained that in so-called 'White' countries, there was a gap between the treatment of 'Whites' and 'coloured'.[105] Despite having reached the status of first-rate nation (*ittō kyōkoku*), the Japanese in the United States were treated worse than the people from European nations. They were being insulted by Gentlemen's Agreements and 'settlement restrictions' (probably a reference to the Alien Land Law). If even Japan, as a first-rate country, was being excluded in that manner, it was hard to even imagine the treatment that other 'coloured nations' like China and the rest were receiving.[106]

For Kamikawa, the war had been the opportunity to make 'coloured' perfectly equal to 'Whites', as it was undeniable that 'coloured people' had played a great role in the conflict. He did not ask for equality because of the service of 'coloured people', but 'I am really just requesting the abolition of racial prejudice as dictated by the laws of morality'.[107] He was convinced that the delegates would thematise the race problem during the peace talks and that 'White people' who 'unjustly colonised the world will have to face the reproach of all of humanity'.[108] This is where Japan had to intervene: 'In regards to the race problem, Japan has to represent the interests of the "coloured races" of the world and relentlessly establish itself as their voice.'[109]

While the idea of a newly found mission for Japan was widespread, there was some disagreement about its nature. Ōkuma Shigenobu's protégé Nagai Ryūtarō (1881–1944), for example, did have a particular vison of Japan's role in the world. After developing a certain idealism for the West (he had studied at Oxford University), Nagai was disappointed by the display of Western racial prejudice. Sharing his disillusionment in a letter to a friend, he wrote of his indignation at the 'attitude of Caucasians toward Orientals' and of his burning with 'an earnest faith in the survival of the Japanese race'.[110] The source of Nagai's indignation was his perceived hypocrisy of Western people: Western people were preaching brotherly love and claiming that God was the father of all mankind, 'but in truth', he wrote, 'belonging to another race is equal to being an inferior animal and brotherly love does not extend to people outside of the White race'.[111] Interestingly also, Nagai pointed to the racial antagonism between Blacks and Whites in the United States as a big stain on civilisation.[112]

From the ruins of Nagai's crushed idealism emerged a sense of national mission. However, he did not see 'yellow imperialism' as an alternative:

> I do not believe, as some argue, that the Japanese race has the divine mission of becoming the leader of Eastern people, then reign over Western people and the whole world. As much as it is not right that the Western people own everything under heaven, it would be equally wrong that people from the East now take over the leadership of the world.[113]

This mission of Japan was different: 'the great task of the Japanese race . . . is to bring about a racial revolution'.[114] The tyranny of the White man had to be overthrown, he continued, and the world's 'coloured' races freed. 'The French Revolution has abolished nobility and liberated the French people . . . But a racial revolution . . . would aim at liberating the millions of coloured people in the world.'[115]

The time when Japanese diplomats were complaining that the Japanese should not be classified with 'Kanakas and Negroes', or when Pan-Asiatic utterances were worth a reprimand, seems far away. The country turned its back on the West to embark on its new mission, a course that would lead it straight into another war. *The Japan Times* published a lengthy article on the failure of the racial equality proposal and especially on the meaning of that failure for the future of Japan's relations with Western countries. It is worth quoting at some length because of its unsettlingly visionary nature:

> The national disappointment may now be considered to verge on disaffection. All [leading thinkers] agree in feeling that the rejection of a demand made by a nation is tantamount to a snub and humiliation . . . There are some whose opinions deserve attention who feel that if Japan's formal demand has failed to accomplish its direct object, it has served the purpose . . . of unearthing and placing on record a hitherto unexpressed but real truth concerning the question and the attitude of whites versus the non-whites. A historic and august congress of the representative white peoples has now formally refused to admit and accept the principle of equality of the non-white people with themselves. It is sincerely to be lamented that this action of the League of Nations Commission will most probably result in erecting a perpetual barrier against a harmonious commingling of the races toward which the world tendency has been thought to have been moving. Instead of removing anything likely to prove a cause of international discord, a seed must now be considered to have been sown by the rejection of Japan's demand that will grow into two groups of peoples irreconcilable in their respective aspirations . . . Japan's admission into the group of the Five Great Powers must be considered to be merely accidental and only for the political convenience of the allies. Her present situation is exactly that of a Negro preacher asked to speak in a church because of his oratorical power. To speak from the pulpit is by no means an admission of equality from a racial standpoint on the part of the white congregation. It is well for Japan to remember this point. It is only by sheer dint of her power and civilization that she is entitled to receive treatment on a footing of equality by those of the white race. The only solution of the question therefore of sustaining Japan's prestige, accidental as it is, must be sought in preparedness to cope with international situations as they may develop from time to time.[116]

Both the West and Japan had indeed changed their priorities. The West did not see the preservation of the racial middle ground worth the risk of upsetting the racial status quo in the world, while the Japanese now turned to Asia. The first major consequence of the loss of the negotiation zone materialised shortly after. In 1924, the American Congress enacted the Immigration Act of 1924, setting quotas for the immigration of Europeans and banning the immigration of non-White people altogether. A provision upholding the terms of the Gentlemen's Agreement of 1908 was discussed in the Senate but defeated by a vote of seventy-six to two.[117] The last remnant of the compromise was gone, and Japanese exclusion became a fixed part of American law. Kimitada Miwa goes as far as saying that 'the train of events that culminated at Pearl Harbor may be said to have been set in motion in 1924 when the United States passed the anti-Japanese immigration bill'.[118] Kimitada may have attached too much importance to that particular event for the Pacific War. However, the Immigration Act of 1924 is a confirmation that the American government was now willing to treat Japanese citizens the same way as other non-Whites.

Notes

1. Kagawa Mari, 'Hai-Nichi tochihō no seitei to Panama taiheiyō bankoku tenrankai: Chinda Sutemi no tai-Bei ninshiki o chūshin to shite', in *Taishōki Nihon no Amerika ninshiki*, ed. Hasegawa Yūichi (Tokyo: Keiō gijuku daigaku shuppankai, 2001), 132.
2. Tosh Minohara, 'The Clash of Pride and Prejudice: The Immigration Issue and US-Japan Relations in the 1910s', in *The Decade of the Great War: Japan and the Wider World in the 1910s*, ed. Tosh Minohara, Tze-ki Hon and Evan Dawley (Leiden: Brill, 2014), 31.
3. Ibid., 32. Wilson is quoted as having said: 'In the matter of Chinese and Japanese coolie immigration I stand for the national policy of exclusion. The whole question is one of assimilation of diverse races. We cannot make a homogeneous population out of a people who do not blend with the Caucasian race. Their lower standard of living as labourers will crowd out the white agriculturist and is, in other fields, a most serious industrial menace . . . Oriental cooleism will give us another race problem to solve and surely we have had our lesson.' As cited in Lake and Reynolds, *Drawing the Global Colour Line*, 271.
4. Nihon gaikō monjo, Oyama to Katsura (22 January 1913), *Kashū no gaikokujin tochi hōan oyobi Nihon seifu no kōgi kankei*, 3–7. The law proposals were aimed at limiting the rights of Japanese immigrants regarding land ownership, fishing and hunting rights, as well as the reintroduction of school segregation. Also see Kagawa, 'Hai-Nichi tochihō no seitei to Panama taiheiyō bankoku tenrankai', 148–9 for more details. For general detailed overviews of anti-Japanese legislation in the United States, see Daniels, *Politics of Prejudice*.
5. Nihon gaikō monjo, Chinda to Katō (5 February 1913), *Kashū no gaikokujin tochi hōan oyobi Nihon seifu no kōgi kankei*, 9. Also see, Minohara, 'The Clash of Pride and Prejudice', 34.
6. For details on the law, see Daniels, *The Politics of Prejudice*; Kagawa, 'Hai-Nichi tochihō no seitei to Panama taiheiyō bankoku tenrankai'; Minohara, 'The Clash of Pride and Prejudice'.
7. Lauren, *Power and Prejudice*, 56–64.
8. Nobuaki Makino, *Kaikoroku (shita)* (Tokyo: Chūō kōronsha, 1978), 85–95.
9. 'Nichi-Bei mondai no konpon kaiketsu', *Taiyō* 19, no. 6 (May 1913): 13.
10. This essay, entitled 'Exclusionists Not True to the Principles of America's Founders', was published in an edited volume of collected papers written by leading Japanese citizen (politicians, diplomats and businessmen). These papers

were a comment on the events in California and the passing of the Alien Land Law. They were edited by Masaoka Naoichi, a journalist who had been news correspondent during the peace conference in Portsmouth (1905) and had also accompanied Japanese businessmen to the United States. See Masaoka Naoichi, ed., *Japan to America: A Symposium of Papers by Political Leaders and Representative Citizens of Japan on Conditions in Japan and on the Relations between Japan and the United States* (New York: G. P. Putnam's Sons, 1914).

11. Seiichiro Terashima, 'Exclusionists Not True to the Principles of America's Founders', in *Japan to America*, 66.
12. Ibid., 67.
13. 'A Japanese Ideal', *The Japan Times*, 23 August 1913.
14. 'Self-Reliance', *The Japan Times*, 6 June 1913.
15. Soroku Ebara, 'Akumade gaikōteki kaiketsu o nozomu', *Taiyō* 20, no. 10 (August 1914): 156.
16. Ibid.
17. Torsten Weber credits the feud between Mahan and Chirol for having brought the issue of Asianism to the Japanese public. For an analysis of the exchange from this perspective, see Torsten Weber, *Embracing 'Asia' in China and Japan: Asianism Discourse and the Contest for Hegemony, 1912–1933* (New York: Palgrave Macmillan, 2018), 89–93.
18. Sir Valentine Chirol, 'Japan Among the Nations: The Bar of Race', *The Times*, 19 May 1913.
19. Ibid.
20. Ibid.
21. Ibid.
22. 'Japan's Place in the World', *The Times*, 19 May 1913.
23. Ibid.
24. Ibid.
25. Alfred T. Mahan, 'Japan Among the Nations: Admiral Mahan's Views', 23 June 1913.
26. Ibid.
27. Ibid.
28. 'America's Attitude towards Japan', *The Times*, 23 June 1913.
29. Minohara, 'The Clash of Pride and Prejudice', 38–9.
30. Shigenobu Okuma, 'Our National Mission', in *Japan to America*, 2.
31. Ibid., 5.
32. Unno Yukinori, 'Kōhaku ryōjinshu hikakuron', *Taiyō* 19, no. 8 (June 1913): 87.
33. Lauren, *Power and Prejudice*, 75.
34. Ibid., 77.
35. Yamamuro Shin'ichi, 'Dai ichiji sekai taisen: Shiten toshite no jūdaisei', *Asahi shinbun*, 24 March 2008. As pointed out in Weber, *Embracing 'Asia' in China and Japan*, 108.
36. Endō Kichisaburō, *Ōshū bunmei no botsuraku* (Tokyo: Fūzanbō, 1914), 109.
37. Ibid., 112.

38. Tokutomi Sohō, *Sekai no henkyoku* (Tokyo: Min'yūsha, 1915), 480.
39. Ibid.
40. Wakanomiya Yūsuke, *Wakanomiya ronshū* (Tokyo: Jitsugyō no seikaisha, 1915), 50.
41. Ibid.
42. Ibid., 50–1.
43. Yamamuro Shin'ichi, 'L'empire du Japon et le choc de la Première Guerre mondiale', *Guerres mondiales et conflits contemporains* 249, no. 1 (2013): 10.
44. Ibid.
45. Yamamuro, *Fukugō sensō*, 12.
46. Iriye, *Across the Pacific*, 131.
47. Yamamuro, *Fukugō sensō*, 97–100; Yamamuro, 'L'empire du Japon et le choc de la Première Guerre mondiale', 7–9. Also see Saeki Shōichi, 'Kasō teki toshite no Amerika no imēji', in *Nihon to Amerika*, 181–224.
48. Yamamuro, *Fukugō sensō*, 41.
49. Yamamuro, 'L'empire du Japon et le choc de la Première Guerre mondiale', 13.
50. Ibid., 15. For details about Japan's relation with the British dominions, see John D. Meehan, 'From Alliance to Conference: The British Empire, Japan, and Pacific Multilateralism, 1911–1921', in *The Decade of the Great War*, 45–63.
51. Yamamuro, *Fukugō sensō*, 42–3; Yamamuro, 'L'empire du Japon et le choc de la Première Guerre mondiale', 13.
52. For details, see for example Sōchi Naraoka, 'A New Look at Japan's Twenty-One Demands: Reconsidering Katō Takaaki's Motives in 1915', in *The Decade of the Great War*.
53. Ibid., 189. Also see Thomas W. Burkman, *Japan and the League of Nations: Empire and World Order, 1914–1938* (Honolulu: University of Hawaii Press, 2008), 19–22.
54. Lauren, *Power and Prejudice*, 57–60.
55. As cited in Yamamuro, *Fukugō sensō*, 20.
56. Takashi Hara, 'Harmony between East and West', in *What Japan Thinks*, ed. K. K. Kawakami (New York: The Macmillan Company, 1921), 135.
57. Ibid.
58. Ibid., 136.
59. Ibid.
60. As cited in Cemil Aydin, 'A Global Anti-Western Moment? The Russo-Japanese War, Decolonization, and Asian Modernity', in *Competing Visions of World Order: Global Moments and Movements, 1880s–1930s*, ed. Sebastian Conrad and Dominic Sachsenmaier (New York: Palgrave Macmillan, 2007), 222.
61. The article was published in the magazine *Taiyō* under Atsumaro Konoe, 'Dōjinshu dōmei, tsuketari Shina mondai kenkyū no hitsuyō', *Taiyō* 24, no. 1 (January 1898): 85–92. For a translation and details on it, see Urs Matthias Zachmann, 'Konoe Atsumaro and the Idea of an Alliance of the Yellow Race, 1898', in *Pan-Asianism: A Documentary History. Vol.1: 1850–1920*, ed. Sven Saaler and Christopher W. A. Szpilman (Lanham, MD: Rowman & Littlefield, 2011), 85–92.

62. Aydin, *The Politics of Anti-Westernism in Asia*, 111. For details on Pan-Asianism, see Weber's *Embracing 'Asia' in China and Japan*.
63. Sven Saaler and Christopher W. A. Szpilman, *Pan-Asianism: A Documentary History. Vol. 1* (Lanham, MD: Rowman & Littlefield, 2011), 16.
64. Weber, *Embracing 'Asia' in China and Japan*, 153.
65. Saaler and Szpilman, *Pan-Asianism*, 17.
66. Sven Saaler, 'Pan-Asianism During and After World War I: Kodera Kenkichi (1916), Sawayanagi Masatarō (1919), and Sugita Teiichi (1920)', in *Pan-Asianism*, 255.
67. Kenkichi Kodera, 'Dai Ajiashugiron [Treatise on Greater Asianism]', in *Pan-Asianism*, 260.
68. Ibid.
69. Ibid., 261.
70. The standard work remains Naoko Shimazu's monograph on the subject, although Lauren's chapter in his *Power and Prejudice* as well as his paper on the subject are equally enlightening. See Naoko Shimazu, *Japan, Race, and Equality: The Racial Equality Proposal of 1919* (London: Routledge, 1998); Paul Gordon Lauren, 'Human Rights in History: Diplomacy and Racial Equality at the Paris Peace Conference', *Diplomatic History* 2, no. 3 (Summer 1978): 257–78; Lauren, *Power and Prejudice*, 82–107. Another short analysis of the controversy surrounding the racial equality proposal can be found in Burkman, *Japan and the League of Nations*, 80–6. Also see Noriko Kawamura, 'Wilsonian Idealism and Japanese Claims at the Paris Peace Conference', *Pacific Historical Review* 66, no. 4 (November 1997): 503–26. The short overview of the events in Paris is based on these works.
71. As cited in Shimazu, *Japan, Race, and Equality*, 16–17.
72. Ibid., 17.
73. As cited in ibid., 20.
74. Ibid., 27.
75. Lauren, *Power and Prejudice*, 99.
76. Ibid., 100.
77. Shimazu has already analysed which words were used for the original text and its subsequent rephrasing. By wording, I mean the meaning of the words used in the proposal inside the greater framework of Japan's complicated racial status.
78. As cited in Lauren, *Power and Prejudice*, 90.
79. 'Phelan Charges Design by Japan', *The New York Times*, 22 March 1919.
80. Ibid.
81. Ibid.
82. 'White Supremacy Menaced by League according to Reed', *The Atlanta Constitution*, 27 May 1919.
83. Ibid.
84. Shimazu, *Japan, Race, and Equality*, 114.
85. Diplomatic Archives of the Ministry of Foreign Affairs, *Kōwa kaigi no ōzei ga Nihon no shōrai no oyobosu eikyō oyobi kore ni shosuru no hōsaku*, 30 November 1918, call number of holding: 1-1-2-77-003.

86. Nihon gaikō monjo, Obata to Uchida (11 March 1919), *Pari kōwa kaigi ni okeru jinshu sabetsu teppai mondai ikken*, 467.
87. Ibid.
88. Ibid.
89. Ibid, 467–8. The aforementioned Senator Phelan used the same device to warn against the Japanese: 'The West is more interested in population than in production, and it seeks to preserve and defend its white population against the incursion of the Japanese particularly, who have been well described as the "Huns of the Orient", having had throughout their development German teaching and training. This is to say, like the Germans, their Government has doubtless planned this peaceful conquest and appointed every man to this task.' 'Phelan Charges Design by Japan'.
90. Nihon gaikō monjo, Obata to Uchida (11 March 1919), *Pari kōwa kaigi ni okeru jinshu sabetsu teppai mondai ikken*, 469–70.
91. Lauren, 'Human Rights in History', 258.
92. Shimazu, *Japan, Race, and Equality*, 61.
93. Ibid., 114.
94. For additional details on the Japanese government's fear that the League was but a Western instrument, see Kawamura, 'Wilsonian Idealism and Japanese Claims at the Paris Peace Conference', 515–16.
95. Tokuzō Fukuda, 'Beikoku ni taisuru shuchō', *Asahi shinbun*, 15 November 1918.
96. Toda Kaiichi, 'Yūshokujin imin haiseki mondai (jō)', *Asahi shinbun*, 1 January 1919.
97. Ibid.
98. Toda Kaiichi, 'Yūshokujin imin haiseki mondai (ge), *Asahi shinbun*, 3 January 1919.
99. Shimazu, *Japan, Race, and Equality*, 51. Burkman argues along the same line. Burkman, *Japan and the League of Nations*, 80–6.
100. Nihon gaikō monjo, Uchida to Saionji (8 February 1919), *Pari kōwa kaigi ni okeru jinshu sabetsu teppai mondai ikken*, 439–40. For details about the *Jinshuteki sabetsu teppai kisei taikai*, see Shimazu, *Japan, Race and Equality*, 51–2.
101. Nihon gaikō monjo, Uchida to Matsui (12 February 1919), *Pari kōwa kaigi ni okeru jinshu sabetsu teppai mondai ikken*, 441.
102. Ibid., 443.
103. Kamikawa Hikomatsu, 'Jinshu mondai kaiketsu no kin'yō ' *Taiyō* 340 (1919): 39.
104. Ibid.
105. I am using brackets as an exception here to stay in accordance with the tone of Kamikawa's text.
106. Kamikawa, 'Jinshu mondai kaiketsu no kin'yō', 33.
107. Ibid., 37.
108. Ibid.
109. Ibid., 38.
110. As cited in Peter Duus, 'Nagai Ryutaro and the "White Peril," 1905–1944', *The Journal of Asian Studies* 31, no. 1 (1971): 44.

111. Nagai Ryūtarō, *Kaizō no risō* (Tokyo: Seikadō, 1920), 188.
112. Ibid., 189.
113. Ibid., 181.
114. Ibid., 187.
115. Ibid.
116. 'Japan and Racial Equality', *The Japan Times*, 19 April 1919.
117. Daniels, *The Politics of Prejudice*, 102–3.
118. Miwa Kimitada, 'Japanese Images of War with the United States', in *Mutual Images: Essays in American-Japanese Relations*, ed. Akira Iriye (Cambridge, MA: Harvard university Press, 1975), 115.

Conclusion: The Elusive Japanese Race

Over the centuries, the alterity of the Japanese island nation never ceased to puzzle Western observers, often in a contradictory manner: Japan was different, because exotic and remote from the West, but also different, because so fundamentally close to Western nations. More than one century after Perry's arrival, in the wake of the Second World War, scholars and laymen alike were still trying to decipher the Japanese mind, be it to understand the enemy or the economic miracle of the country.[1] The uniqueness of Japan was also a beloved topic in Japan itself, as testified by the popularity of *Nihonjinron* (theory of Japaneseness) in the post-war years.[2]

In the Meiji period, however, it was before all Japan's resemblance with the West in civilisational terms that made it truly special. According to the scientific and political logic of the time, this closeness led to a profound dissonance. Political and military achievements such as a 'modern' form of government might have seemed to be objective factors attainable by any nation. Yet, by the nineteenth century, racial categories were clearly overlapping with civilisational achievements, causing the racial category 'White' to be synonymous with 'civilisation' and 'coloured' with 'barbarity'. That Japan, classified as 'yellow', could pretend to a place amongst the civilised White nations must therefore truly be seen as an anomaly.

As explained in the introduction to this work, historians of Japan today, while having the clear advantage of hindsight, find themselves facing the same dilemma as the individuals concerned with Japan's racial identity at the turn of the twentieth century: how to fit the Japanese into the ideological framework of the nineteenth and early twentieth centuries. The idea of the Racial Middle Ground can be an answer to that question, as it not only recreates the process through which Japan escaped the usual dichotomy, but also offers a conceptual approach to understand how and why this process was launched and made possible. I hope to have shown that when considering the case of Japan at the turn of the twentieth century, thinking in binary terms of 'White' and 'coloured' is not meaningful. In addition to making the explicit formulation of the standard of civilisation necessary, Japan's modernisation along Western lines eroded the foundations of White supremacist thinking and made a compromise necessary to uphold the racial status quo. This compromise took the form of a racial middle ground.

There have been several of these in the history of Western and Japanese interactions. The most astonishing one is probably the one built between Nazi Germany and the Japanese Empire. The Nazi ideology was, after all, extreme in its belief in White supremacy. Reconciling it with a political alliance with a 'yellow' nation must have needed a more than solid negotiation zone.[3] The US Occupation of Japan (1945–52) offers a small-scale replica of the middle ground portrayed in these pages, with the American racial system transferred to Japan and reproducing the constellation of White Americans as the 'upper race', Japanese in the middle, and African Americans as the 'race at the bottom'.[4] In more recent decades, Japan made the racial policy of another racist regime uncertain: despite its policy of apartheid, the economic importance of Japan as a trading partner made South Africa grant the status of 'honorary Whites' to the Japanese in the 1960s.[5] One could even argue that Japan is continuously walking on a middle ground in present times, with descendants of Japanese immigrants lauded as 'model minorities' in their host countries.[6]

Each of these middle grounds is singular in its nature and was built inside a specific context. Yet, the one described in this work has some specificities that make it particularly interesting. First, it can be said to have been the 'original' one negotiated between the West and Japan, and, as such, as posing the basis for all subsequent ones to come. Second, its longevity makes it the most enduring one. Third, its scope also makes it the most encompassing example. The focus in this book was US–Japan relations, but the problem of accepting Japan as 'more than coloured' was of global relevance.

A racial ideology was foreign to Japan prior to the arrival of the Western nations. Yet its acceptance was fostered by the existence of patterns of differentiation available in Japan long before the forced end to the seclusion policy in the nineteenth century. One of the pillars of Tokugawa society was, after all, the separation of individuals into distinct status groups, with each of these groups having defined functions and a certain amount of social prestige. But unlike the racial categories developed by Western scientists, the creation of the early modern Japanese status groups was not based on alleged unchangeable and inheritable characteristics. It was informed by social, political and religious incentives, leading to the formation of a societal order in which each member had a proper place.

The idea of a 'proper place' was also at the heart of the racial ideology that Fukazawa Yukichi introduced to his readership through the translation of Western works of geography. The rather gentle adaptation of the concept of race in Fukuzawa's works shows that the separation of mankind into superior and inferior people did not appear particularly surprising to him. What did dismay him, however, was the place attributed to Japan inside this hierarchy: at the bottom, as a 'coloured' race. Fukuzawa's omission of Japan in his adaptation of the Western racial hierarchy as well as his rejection of biological determinism were at the same time a representation of Japan's newly set course as well as a premonition of the attitude the nation was to take in the decades to come: the

Japanese believed, and aimed to prove, that they were different, and better, than the rest of the other non-Whites.

Pointing to a particular event as the beginning of the negotiation zone is difficult. The First Sino-Japanese War, however, with its quality as a civilisational test, made the issue of the Japanese anomaly apparent and gave it a certain urgency. Japan entered the war as an underdog but emerged from it as a great power. The reaction to the Port Arthur Massacre illustrates that the Western nations were ready to set the Japanese nation apart from its eternal reference point, China. For the brief span of a few months, the Japanese soldiers received licence to kill and abuse people considered inferior under the approving eyes of the West. There were elements inside the Western press that emitted some reservations regarding the new power. But that the unequal treaties were revised in the wake of the war is proof that at least when opposed to the Chinese, the Japanese were accepted as being part of a superior race.

Things could have escalated swiftly only a decade later. The real test for Japan, and especially for the racial middle ground, was made once again on the battlefield. Only this time, the opponents were White. In hindsight, strictly speaking in terms of race, the war against Russia was quite the gamble. Nothing guaranteed that the Western enthusiasm for the Japanese prowess against China would extend to a war against White people. The Japanese government was conscious of the explosive potential of race in this matter and prepared itself accordingly even before the first troops were sent abroad. Agents were hired to build the racial middle ground by convincing Western public opinion that the war had no relation to race. Relentlessly publishing in American papers and giving talks on the subject, Kaneko Kentarō for example tried to depict Japan as the vanguard of Western civilisation in the East. His mission was facilitated by the fact that the West itself had willing agents: none other than the American President Theodore Roosevelt became one of them, motivated by a blend of political realism and genuine sympathy for Japan. Through these agents' actions, the racial middle ground of the Russo-Japanese War almost completely stripped race of its relevance and prevented the emergence of a racially-based solidarity between Western nations.

Only one year after the victory against Russia, Roosevelt confirmed his role as an agent of the middle ground by negotiating the end of the San Francisco school segregation order. That the Californians were willing to risk a conflict with Japan to preserve their racial order is proof of how limited in scope the racial middle ground could be. In the case of the Californians, the enthusiasm for the Japanese nation did evidently not extend to its individual people. On the Pacific Coast, the modernisation of Japan, as well as the potential threat deriving from it, were secondary to the racial purity of the state. In the American domestic context, therefore, Japanese immigrants were interpreted as another kind of non-White. Roosevelt's intervention on behalf of them reflects a difference in priorities that directly influenced the success of the middle ground.

That the improvements inherent to the negotiation zone were reserved solely to the Japanese becomes apparent when considering the situation of other non-Whites in the United States. Be it African Americans, Native Americans or Chinese, none was granted a special treatment; foremost because none of them had the bargaining power of the Japanese: a strong government to back them up. Roosevelt did not intervene on their behalf, nor had he any incentive to do so. The ambivalent reaction of African Americans to the racial middle ground is a measure of its success: indeed, the negotiation zone resolved an issue that was well known by African Americans, and their feelings towards the special treatment of the Japanese were accordingly complicated.

Japan lost its most powerful agent with the end of Roosevelt's presidency. Woodrow Wilson, who came into power in 1912, did not have the same priorities as Roosevelt: using the middle ground to its own advantage, he had based his campaign in California on anti-Japanese sentiments. The first serious failure of the middle ground, the Alien Land Law, occurred during his presidency. Besides its domestic implication, the law exposed American hypocrisy to the Japanese and led to a loss of prestige of the United States. The American case, however, was only mirroring the simultaneous global events: despite the Anglo-Japanese Alliance from 1902, every British Dominion had enacted laws barring Oriental immigration.

The mass slaughter of the First World War further increased doubts about the legitimacy of the Eurocentric model. Japanese critics grew louder and Pan-Asianism became a viable alternative to a 'declining' West. The anti-Oriental movements of the previous decades had taken their toll even on statesmen. And while the beginning of the middle ground is blurred, its ending is well defined: the moment the Japanese delegates presented the racial equality proposal during the Paris Peace Conference in 1919, they also conceded that Japan was 'coloured' and acknowledged that the Japanese would probably not be accepted as 'honorary Whites' anymore. The collapse of the negotiation zone on the Western side occurred simultaneously with the rejection of the said proposal: it made the one factor that had enabled the relatively long maintenance of the middle ground possible – the differentiation between Japan as a nation and the Japanese as individual – unsustainable. Without this differentiation, the middle ground would have been a direct threat to the racial order of several of the countries assembled at Paris.

No study can pretend to be without limitations and in the case of this book, too, there are certain aspects that deserve further research. The 'class aspect' of the racial middle ground is certainly one of these. We have briefly discussed that upper middle class people from the early anti-Japanese movement in the United States were not against the immigration of qualified Japanese and that their contempt was direct against unskilled labourers. Likewise, the Japanese intellectuals and the immigrant elite did agree that most unskilled Japanese immigrants were inferior. The former even racialised the latter, by comparing them to Chinese labourers and trying to suppress their 'Sinification'. Social and economic status could therefore directly influence the appraisal of Japanese immigrants as a race. In terms of the Racial Middle Ground, we would have the following constellation: upper-middle-class Whites as the 'upper race', the Japanese elite (intellectuals, immigrant leaders) as the 'race in the middle', and unskilled Japanese labourers as the 'race at the bottom'. This aspect is clearly not restricted to this study: the Japanese minority in Brazil, for example, made the shift from a socially low and discriminated ethnic group before the Second World War to a respected urban middle-class model minority. This change in prestige followed the rise in social mobility of the younger generation of ethnic Japanese, as well as the economic growth of Japan after the Second World War.[7] There remains great potential to broaden the study of the middle ground described in this book, and the class aspect of it is a step in that direction.

Furthermore, while outside the scope of this study, it is noteworthy that while the Japanese were negotiating their racial identity with the Western powers, they were also establishing a middle ground of their own in Asia: a colonial power since the acquisition of Taiwan in 1895, Japan constructed an order closely modelled on the Western one. This included not only a racial chauvinism that legitimised the mistreatment of people considered inferior, but also 'scientific' ventures that tried to prove the superiority of the Japanese race over the people under its governance. The lynching of ethnic Koreans as scapegoats in the aftermath of the Great Kantō earthquake in 1923 is an example of the former that bears an uncanny and sad resemblance to the lynching of African Americans in the US.[8] The measurement of Ainu skulls is but one aspect of the latter.[9]

What does the Racial Middle Ground tell us about race in the context of Japanese history? The most significant insight is that through the negotiation zone there was no single Japanese race, but that the Japanese possessed multiple racial identities at the same time. Kowner points to the fluidity of the 'Japanese race' by arguing that the more the Japanese were perceived as a threat, the more concrete was their definition as an inferior race.[10] While the changing nature of the Japanese racial identity is a fact, I would argue that it was because the Japanese were becoming threatening that they had to be elevated to the 'race in the middle'. Where the distinction has to be made is whether one is considering Japan as a nation or the Japanese as individuals, as both represented different things and as such were assessed in different ways. In this vein, the usual dichotomic view of race relations cannot be uncritically applied to Japanese history, especially when considered in a global framework: on the racial middle ground, Japan was neither White nor 'yellow', but something in between that was subjected to a multitude of interpretations. That the racial equality proposal voided the possibility of the multiple interpretations of Japan only strengthens this understanding. The demand for universal racial equality left only one possible interpretation of Japan: that of a 'coloured' race.

There is one individual's personal fate that can serve as a metaphor for the developments described in this book, from the inception of the racial middle ground, over the reasons for its maintenance and its shortcomings, to its final demise: on 13 November 1922, the Supreme Court of the United States decided that Ozawa Takao, a Japanese citizen who had applied for American citizenship, was ineligible for naturalisation because he was not Caucasian. Ozawa told the court that he was properly assimilated into American society, spoke English fluently, was a University of California alumni, and was of Christian confession. As such, he argued that he had all the rights to become a citizen of the United States. He did not challenge the naturalisation restrictions that limited citizenship to free White people and people of African ancestry. He did only try to pass himself off as White. The court conceded that he was 'qualified by character and education for citizenship'. But the crucial question was another one: who was included in the category 'free White person'? According to the Supreme Court, 'White person' was synonym with 'a person of the Caucasian race':

> The appellant, in the case now under consideration, however, is clearly of a race which is not Caucasian . . . The briefs filed on behalf of appellant refer in complimentary terms to the culture and enlightenment of the Japanese people, and with this estimate we have no reason to disagree; but these are matters which cannot enter into our consideration of the questions here at issue.[11]

The same old rhetoric: Japan as a nation was surely admirable, the Japanese as individuals not so much. In the end, for Ozawa, being Japanese was too much and not enough at the same time.

Notes

1. For two famous examples, see Ruth Benedict, *The Chrysanthemum and the Sword: Patterns of Japanese Culture* (Rutland, VT: Tuttle, 1946; repr., 1986); Ezra F. Vogel, *Japan as Number One: Lessons for America* (Cambridge, MA: Harvard University Press, 1979).
2. For a concise introduction to *Nihonjinron*, see Yoshio Sugimoto, 'Making Sense of Nihonjinron', *Thesis Eleven* 57, no. 1 (1999): 81–96. For further details, see Harumi Befu, *Hegemony of Homogeneity: An Anthropological Analysis of 'Nihonjinron'* (Melbourne: Trans Pacific Press, 2001); Rotem Kowner and Harumi Befu, 'Ethnic Nationalism in Postwar Japan: Nihonjinron and Its Racial Facets', in *Race and Racism in Modern East Asia: Interactions, Nationalism, Gender and Lineage*, ed. Rotem Kowner and Walter Demel (Leiden: Brill, 2015), 389–412.
3. For the relationship between the Third Reich and the Japanese Empire, see Hans-Joachim Bieber, *SS und Samurai: deutsch-japanische Kulturbeziehungen 1933–1945* (München: Iudicium, 2014). Also see Krebs, 'Racism under Negotiation'.
4. For racism during the Occupation of Japan, see Koshiro, *Trans-Pacific Racisms and the U.S. Occupation of Japan*.
5. For details, see Masako Osada, *Sanctions and Honorary Whites: Diplomatic Policies and Economic Realities in Relations between Japan and South Africa* (Westport, CT:

Greenwood Press, 2002). Henning mentions this too. See Henning, *Outposts of Civilization*, 167.

6. For an example from the American context, see Michael Thornton and Atsushi Tajima, 'A "Model" Minority: Japanese Americans as References and Role Models in Black Newspapers, 2000–2010', *Communication and Critical/Cultural Studies* 11, no. 2 (April 2014): 139–57.
7. Takeyuki Gaku Tsuda, 'When Identities Become Modern: Japanese Emigration to Brazil and the Global Contextualization of Identity', *Ethnic and Racial Studies* 24, no. 3 (January 2001): 426–30.
8. For details on the lynchings, see Kenji Hasegawa, 'The Massacre of Koreans in Yokohama in the Aftermath of the Great Kanto Earthquake of 1923', *Monumenta Nipponica* 75, no. 1 (2020): 91–122.
9. On the 'scientific' research surrounding Ainu, see for example Siddle, *Race, Resistance, and the Ainu of Japan*.
10. Kowner, '"Lighter than Yellow, but not Enough"', 105.
11. For the text of the decision, see for example: Legal Information Institute, '*Takao Ozawa* vs *United States*': https://www.law.cornell.edu/supremecourt/text/260/178

References

'A Japanese Ideal'. *The Japan Times*, 23 August 1913.
'America's Attitude towards Japan'. *The Times*, 23 June 1913.
'Awful if True'. *Los Angeles Times*, 29 November 1894.
'Beikoku daitōryō no kokujin tōyō'. *Gaikō jihō* 63 (April 1903): 72.
'Beikoku no kokujin'. *Kyōkai hyōron* 48 (January 1896): 25–8.
'Beikoku-dan'. *Yomiuri shinbun*, 9 September 1887.
'Beikokujin no ijinshu ken'o'. *Asahi shinbun*, 2 December 1902.
'Capture of Port Arthur'. *Chicago Daily Tribune*, 27 November 1894.
'Chinese and Japanese in America'. *The Annals of the American Academy of Political and Social Science* 34, no. 2 (September 1909): i–155.
'Gasshūkoku daitōryō kokujin o shōtai shite nanbō no jinbō o ushinau'. *Gaikō jihō* 47 (December 1901): 48.
'Gasshūkoku shindaitōryō no ronkoku'. *Yomiuri shinbun*, 1 January 1885.
'Horrors of Oriental Barbarity'. *The Washington Post*, 8 January 1895.
'How It Was Done'. *Chicago Daily Tribune*, 5 December 1894.
'How the Japs Did It'. *The Atlanta Constitution*, 30 November 1894.
'Japan and China'. *Los Angeles Times*, 19 December 1894.
'Japan and the Color Line'. *The Boston Daily Globe*, 28 October 1906.
'Japan and Racial Equality'. *The Japan Times*, 19 April 1919.
'Japan and San Francisco Discrimination'. *The Colored American Magazine* 11, no. 5 (November 1906).
'Japan on Its Behavior'. *The New York Times*, 18 December 1894.
'Japan's Place in the World'. *The Times*, 19 May 1913.
'Japanese Accused Unjustly'. *The New York Times*, 20 December 1894.
'Japanese Situation'. *The American Journal of International Law* 1, no. 2 (April 1907): 449–52.
'Japs on the Cross'. *Los Angeles Times*, 18 December 1894.
'Kokujin mondai to Beikoku daitōryō'. *Asahi shinbun*, 10 January 1903.
'Nakamura Tadao-shi'. *Yomiuri shinbun*, 3 September 1887.
'Negro and Japanese Pupils'. *The Broad Ax*, 13 February 1909.
'Nichi-Ei dōmei no happyō'. *Asahi shinbun*, 13 February 1902.
'Nichi-Bei mondai no konpon kaiketsu'. *Taiyō* 19, no. 6 (May 1913): 11–15.
'Phelan Charges Design by Japan'. *The New York Times*, 22 March 1919.

'President Demands Citizenship for Japanese'. *The New York Times*, 5 December 1906.
'Problems of the Pacific'. *Blackwood's Edinburgh Magazine* 171, no. 1040 (June 1902): 852–70.
'Race Question Great Problem before the Nation'. *The Atlanta Constitution*, 8 February 1909.
'Rev. J. M. Foster in the Christian Nation, New York'. *The Broad Ax*, 5 January 1907.
'Rights of the Japanese in California Schools'. *Harvard Law Review* 20, no. 4 (February 1907): 337–40.
'Self-Reliance'. *The Japan Times*, 6 June 1913.
'Shōjo no ōshi'. *Yomiuri shinbun*, 27 January 1886.
'Some of Them Crucified'. *The Atlanta Consitution*, 18 December 1894.
'Speech of Foreign Minister Mutsu Munemitsu in the House of Representatives'. In *The Meiji Japan through Contemporary Sources*. Vol. 3: 1869–1894. Edited by Center for East Asian Cultural Studies, 185–6. Tokyo, 1972.
'The California Muddle'. *The Colored American Magazine* 12, no. 3 (March 1907).
'The Controversy with Japan'. *The Voice of the Negro* 4, no. 2 (March 1907).
'The Jap and the Negro'. *The Atlanta Consitution*, 9 February 1909.
'The Japanese Question'. *The Voice of the Negro* 4, no. 7 (July 1907).
'The Other Side of the Story'. *The Washington Post*, 1 December 1894.
'The Port Arthur Massacre'. *The Atlanta Constitution*, 14 December 1894.
'The Press on the Anglo-Japanese Alliance'. *The Japan Times*, 14 Februrary 1902.
'The Truth about Port Arthur'. *The Atlanta Constitution*, 10 January 1895.
'Tortured by Chinese'. *The Washington Post*, 18 December 1894.
'Treaty of Commerce and Navigation between the United States and Japan'. *The American Journal of International Law* 5, no. 2 (April 1911): 106–16.
'White Schools Shut to Japs; Roosevelt Mad'. *The Atlanta Constitution*, 5 February 1909.
'White Supremacy Menaced by League according to Reed'. *The Atlanta Constitution*, 27 May 1919.
'Zangyaku naru shikei'. *Yomiuri shinbun*, 8 January 1900.

Ameda Eiichi. 'Fukuzawa Yukichi no "maruhadaka no kyōsō" to "jinshu kairyō" no shisō'. *Tōyō bunka kenkyū* 2 (2000): 385–418.
Amos, Timothy D. *Embodying Difference: The Making of Burakumin in Modern Japan*. Honolulu: University of Hawaii Press, 2011.
Anand, R. P. 'Family of "Civilized" States and Japan: A Story of Humiliation, Assimilation, Defiance and Confrontation'. *Journal of the History of International Law* 5 (2003): 1–75.
Anghie, Antony. 'Francisco De Vitoria and the Colonial Origins of International Law'. *Social & Legal Studies* 5, no. 3 (September 1996): 321–36.
Anghie, Antony. *Imperialism, Sovereignty, and the Making of International Law*. Cambridge: Cambridge University Press, 2005.
Asaka, Ikuko. '"Colored Men of the East": African Americans and the Instability of Race in US-Japan Relations'. *American Quarterly* 66, no. 4 (December 2014): 971–97.

Auslin, Michael R. *Negotiating with Imperialism: The Unequal Treaties and the Culture of Japanese Diplomacy*. Cambridge, MA: Harvard University Press, 2004.

Aydin, Cemil. 'A Global Anti-Western Moment? The Russo-Japanese War, Decolonization, and Asian Modernity'. In *Competing Visions of World Order: Global Moments and Movements, 1880s–1930s*, edited by Sebastian Conrad and Dominic Sachsenmaier, 213–36. New York: Palgrave Macmillan, 2007.

Aydin, Cemil. *The Politics of Anti-Westernism in Asia: Visions of World Order in Pan-Islamic and Pan-Asian Thought*. Columbia Studies in International and Global History. New York: Columbia University Press, 2007.

Azuma, Eiichiro. *Between Two Empires: Race, History, and Transnationalism in Japanese America*. New York: Oxford University Press, 2005.

Bailey, Thomas Andrew. *Theodore Roosevelt and the Japanese-American Crises: An Account of the International Complications Arising from the Race Problem on the Pacific Coast*. Stanford, CA: Stanford University Press, 1934.

Balibar, Étienne. 'Le racisme de classe'. In *Race, nation, classe: les identités ambiguës*, edited by Étienne Balibar and Immanuel Wallerstein, 272–88. Paris: La Découverte, 1997.

Balibar, Étienne. 'Y a-t-il un "néo-racisme"?'. In *Race, nation, classe: les identités ambiguës*, edited by Étienne Balibar and Immanuel Wallerstein, 24–41. Paris: La Découverte, 1997.

Befu, Harumi. *Hegemony of Homogeneity: An Anthropological Analysis of 'Nihonjinron'*. Melbourne: Trans Pacific Press, 2001.

Benedict, Ruth. *The Chrysanthemum and the Sword: Patterns of Japanese Culture*. Rutland, VT: Tuttle, 1986. 1946.

Benfey, Christopher. *The Great Wave: Gilded Age Misfits, Japanese Eccentrics, and the Opening of Old Japan*. New York: Random House, 2003.

Berg, Manfred. '"A Great Civilized Power of a Formidable Type": Theodore Roosevelt, die USA und der Russisch-Japanische Krieg'. In *Der Russisch-Japanische Krieg 1904/05: Anbruch einer neuen Zeit*. Wiesbaden: Harrassowitz Verlag, 2007.

Best, Antony. 'Race, Monarchy, and the Anglo-Japanese Alliance, 1902–1922'. *Social Science Japan Journal* 9, no. 2 (October 2006): 171–86.

Bhabha, Homi K. *The Location of Culture*. 2nd ed. London: Routledge, 2004.

Biddiss, Michael Denis. 'The Politics of Anatomy: Dr Robert Knox and Victorian Racism'. *Journal of the Royal Society of Medicine* 69, no. 4 (1975): 245–50.

Bieber, Hans-Joachim. *SS und Samurai: deutsch-japanische Kulturbeziehungen 1933–1945*. München: Iudicium, 2014.

Blind, Karl. 'Does Russia Represent Aryan Civilization?'. *The North American Review* 178, no. 571 (June 1904): 801–11.

Bonnet, Alastair. 'How the British Working Class Became White: The Symbolic (Re)formation of Racialized Capitalism'. *Journal of Historical Sociology* 11, no. 3 (1998): 316–40.

Boot, Willem. 'Confucianism in the Early Tokugawa Period'. In *Sources of Japanese Tradition*, edited by Wm. Theodore de Bary, Carol Gluck and Arthur E. Tiedemann. New York: Columbia University Press, 2005.

Botsman, Daniel V. *Punishment and Power in the Making of Modern Japan*. Princeton, NJ: Princeton University Press, 2005.

Bowden, Brett. 'The Colonial Origins of International Law. European Expansion and the Classical Standard of Civilization'. *Journal of the History of International Law* 7 (January 2005): 1–23.

Bowden, Brett. *The Empire of Civilization: The Evolution of an Imperial Idea*. Chicago: University of Chicago Press, 2009.

Boxer, Charles Ralph. *The Christian Century in Japan, 1549–1650*. Berkeley: University of California Press, 1951.

Burkman, Thomas W. *Japan and the League of Nations: Empire and World Order, 1914–1938*. Honolulu: University of Hawaii Press, 2008.

Burnett, Albert G. 'Misunderstanding of Eastern and Western States regarding Oriental Immigration'. *The Annals of the American Academy of Political and Social Science* 34, no. 2 (September 1909): 37–41.

Campbell, John T. 'Chance for the Afro-Americans to Join Hands with the Japanese and Bring on a Bloody War in this Country'. *The Broad Ax*, 15 April 1911.

Campbell, John T. 'What May Result if the Persecution of the Negro Continues'. *The Broad Ax*, 19 January 1907.

Cassini, Comte. 'Russia in the Far East'. *The North American Review* 178, no. 570 (1904): 681–89.

Chambers, Sarah C. 'Little Middle Ground: The Instability of a Mestizo Identity in the Andes, Eighteenth and Nineteenth Centuries'. In *Race and Nation in Modern Latin America*, edited by Nancy P. Appelbaum, Anne S. Macpherson and Karin A. Rosemblatt, 32–55. Chapel Hill: University of North Carolina Press, 2003.

Chirol, Sir Valentine. 'Japan Among the Nations: The Bar of Race'. *The Times*, 19 May 1913.

Cortambert, Eugène. *Cours de géographie comprenant la description physique et politique et la géographie historique des diverses contrées du globe*. 13th ed. Paris: Librairie Hachette et Cie., 1876. 1846.

Creelman, James. 'A Japanese Massacre'. *New York World*, 12 December 1894.

Daniels, Roger. 'Japanese Immigrants on a Western Frontier: The Issei in California, 1890–1940'. In *East across the Pacific: Historical and Sociological Studies of Japanese Immigration and Assimilation*, edited by Hilary Conroy and T. Scott Miyakawa, 76–91. Santa Barbara, CA: American Bibliographical Center-Clio Press, 1972.

Daniels, Roger. *The Politics of Prejudice: The Anti-Japanese Movement in California and the Struggle for Japanese Exclusion*. 2nd ed. Berkeley: University of California Press, 1977.

Davis, Deborah. *Guest of Honor: Booker T. Washington, Theodore Roosevelt, and the White House Dinner that Shocked a Nation*. New York: Atria Books, 2012.

Dikötter, Frank, ed. *The Construction of Racial Identities in China and Japan*. Hong Kong: Hong Kong University Press, 1997.

Diplomatic Archives of the Ministry of Foreign Affairs. *Kōwa kaigi no ōzei ga Nihon no shōrai no oyobosu eikyō oyobi kore ni shosuru no hōsaku*. 30 November 1918, call number of holding: 1-1-2-77-003.

Diplomatic Archives of the Ministry of Foreign Affairs. Makino to Komura (30 May 1904). *Hikōkaron henjutsu hakkō no gi ni kanshi ōkoku kōshi yori hinshin ikken*, call number of holding: 7-2-2-16.

Diplomatic Archives of the Ministry of Foreign Affairs. Takahira to Komura (29 March 1904). *Kaneko Kentarō*, call number of holding: 5-2-18-0-33.

Dore, R. P. 'The Prestige Factor in International Relations'. *International Affairs* 51, no. 2 (April 1975): 190–207.

Dore, Ronald P. *Education in Tokugawa Japan*. London: The Athlone Press, 1984.

Dorwart, Jeffery M. 'James Creelman, the New York World and the Port Arthur Massacre'. *Journalism Quarterly* 50, no. 4 (1973): 697–701.

Dower, John W. *Embracing Defeat: Japan in the Wake of World War II*. New York: W. W. Norton & Co., 1999.

Dower, John W. *War Without Mercy: Race and Power in the Pacific War*. New York: Pantheon Books, 1986.

Dyer, Thomas G. *Theodore Roosevelt and the Idea of Race*. Baton Rouge: Louisiana State University Press, 1980.

Ebara Soroku. 'Akumade gaikōteki kaiketsu o nozomu'. *Taiyō* 20, no. 10 (August 1914): 155–8.

Elison, George. *Deus Destroyed: The Image of Christianity in Early Modern Japan*. Cambridge, MA: Harvard University Press, 1988.

Endō Kichisaburō. *Ōshū bunmei no botsuraku*. Tokyo: Fūzanbō, 1914.

Esthus, Raymond A. *Double Eagle and Rising Sun: The Russians and Japanese at Portsmouth in 1905*. Durham, NC: Duke University Press, 1988.

Fairbank, John K., ed. *The Chinese World Order: Traditional China's Foreign Relations*. Cambridge, MA: Harvard University Press, 1968.

Fanon, Frantz. *Peau noire, masques blancs*. Paris: Éditions du Seuil, 2015. 1952.

Faure, Bernard. *The Power of Denial: Buddhism, Purity, and Gender*. Princeton, NJ: Princeton University Press, 2009.

Franklin, John Hope and Evelyn Brooks Higginbotham. *From Slavery to Freedom: A History of African Americans*. 10th ed. New York: McGraw Hill, 2021.

Fredrickson, George M. 'Racism, History of'. In *International Encyclopedia of the Social & Behavioral Sciences*, edited by James D. Wright, 852–6. Amsterdam: Elsevier, 2015.

Fredrickson, George M. *Racism: A Short History*. Princeton, NJ: Princeton University Press, 2015.

Fredrickson, George M. *White Supremacy: A Comparative Study in American and South African History*. New York: Oxford University Press, 1981.

Fuess, Harald. *Divorce in Japan: Family, Gender, and the State, 1600–2000*. Stanford, CA: Stanford University Press, 2004.

Fujita Midori. *Afurika hakken: Nihon ni okeru Afurika-zō no hensen*. Tokyo: Iwanami shoten, 2005.

Fukamauchi Motoi. *Yochi shōgaku*. Vol. 1. Tokyo: Meizankaku, 1874.

Fukuda Tokuzō. 'Beikoku ni taisuru shuchō'. *Asahi shinbun*, 15 November 1918.

Fulton, C. W. 'American Schools and Japanese Pupils'. *The North American Review* 183, no. 605 (December 1906): 1225–8.

Fumiko, Miyazaki. 'Female Pilgrims and Mt. Fuji: Changing Perspectives on the Exclusion of Women'. *Monumenta Nipponica* 60, no. 3 (2005): 339–91.

Furukawa Hiromi. 'Black Presence in Japan-U.S. Relations'. *Kokujin kenkyū* 64 (1994): 10–19.

Gallicchio, Marc. *The African American Encounter with Japan & China: Black Internationalism in Asia, 1895–1945*. Chapel Hill: University of North Carolina Press, 2000.

Gerstle, Gary. *American Crucible: Race and Nation in the Twentieth Century*. Princeton, NJ: Princeton University Press, 2001.

Gluck, Carol. 'Re-Présenter Meiji'. In *La nation en marche: Études sur le Japon impérial de Meiji*, edited by Jean-Jacques Tschudin and Claude Hamon, 9–40. Paris: Philippe Picquier, 2007.

Godart, G. Clinton. *Darwin, Dharma, and the Divine: Evolutionary Theory and Religion in Modern Japan*. Honolulu: University of Hawaii Press, 2017.

Gollwitzer, Heinz. *Die Gelbe Gefahr: Geschichte eines Schlagwortes. Studien zum imperialistischen Denken*. Göttingen: Vandenhoeck & Ruprecht, 1962.

Gomi Toshiki. 'Anguro-sakuzonizumu to sen kyūhyaku nijūyo nen iminhō'. In *Nichi-Bei kiki no kigen to hai-Nichi iminhō*, edited by Kimitada Miwa, 183–218. Tokyo: Ronsōsha, 1997.

Gong, Gerrit W. *The Standard of 'Civilization' in International Society*. Oxford: Clarendon Press, 1984.

Goto-Shibata, Harumi. 'Internationalism and Nationalism: Anti-Western Sentiments in Japanese Foreign Policy Debates, 1918–22'. In *Nationalisms in Japan*, edited by Naoko Shimazu, 66–84. London: Routledge, 2006.

Gould, Stephen Jay. *The Mismeasure of Man*. New York: Norton, 1981.

Guillaumin, Colette. 'Avec ou sans race?'. *Le Genre Humain* 2, no. 11 (1984): 215–22.

Gulick, Sidney L. *The American Japanese Problem: A Study of the Racial Relations of the East and the West*. New York: Charles Scribner's Sons, 1914.

Gulick, Sidney L. *Evolution of the Japanese: Social and Psychic*. New York: Fleming H. Revell, 1903.

Hall, John W. 'Rule by Status in Tokugawa Japan'. *The Journal of Japanese Studies* 1, no. 1 (Autumn 1974): 39–49.

Hane, Mikiso. *Modern Japan: A Historical Survey*. 3rd ed. Boulder, CO: Westview Press, 2001.

Hane, Mikiso. *Peasants, Rebels, and Outcastes: The Underside of Modern Japan*. New York: Pantheon, 1982.

Hannaford, Ivan. *Race: The History of an Idea in the West*. Baltimore, MD: The John Hopkins University Press, 1996.

Hara Takashi. 'Harmony between East and West'. In *What Japan Thinks*, edited by K. K. Kawakami, 132–42. New York: The Macmillan Company, 1921.

Hardin, Thomas L. 'American Press and Public Opinion in the First Sino-Japanese War'. *Journalism Quarterly* 50, no. 1 (1973): 54–9.

Harootunian, Harry D. 'The Functions of China in Tokugawa Thought'. In *The Chinese and the Japanese: Essays in Political and Cultural Interactions*, edited by Akira Iriye, 9–36. Princeton, NJ: Princeton University Press, 1980.

Hasegawa, Kenji. 'The Massacre of Koreans in Yokohama in the Aftermath of the Great Kanto Earthquake of 1923'. *Monumenta Nipponica* 75, no. 1 (2020): 91–122.

Hawks, Francis L. *Narrative of the Expedition of an American Squadron to the China Seas and Japan, Performed in the Years 1852, 1853, and 1854, under the Command of Commodore M. C. Perry, United States Navy, by Order of the Government of the United States.* Washington: Beverley Tucker, 1856.

Heco, Joseph. *The Narrative of a Japanese: What He Has Seen and the People He Has Met in the Course of the Last Forty Years.* Edited by James M. A. Murdoch. 2 vols. Yokohama Printing and Publishing, 1892. 1895.

Heere, Cees. *Empire Ascendant: The British World, Race, and the Rise of Japan, 1894–1914.* Oxford: Oxford University Press, 2020.

Heere, Cornelis. '"That Racial Chasm That Yawns Eternally in our Midst": The British Empire and the Politics of Asian Migration, 1900–14'. *Historical Research* 90, no. 249 (2017): 591–612.

Hellwig, David J. 'Afro-American Reactions to the Japanese and the Anti-Japanese Movement, 1906–1924'. *Phylon* 38, no. 1 (1977): 93–104.

Henderson, Dan Fenno. 'The Evolution of Tokugawa Law'. In *Studies in the Institutional History of Early Modern Japan*, edited by John Whitney Hall and Marius B. Jansen, 203–30. Princeton, NJ: Princeton University Press, 1968.

Henning, Joseph M. *Outposts of Civilization: Race, Religion, and the Formative Years of American-Japanese Relations.* New York: New York University Press, 2000.

Henning, Joseph M. 'White Mongols? The War and American Discourses on Race and Religion'. In *The Impact of the Russo-Japanese War*, edited by Rotem Kowner, 153–66. London: Routledge, 2006.

Hershey, Amos S. 'The Japanese School Question and the Treaty-Making Power'. *The American Political Science Review* 1, no. 3 (1907): 393–409.

Higashibaba, Ikuo. *Christianity in Early Modern Japan: Kirishitan Belief and Practice.* Leiden: Brill, 2001.

Holt, Thomas C. *Children of Fire: A History of African Americans.* New York: Hill and Wang, 2010.

Horikawa Kensai. *Chikyū sanbutsu zasshi.* Tokyo: Izumiya ichibei, 1872.

Horsman, Reginald. *Race and Manifest Destiny: The Origins of American Racial Anglo-Saxonism.* Cambridge, MA: Harvard University Press, 1981.

Howell, David L. 'Ainu Ethnicity and the Boundaries of the Early Modern Japanese State'. *Past & Present* 142 (February 1994): 69–93.

Howell, David L. *Geographies of Identity in Nineteenth-Century Japan.* Berkeley: University of California Press, 2005.

Howland, Douglas. 'Japan's Civilized War: International Law as Diplomacy in the Sino-Japanese War (1894–1895)'. *Journal of the History of International Law* 9, no. 2 (January 2007): 179–201.

Howland, Douglas. *Translating the West: Language and Political Reason in Nineteenth-Century Japan.* Honolulu: University of Hawaii Press, 2002.

Hsu, Hsuan L. 'Personality, Race, and Geopolitics in Joseph Heco's "Narrative of a Japanese"'. *Biography* 29, no. 2 (Spring 2006): 273–306.

Ignatiev, Noel. *How the Irish Became White.* New York: Routledge, 1995.

Iikura Akira. 'The Anglo-Japanese Alliance and the Question of Race'. In *The Anglo-Japanese Alliance, 1902–1922*, edited by Phillips Payson O'Brien, 158–66. London: Routledge, 2004.

Iikura Akira. *Ierō periru no shinwa: Teikoku Nihon to kōka no gyakusetsu.* Tokyo: Sairyūsha, 2004.

Inō Tentarō. *Naichi zakkyoron shiryō shūsei.* Tokyo: Hara shobō, 1992.

Inoue Tetsujirō. *Naichi zakkyoron.* Tokyo: Tetsugaku shoin, 1889.

Iriye, Akira. *Across the Pacific: An Inner History of American-East Asian Relations.* Rev. ed. Chicago: Imprint Publications, 1992.

Iriye, Akira. 'Kyōsō aite Nihon: Sen happyaku kyūjūgo nen kara sen kyūhyaku jūnana nen'. In *Nihon to Amerika: Aite koku no imēji kenkyū*, edited by Hidetoshi Katō and Kamei Shunsuke, 145–80. Tokyo: Nihon gakujutsu shinkōkai, 1993.

Iriye, Akira. *Pacific Estrangement: Japanese and American expansion, 1897–1911.* Cambridge, MA: Harvard University Press, 1972.

Jernigan, T. R. 'Japan's Entry into the Family of Nations'. *The North American Review* 169, no. 513 (August 1899): 218–26.

Kagawa Mari. 'Hai-Nichi tochihō no seitei to Panama taiheiyō bankoku tenrankai: Chinda Sutemi no tai-Bei ninshiki wo chūshin to shite'. In *Taishōki Nihon no Amerika ninshiki*, edited by Hasegawa Yūichi. Tokyo: Keiō gijuku daigaku shuppankai, 2001.

Kaibara Ekken. 'The Great Learning for Women'. In *Sources of Japanese Tradition: Volume 2, 1600–2000*, 2nd ed., edited by Wm. Theodore de Bary, Carol Gluck and Arthur E. Tiedemann, 261–7. New York: Columbia University Press, 2005.

Kamata Ekichi. 'Jinshu sabetsu teppai mondai'. *Nihon no kanmon* 4, no. 45 (June 1919): 17–18.

Kamei Shunsuke, ed. *Kindai Nihon no hon'yaku bunka.* Tokyo: Chūō kōronsha, 1994.

Kamikawa Hikomatsu. 'Jinshu mondai kaiketsu no kin'yō'. *Taiyō* 340 (1919): 32–40.

Kaneko, Kentaro. *The Situation in the Far East.* Cambridge, MA: The Japan Club of Harvard University, 1904.

Kaneko, Kentaro. 'The Yellow Peril Is the Golden Opportunity for Japan'. *The North American Review* 179, no. 576 (1904): 641–8.

Katō Hiroyuki. 'Nihon jinshu kairyōron no ben'. *Tōkyō gakushi kaiin zasshi* 8, no. 1 (1886): 1–46.

Kawamura, Noriko. 'Wilsonian Idealism and Japanese Claims at the Paris Peace Conference'. *Pacific Historical Review* 66, no. 4 (November 1997): 503–26.

Kayaoglu, Turan. *Legal Imperialism: Sovereignty and Extraterritoriality in Japan, the Ottoman Empire, and China.* Cambridge: Cambridge University Press, 2010.

Kazui, Tashiro. 'Foreign Relations during the Edo Period: Sakoku Reexamined'. *Journal of Japanese Studies* 8, no. 2 (1982): 283–306.

Kearney, Reginald. *African American Views of the Japanese: Solidarity or Sedition?* Albany: State University of New York Press, 1998.

Keene, Donald. *Emperor of Japan: Meiji and his World, 1852–1912*. New York: Columbia University Press, 2002.

Keevak, Michael. *Becoming Yellow: A Short History of Racial Thinking*. Princeton, NJ: Princeton University Press, 2011.

Keiō gijuku, ed. *Fukuzawa Yukichi zenshū*. Vol. 1. Tokyo: Iwanami shoten, 1969–71.

Keith, Jeffrey A. 'Civilization, Race, and the Japan Expedition's Cultural Diplomacy, 1853–1854'. *Diplomatic History* 35, no. 2 (2011): 179–202.

Kikue, Yamakawa. *Women of the Mito Domain; Recollections of Samurai Family Life*. Translated by Kate Wildman Nakai. Tokyo: University of Tokyo Press, 1992.

Kimitada Miwa. 'Japanese Images of War with the United States'. In *Mutual Images: Essays in American-Japanese Relations*, edited by Akira Iriye, 115–37. Cambridge, MA: Harvard university Press, 1975.

Kiyama Henry (Yoshitaka). *Yonin shosei manga*. San Francisco, CA: The Yoshitaka Kiyama Studio, 1931.

Knox, Robert. *Races of Men: A Fragment*. Philadelphia, PA: Lea and Blanchard, 1850.

Ko, Dorothy, JaHyun Kim Haboush and Joan R. Piggot, eds. *Women and Confucian Cultures in Premodern China, Korea, and Japan*. Los Angeles: University of California Press, 2003.

Kodera Kenkichi. 'Dai Ajiashugiron'. Translated by Sven Saaler. In *Pan-Asianism: A Documentary History*. Vol 1: 1859–1920. Edited by Sven Saaler and Christopher W. A. Szpilman, 260–2, 2011.

Konoe Atsumaro. 'Dō-jinshu dōmei, tsuketari Shina mondai kenkyū no hitsuyō'. *Taiyō* 24, no. 1 (January 1898).

Koshiro, Yukiko. 'Beyond an Alliance of Color: The African American Impact on Modern Japan'. *positions: East Asia Cultures Critique* 11, no. 1 (Spring 2003): 183–215.

Koshiro, Yukiko. *Trans-Pacific Racisms and the U.S. Occupation of Japan*. New York: Columbia University Press, 1999.

Kowner, Rotem. 'Becoming an Honorary Civilized Nation: Remaking Japan's Military Image during the Russo-Japanese War, 1904–1905'. *The Historian* 64, no. 1 (Fall 2001): 19–38.

Kowner, Rotem. 'Between Contempt and Fear: Western Racial Constructions of East Asians since 1800'. In *Race and Racism in Modern East Asia: Western and Eastern Constructions* edited by Rotem Kowner and Walter Demel, 87–125. Leiden: Brill, 2013.

Kowner, Rotem, ed. *The Impact of the Russo-Japanese War*. New York: Routledge, 2007.

Kowner, Rotem. '"Lighter than Yellow, but not Enough": Western Discourse on the Japanese "Race", 1854–1904'. *The Historical Journal* 43, no. 1 (2000): 103–31.

Kowner, Rotem and Harumi Befu. 'Ethnic Nationalism in Postwar Japan: Nihonjinron and Its Racial Facets'. In *Race and Racism in Modern East Asia: Interactions, Nationalism, Gender and Lineage*, edited by Rotem Kowner and Walter Demel, 389–412. Leiden: Brill, 2015.

Kowner, Rotem and Walter Demel. 'Modern East Asia and the Rise of Racial Thought: Possible Links, Unique Features and Unsettled Issues'. In *Race and Racism in Modern*

East Asia: Western and Eastern Constructions, edited by Rotem Kowner and Walter Demel, 1–37. Leiden: Brill, 2013.

Kowner, Rotem and Walter Demel. *Race and Racism in Modern East Asia: Western and Eastern Constructions*. Leiden: Brill, 2013.

Krebs, Gerhard. 'Racism under Negotiation: The Japanese Race in the Nazi-German Perspective'. In *Race and Racism in Modern East Asia: Interactions, Nationalism, Gender and Lineage*, edited by Rotem Kowner and Walter Demel, 217–41. Leiden: Brill, 2015.

Krenn, Michael L. *The Color of Empire: Race and American Foreign Relations*. Washington, DC: Potomac Books, 2006.

Kuo, Joyce. 'Excluded, Segregated and Forgotten: A Historical View of the Discrimination of Chinese Americans in Public Schools'. *Asian American Law Journal* 5 (January 1998): 181–212.

Kurino, S. 'The Future of Japan'. *The North American Review* 160, no. 462 (May 1895): 621–31.

Kurino, S. 'The Oriental War'. *The North American Review* 159, no. 456 (November 1894): 529–36.

LaFeber, Walter. *The Clash: U.S.-Japan Relations Throughout History*. New York: W. W. Norton & Company, 1997.

Lake, Marilyn and Henry Reynolds. *Drawing the Global Colour Line: White Men's Countries and the International Challenge of Racial Equality*. Cambridge: Cambridge University Press, 2008.

Langer-Kaneko, Christiane. 'Zur Geschichte der Erziehung und Bildung der Frau in Japan, reflektiert an ihrer Rolle in der Gesellschaft'. In *Japan – Ein Land der Frauen?*, edited by Elisabeth Gössman, 81–116. München: Iudicium Verlag, 1991.

Lauren, Paul Gordon. 'Human Rights in History: Diplomacy and Racial Equality at the Paris Peace Conference'. *Diplomatic History* 2, no. 3 (Summer 1978): 257–78.

Lauren, Paul Gordon. *Power and Prejudice: The Politics and Diplomacy of Racial Discrimination*. 2nd ed. Boulder, CO: Westview Press, 1996.

Legal Information Institute. '*Takao Ozawa* vs *United States*'. https://www.law.cornell.edu/supremecourt/text/260/178 (accessed 28 May 2022).

Letter from Theodore Roosevelt to Albion W. Tourgée, 8 November 1901. Theodore Roosevelt Digital Library. Dickinson State University. http://www.theodorerooseveltcenter.org/Research/Digital-Library/Record?libID=o180529 (accessed 28 May 2022).

Letter from Theodore Roosevelt to Cecil Spring Rice, June 13, 1904. Theodore Roosevelt Papers. Library of Congress Manuscript Division. https://www.theodorerooseveltcenter.org/Research/Digital-Library/Record?libID=o267973 (accessed 28 May 2022).

Letter from Theodore Roosevelt to John Hay, September 2, 1904. Theodore Roosevelt Papers. Library of Congress Manuscript Division. http://www.theodorerooseveltcenter.org/Research/Digital-Library/Record?libID=o189070 (accessed 28 May 2022).

Letter from Theodore Roosevelt to Kaneko Kentarō, April 23, 1904. Theodore Roosevelt Papers. Library of Congress Manuscript Division. https://www.theodorerooseveltcenter.org/Research/Digital-Library/Record/ImageViewer?libID=o187994&imageNo=1 (accessed 28 May 2022).

Letter from Theodore Roosevelt to Kermit Roosevelt, October 27, 1906. Theodore Roosevelt Papers. Library of Congress Manuscript Division. http://www.theodorerooseveltcenter.org/Research/Digital-Library/Record?libID=o280819 (accessed 28 May 2022).

Louis, Brett St. 'Post-Race/Post-Politics? Activist-Intellectualism and the Reification of Race'. *Ethnic and Racial Studies* 25, no. 4 (2002): 652–75.

McFarland, Brian James. 'From Publisher to Pocket: Interpreting Nineteenth Century American History through the Pocket Maps of Samuel Augustus Mitchell'. MA thesis, University of Texas at Arlington, 2002.

Mahan, Alfred T. 'Japan Among the Nations: Admiral Mahan's Views'. 23 June 1913.

Mahan, Alfred T. 'A Twentieth Century Outlook'. *Harper's New Monthly Magazine* 95 (June 1897): 521–33.

Majima Ayu. *Hadairo no yūutsu: Kindai Nihon no jinshu taiken.* Tokyo: Chūō kōron shinsha, 2014.

Majima Ayu. 'Skin Color Melancholy in Modern Japan: Male Elites' Racial Experiences Abroad, 1880s–1950s'. In *Race and Racism in Modern East Asia: Western and Eastern Constructions*, edited by Rotem Kowner and Walter Demel, 391–410. Leiden: Brill, 2013.

Makino Nobuaki. *Kaikoroku (shita).* Tokyo: Chūō kōronsha, 1978.

Manela, Erez. *The Wilsonian Moment: Self-Determination and the International Origins of Anticolonial Nationalism.* Oxford: Oxford University Press, 2007.

Maruyama Masao. *Studies in the Intellectual History of Tokugawa Japan.* Translated by Mikiso Hane. Princeton, NJ: Princeton University Press, 1974.

Maruyama Masao and Katō Shūichi. *Hon'yaku to Nihon no kindai.* Tokyo: Iwanami shoten, 1998.

Matsumura Masayoshi. 'Nihon ni kita saisho no Amerika kokujin'. *Gaikō Jihō* 1185 (July 1981): 18–26.

Matsuo, Kenji. *A History of Japanese Buddhism.* Kent: Global Oriental, 2007.

Meehan, John D. 'From Alliance to Conference: The British Empire, Japan, and Pacific Multilateralism, 1911–1921'. In *The Decade of the Great War: Japan and the Wider World in the 1910s*, edited by Tosh Minohara, Tze-ki Hon and Evan Dawley, 45–63. Leiden: Brill, 2014.

Mehnert, Ute. *Deutschland, Amerika und die 'Gelbe Gefahr': zur Karriere eines Schlagworts in der grossen Politik, 1905–1917.* Stuttgart: Steiner, 1995.

Miles, Robert. *Racism after 'Race Relations'.* London: Routledge, 1993.

Miles, Robert and Malcolm Brown. *Racism.* 2nd ed. London: Routledge, 2003.

Mills, Charles W. '"But What Are You Really?": The Metaphysics of Race'. In *Blackness Visible: Essays on Philosophy and Race*, 41–66. Ithaca, NY: Cornell University Press, 2015.

Mills, Charles W. *The Racial Contract.* Ithaca, NY: Cornell University Press, 1997.

Minohara, Tosh. 'The Clash of Pride and Prejudice: The Immigration Issue and US-Japan Relations in the 1910s'. In *The Decade of the Great War: Japan and the Wider World in the 1910s*, edited by Tosh Minohara, Tze-ki Hon and Evan Dawley, 19–44. Leiden: Brill, 2014.

Mishima Yatarō. *Mishima Yatarō no tegami: Amerika e watatta Meiji shoki no ryūgakusei.* Edited by Mishima Yoshiyasu. Tokyo: Gakuseisha, 1994.

Mitchell, Samuel Augustus. *A System of Modern Geography: Political, Physical and Descriptive.* Philadelphia, PA: E. H. Butler and Co., 1865. 1843.

Miyoshi, Masao. *As We Saw Them: The First Japanese Embassy to the United States (1860).* Berkeley: University of California Press, 1979.

Montagu, Ashley. *Man's Most Dangerous Myth: The Fallacy of Race.* 6th ed. Walnut Creek, CA: AltaMira Press, 1997.

Mori Rintarō. *Kōkaron kōgai.* Tokyo: Shun'yōdō, 1904.

Mori Toyokichi. *Nichi-Ei dōmei.* Tokyo: Kōbunsha, 1902.

Moriyama Tokō. 'Nichi-Ei no dōmei'. Taiyō 3, no. 3 (March 1902): 59–62.

Morris-Suzuki, Tessa. 'A Descent into the Past: The Frontier in the Construction of Japanese History'. In *Multicultural Japan: Palaeolithic to Postmodern*, edited by Donald Denoon, Mark Hudson, Gavan McCormack and Tessa Morris-Suzuki, 81–94. Cambridge: Cambridge Universtity Press, 2001.

Morris-Suzuki, Tessa. *Re-Inventing Japan: Time, Space, Nation.* New York: M. E. Sharpe, 1998.

Morris-Suzuki, Tessa. *The Technological Transformation of Japan: From the Seventeenth to the Twenty-First Century.* Cambridge: Cambridge University Press, 1994.

Myers, Ramon Hawley and Mark R. Peattie. *The Japanese Colonial Empire, 1895–1945.* Princeton, NJ: Princeton University Press, 1984.

Nagai Ryūtarō. *Kaizō no risō.* Tokyo: Seikadō, 1920.

Nagai, Michio. 'Herbert Spencer in Early Meiji Japan'. *Far Eastern Quarterly* 14, no. 1 (November 1954): 55–64.

Naoichi Masaoka, ed. *Japan to America: A Symposium of Papers by Political Leaders and Representative Citizens of Japan on Conditions in Japan and on the Relations between Japan and the United States.* New York: G. P. Putnam's Sons, 1914.

Napier, Susan Jolliffe. *From Impressionism to Anime: Japan as Fantasy and Fan Cult in the Mind of the West.* New York: Palgrave Macmillan, 2007.

Naraoka, Sōchi. 'A New Look at Japan's Twenty-One Demands: Reconsidering Katō Takaaki's Motives in 1915'. In *The Decade of the Great War: Japan and the Wider World in the 1910s*, edited by Tosh Minohara, Tze-ki Hon and Evan Dawley, 189–210. Leiden: Brill, 2014.

National Center for Education Statistics. '120 Years of American Education: A Statistical Portrait'. 1993. https://nces.ed.gov/naal/lit_history.asp#illiteracy (accessed 28 May 2022).

Nenzi, Laura. *Excursions in Modernity: Travel and the Intersection of Place, Gender, and Status in Edo Japan.* Honolulu: University of Hawaii Press, 2008.

Newlands, Francis G. 'A Western View of the Race Question'. *The Annals of the American Academy of Political and Social Science* 34, no. 2 (1909): 49–51.

Nihon gaikō monjo. 'Kakugi kettei: tai-Ro kōshō ketsuretsu no sai Nihon no toru beki tai-Shin-Kan hōshin'. Man-Kan ni kansuru Nichi-Ro kōshō ikken (30 December 1903): 44.

Nihon gaikō monjo. Aoki to Hayashi (1 November 1906). *Nihon ni oite honbō imin tokō seigen narabi Sōkō hai-Nichi undō no ken*, 455.

Nihon gaikō monjo. Chinda to Katō (5 February 1913). *Kashū no gaikokujin tochi hōan oyobi Nihon seifu no kōgi kankei*, 9.

Nihon gaikō monjo. Hioki to Saionji (30 March 1906). *Nihon ni oite honbō imin tokō seigen narabi Sōkō hai-Nichi undō no ken*, 377–94.

Nihon gaikō monjo. Obata to Uchida (11 March 1919). *Pari kōwa kaigi ni okeru jinshu sabetsu teppai mondai ikken*, 469–70, 467.

Nihon gaikō monjo. Oyama to Katsura (22 January 1913). *Kashū no gaikokujin tochi hōan oyobi Nihon seifu no kōgi kankei*, 3–7.

Nihon gaikō monjo. Uchida to Matsui (12 February 1919). *Pari kōwa kaigi ni okeru jinshu sabetsu teppai mondai ikken*, 441.

Nihon gaikō monjo. Uchida to Saionji (8 February 1919). *Pari kōwa kaigi ni okeru jinshu sabetsu teppai mondai ikken*, 439–40.

Nish, Ian. *The Anglo-Japanese Alliance: The Diplomacy of Two Island Empires, 1894–1907*. London: Bloomsbury, 2012.

Oguma Eiji. *A Genealogy of 'Japanese' Self-Images*. Translated by David Askew. Melbourne: Trans Pacific Press, 2002.

Oka, Yoshitake. 'The First Anglo-Japanese Alliance in Japanese Public Opinion'. In *Themes and Theories in Modern Japanese History: Essays in Memory of Richard Storry*, edited by Susan Henny and Jean-Pierre Lehmann, 185–93. London: Bloomsbury. Reprint, 2012.

Okuma Shigenobu. 'Our National Mission'. In *Japan to America, Japan to America: A Symposium of Papers by Political Leaders and Representative Citizens of Japan on Conditions in Japan and on the Relations between Japan and the United States*, edited by Naoichi Masaoka, 1–5. New York: G. P. Putnam's Sons, 1914.

Onishi, Yuichiro. *Transpacific Antiracism: Afro-Asian Solidarity in Twentieth-Century Black America, Japan, and Okinawa*. New York: New York University Press, 2013.

Ooms, Herman. *Tokugawa Village Practice: Class, Status, Power, Law*. Berkeley: University of California Press, 1996.

Osada, Masako. *Sanctions and Honorary Whites: Diplomatic Policies and Economic Realities in Relations between Japan and South Africa*. Westport, CT: Greenwood Press, 2002.

Paine, Sarah C. M. *The Sino-Japanese War of 1894–1895: Perceptions, Power, and Primacy*. Cambridge: Cambridge University Press, 2002.

Pascoe, Peggy. *What Comes Naturally: Miscegenation Law and the Making of Race in America*. Oxford: Oxford University Press, 2009.

Pearson, Charles H. *National Life and Character: A Forecast*. London: Macmillan and Co., 1893.

Peter, Duus. 'Nagai Ryutaro and the "White Peril," 1905–1944'. *The Journal of Asian Studies* 31, no. 1 (1971): 41–8.

Pinon, René. 'La guerre russo-japonaise et l'opinion européenne'. *Revue des Deux Mondes* 21 (May 1904): 186–219.

Reid, Wemyss. 'Last Month'. *The Nineteenth Century and After* 51 (March 1902): 506–20.

Robertson, Jennifer. 'Blood Talks: Eugenic Modernity and the Creation of New Japanese'. *History and Anthropology* 13, no. 3 (2002): 191–216.

Rowell, Chester H. 'Chinese and Japanese Immigrants: A Comparison'. *The Annals of the American Academy of Political and Social Science* 34, no. 2 (September 1909): 3–10.

Russel, John G. 'The Other Other: The Black Presence in the Japanese Experience'. In *Japan's Minorities: The Illusion of Homogeneity*, edited by Michael Weiner, 84–115. London: Routledge, 2009.

Saaler, Sven. 'Pan-Asianism during and after World War I: Kodera Kenkichi (1916), Sawayanagi Masatarō (1919), and Sugita Teiichi (1920)'. In *Pan-Asianism: A Documentary History. Vol. 1: 1850–1920*, edited by Sven Saaler and Christopher W. A. Szpilman, 255–70. Lanham, MD: Rowman & Littlefield, 2011.

Saaler, Sven and Christopher W. A. Szpilman. *Pan-Asianism: A Documentary History*. Vol. 1. Lanham, MD: Rowman & Littlefield, 2011.

Saeki Shōichi. 'Kasō teki toshite no Amerika no imēji'. In *Nihon to Amerika: Aite koku no imēji kenkyū*, edited by Hidetoshi Katō and Shunsuke Kamei, 181–224. Tokyo: Nihon gakujutsu shinkōkai, 1991.

Saitō Yōichi and Ōishi Shinzaburō. *Mibun sabetsu shakai no shinjitsu*. Tokyo: Kodansha, 1995.

Sakano Tōru. *Teikoku Nihon to jinruigakusha: 1884–1952 nen*. Tokyo: Keisō shobō, 2005.

Sato, Kazuki. '"Same Language, Same Race": The Dilemma of *Kanbun* in Modern Japan'. In *The Construction of Racial Identities in China and Japan*, edited by Frank Dikötter, 118–35. Hong Kong: Hong Kong University Press, 1997.

Shankman, Arnold. '"Asiatic Ogre" or "Desirable Citizen"? The Image of Japanese Americans in the Afro-American Press, 1867–1933'. *Pacific Historical Review* 46, no. 4 (November 1977): 567–87.

Shimao, Eikoh. 'Darwinism in Japan, 1877–1927'. *Annals of Science* 38, no. 1 (1981): 93–102.

Shimazu, Naoko. *Japan, Race, and Equality: The Racial Equality Proposal of 1919*. London: Routledge, 1998.

Shively, Donald H. 'Sumptuary Regulation and Status in Early Tokugawa Japan'. *Harvard Journal of Asiatic Studies* 25 (1964–5): 123–64.

Siddle, Richard. *Race, Resistance, and the Ainu of Japan*. London: Routledge, 1996.

Sinkler, George. *The Racial Attitudes of American Presidents: From Abraham Lincoln to Theodore Roosevelt*. New York: Doubleday, 1971.

Smyers, Karen Ann. 'Women and Shinto: The Relation Between Purity and Pollution'. *Japanese Religions* 12, no. 4 (July 1983): 7–18.

Sprotte, Maik Hendrik, Wolfgang Seifert and Heinz-Dietrich Löwe, eds. *Der Russisch-Japanische Krieg 1904/05: Anbruch einer neuen Zeit?* Wiesbaden: Harrassowitz Verlag, 2007.

Stanley, Amy. 'Adultery, Punishment, and Reconciliation in Tokugawa Japan'. *The Journal of Japanese Studies* 33, no. 2 (Summer 2007): 309–35.

Starling, Jessica. 'Domestic Religion in Late Edo-Period Sermons for Temple Wives'. *The Eastern Buddhist* 43, no. 1/2 (2012): 271–97.

Steinberg, John, David Wolff, Steve Marks, Bruce Menning, David Schimmelpenninck van der Oye and Shinji Yokote, eds. *The Russo-Japanese War in Global Perspective: World War Zero, Volume II*. Leiden: Brill, 2006.

Sugimoto, Yoshio. 'Making Sense of Nihonjinron'. *Thesis Eleven* 57, no. 1 (1999): 81–96.

Suzuki Hanzaburō. *Beikoku kokuminsei no shinkenkyū*. Tokyo: Rakuyōdō, 1916.

Suzuki, Keiko. 'The Making of *Tōjin*: Construction of the Other in Early Modern Japan'. *Asian Folklore Studies* 66, no. 1/2 (2007): 83–105.

Suzuki, Shogo. *Civilization and Empire: China and Japan's Encounter with European International Society*. London: Routledge, 2009.

Tajima, Atsushi and Michael Thornton. 'Strategic Solidarity: Japanese Imaginings of Blacks and Race in Popular Media'. *Inter-Asia Cultural Studies* 13, no. 3 (2012): 345–64.

Takahashi Korekiyo. *Takahashi Korekiyo jiden (jō)*. Edited by Uetsuka Tsukasa. Tokyo: Chūō kōron shinsha, 2013.

Takahashi Yoshio. *Nihon jinshu kairyōron*. Tokyo: Ishikawa Hanjirō, 1884.

Takemi, Momoko. '"Menstruation Sutra" Belief in Japan'. *Japanese Journal of Religious Studies* 10, no. 2–3 (1983): 229–46.

Takezawa Yasuko, ed. *Jinshu gainen no fuhensei o tou: Seiyōteki paradaimu o koete*. Tokyo: Jimbunshoin, 2005.

Takezawa Yasuko. 'Transcending the Western Paradigm of the Idea of Race'. *The Japanese Journal of American Studies* 16 (2005): 5–30.

Takezawa Yasuko. 'Translating and Transforming "Race": Early Meiji Period Textbooks'. *Japanese Studies* 35, no. 1 (2015): 5–21.

Tamura Shōgyo. *Hokubei sezokukan*. Tokyo: Hakubunkan, 1909.

Tanaka, Stefan. *Japan's Orient: Rendering Pasts into History*. Berkeley: University of California Press, 1993.

Terashima, Seiichiro. 'Exclusionists Not True to the Principles of America's Founders'. In *Japan to America: A Symposium of Papers by Political Leaders and Representative Citizens of Japan on Conditions in Japan and on the Relations between Japan and the United States*, edited by Naoichi Masaoka. New York: G. P. Putnam's Sons, 1914.

Terre, Jean sans. 'La Chine ouverte'. *Le Petit Journal*, 28 November 1894.

Thornton, Michael and Atsushi Tajima. 'A "Model" Minority: Japanese Americans as References and Role Models in Black Newspapers, 2000–2010'. *Communication and Critical/Cultural Studies* 11, no. 2 (April 2014): 139–57.

Toby, Ronald P. 'Imagining and Imaging "Anthropos" in Early-Modern Japan'. *Visual Anthropology Review* 14, no. 1 (Spring–Summer 1998): 19–44.

Toby, Ronald P. *State and Diplomacy in Early Modern Japan: Asia in the Development of the Tokugawa Bakufu*. Princeton, NJ: Princeton University Press, 1984.

Toby, Ronald P. 'Three Realms/Myriad Countries: An "Ethnography" of Other and the Re-bounding of Japan, 1550–1750'. In *Constructing Nationhood in Modern East Asia*, edited by Kai-wing Chow, Kevin M. Doak and Poshek Fu, 15–45. Ann Harbor: University of Michigan Press, 2001.

Tocco, Martha C. 'Norms and Texts for Women's Education in Tokugawa Japan'. In *Women and Confucian Cultures in Premodern China, Korea, and Japan*, edited by Dorothy Ko, JaHyun Kim Haboush and Joan R. Piggot, 193–218. Los Angeles: University of California Press, 2003.

Toda Kaiichi. 'Yūshokujin imin haiseki mondai (ge)'. *Asahi shinbun*, 3 January 1919.

Toda Kaiichi. 'Yūshokujin imin haiseki mondai (jō)'. *Asahi shinbun*, 1 January 1919.

Tokutomi, Sohō. *Sekai no henkyoku*. Tokyo: Min'yūsha, 1915.

Tsuchida, Motoko. 'A History of Japanese Emigration from the 1860s to the 1990s'. In *Temporary Workers or Future Citizens?: Japanese and U.S. Migration Policies*, edited by Myron Weiner and Tadashi Hanami, 77–119. London: Palgrave Macmillan, 1998.

Tsuda, Takeyuki Gaku. 'When Identities Become Modern: Japanese Emigration to Brazil and the Global Contextualization of Identity'. *Ethnic and Racial Studies* 24, no. 3 (January 2001): 412–32.

Uchiyama, Akiko. 'Translation as Representation: Fukuzawa Yukichi's Representation of the "Others"'. In *Agents of Translation*, edited by John Milton and Paul Bandia, 63–83. Amsterdam: John Benjamins Publishing Company, 2009.

Unno Yukinori. 'Kōhaku ryōjinshu hikakuron'. *Taiyō* 19, no. 8 (June 1913): 87–94.

Unoura Hiroshi. 'Samurai Darwinism: Hiroyuki Katō and the Reception of Darwin's Theory in Modern Japan from the 1880s to the 1900s'. *History and Anthropology* 11, no. 2–3 (1999): 235–55.

Unoura Hiroshi. 'Shinkaron to naichi zakkyoron: Shinkaron juyō no ichi sokumen'. *Kisato daigaku kiyōbu kiyō* (March 1988): 82–99.

Valliant, Robert B. 'The Selling of Japan: Japanese Manipulation of Western Opinion, 1900–1905'. *Monumenta Nipponica* 29, no. 4 (1974): 415–38.

Vámbéry, H. *Die Gelbe Gefahr: Eine Kulturstudie.* Budapest: Königliche Universitäts-Buchhandlung, 1904.

Vogel, Ezra F. *Japan as Number One: Lessons for America.* Cambridge, MA: Harvard University Press, 1979.

Wagatsuma, Hiroshi. 'The Social Perception of Skin Color in Japan'. *Daedalus* 96, no. 2 (Spring 1967): 407–43.

Wakabayashi, Bob Tadashi. *Anti-Foreignism and Western Learning in Early-Modern Japan: The New Theses of 1825*. Cambridge, MA: Harvard University Press, 1992.

Wakabayashi, Bob Tadashi. 'Opium, Expulsion, Sovereignty: China's Lessons for Bakumatsu Japan'. *Monumenta Nipponica* 47, no. 1 (Spring 1992): 1–25.

Wakanomiya Yūsuke. *Wakanomiya ronshū.* Tokyo: Jitsugyō no seikaisha, 1915.

Walker, Brett L. *The Conquest of Ainu Lands: Ecology and Culture in Japanese Expansion, 1590–1800*. Berkeley: University of California Press, 2001.

Wallerstein, Immanuel. 'Universalisme, racisme, sexisme: les tensions idéologiques du capitalisme'. In *Race, nation, classe: Les identités ambiguës*, edited by Étienne Balibar and Immanuel Wallerstein, 42–53. Paris: La Découverte, 1997.

Watanabe Hiroshi. *A History of Japanese Political Thought, 1600–1901*. Translated by David Noble. Tokyo: I-House Press, 2012.

Weber, Torsten. *Embracing 'Asia' in China and Japan: Asianism Discourse and the Contest for Hegemony, 1912–1933*. New York: Palgrave Macmillan, 2018.

Weiner, Michael. 'The Invention of Identity: Race and Nation in Pre-War Japan'. In *The Constructions of Racial Identities in China and Japan: Historical and Contemporary Perspectives*, edited by Frank Dikötter, 96–116. Hong Kong: Hong Kong University Press, 1997.

Weiner, Michael. *Race and Migration in Imperial Japan.* London: Routledge, 1994.

Weiner, Michael. '"Self" and "Other" in Imperial Japan'. In *Japan's Minorities: The Illusion of Homogeneity*, edited by Michael Weiner, 1–20. London: Routledge, 2009.
White, Richard. *The Middle Ground: Indians, Empires, and Republics in the Great Lakes Region, 1650–1815*. 2nd ed. New York: Cambridge University Press, 2011.
Wildman Nakai, Kate. 'The Naturalization of Confucianism in Tokugawa Japan: The Problem of Sinocentrism'. *Harvard Journal of Asiatic Studies* 40, no. 1 (June 1980): 157–99.
Wiley, Peter Booth. *Yankees in the Land of the Gods: Commodore Perry and the Opening of Japan*. New York: Viking, 1990.
Wippich, Rolf-Harald, ed. *'Haut Sie, dass die Lappen fliegen!': Briefe von Deutschen an das japanische Kriegsministerium während des Chinesich-Japanischen Krieges 1894/1895*. Vol. 067, OAG Taschenbuch. München: Iudicium, 1997.
Wm. Draper, Lewis. 'Can the United States by Treaty Confer on Japanese Residents in California the Right to Attend the Public Schools?'. *The American Law Register (1898–1907)* 55, no. 2 (February 1907): 73–90.
Wright, David. 'The Use of Race and Racial Perceptions among Asians and Blacks: The Case of the Japanese and African Americans'. *Hitotsubashi Journal of Social Studies* 30, no. 2 (1998): 135–52.
Wright, Diana E. 'Female Crime and State Punishment in Early Modern Japan'. *Journal of Women's History* 16, no. 3 (Fall 2004): 10–29.
Yamamoto Hidemasa. 'Shoki nihonjin tobeishi ni okeru gakusei kanai rōdōsha'. *Eigakushi kenkyū* 19 (1987): 141–56.
Yamamuro Shin'ichi. 'Dai ichiji sekai taisen: Shiten toshite no jūdaisei'. *Asahi shinbun*, 24 March 2008.
Yamamuro Shin'ichi. 'L'empire du Japon et le choc de la Première Guerre mondiale'. *Guerres mondiales et conflits contemporains* 249, no. 1 (2013): 5–32.
Yamamuro Shin'ichi. *Fukugō sensō to sōryokusen no dansō: Nihon ni totte no daiichiji sekai taisen*. Tokyo: Jinbun shoin, 2011.
Yoell, A. E. 'Oriental vs. American Labor'. *The Annals of the American Academy of Political and Social Science* 34, no. 2 (September 1909): 27–36.
Yokoyama Matajirō. *Sekai ni okeru shizen no kikan*. Tokyo: Kōbun shoten, 1915.
Yonaha Jun. 'Kindai Nihon ni okeru "jinshu" kannen no hen'yō: Tsuboi Shōgorō no "jinruigaku" to no kakawari o chūshin ni'. *Minzoku kenkyū* 68, no. 1 (2003): 85–97.
Yoshino Sakuzō, ed. *Gendai Beikoku*. Tokyo: Min'yūsha, 1916.
Young, John P. 'The Support of the Anti-Oriental Movement'. *The Annals of the American Academy of Political and Social Science* 34, no. 2 (September 1909): 11–18.
Young, Louise. 'Rethinking Race for Manchukuo: Self and Other in the Colonial Context'. In *The Construction of Racial Identities in China and Japan: Historical and Contemporary Perspectives*, edited by Frank Dikötter, 158–76. Hong Kong: Hong Kong University Press, 1997.
Yuhara Motoichi. 'Jinshu mondai yori miru kōkyū heiwa no yōken'. *Taiyō* 25, no. 2 (February 1919): 88–94.
Zachmann, Urs Matthias, ed. *Asia after Versailles: Asian Perspectives on the Paris Peace*

Conference and the Interwar Order, 1919–33. Edinburgh: Edinburgh University Press, 2017.

Zachmann, Urs Matthias. *China and Japan in the Late Meiji Period: China Policy and the Japanese Discourse on National Identity, 1895–1904*. London: Routledge, 2009.

Zachmann, Urs Matthias. 'Konoe Atsumaro and the Idea of an Alliance of the Yellow Race, 1898'. In *Pan-Asianism: A Documentary History. Vol. 1: 1850–1920*, edited by Sven Saaler and Christopher W. A. Szpilman, 85–92. Lanham, MD: Rowman & Littlefield, 2011.

Zachmann, Urs Matthias. 'Race Without Supremacy: On Racism in the Political Discourse of Late Meiji Japan, 1890–1912'. In *Racism in the Modern World: Historical Perspectives on Cultural Transfer and Adaptation*, edited by Manfred Berg and Simon Wendt, 255–79. New York: Berghahn Books, 2011.

Index

EU representative:
Easy Access System Europe
Mustamäe tee 50, 10621 Tallinn, Estonia
Gpsr.requests@easproject.com

www.ingramcontent.com/pod-product-compliance
Lightning Source LLC
Chambersburg PA
CBHW061734270326
41928CB00011B/2230
* 9 7 8 1 3 9 9 5 0 6 9 0 8 *